BOUNDARY PROBLEMS IN WESTERN NIGERIA

Location of Boundary Disputes in the text

Boundary Problems in Western Nigeria

A Geographical Analysis

By

ỌMỌLADE ADEJUYIGBE, B.A., PH.D.

Senior Lecturer,
Department of Geography,
University of Ife,
Ile-Ife

UNIVERSITY OF IFE PRESS
ILE—IFE NIGERIA

O02069252

ISBN 978—136—001—1

Printed by
The Caxton Press (West Africa) Limited, Ibadan

To My Father

and

The Entire Adejuyigbe Family

Contents

Preface

There is scarcely any major community in Western Nigeria which has not been involved in boundary disputes with its neighbours during the twentieth century. At present more than fifty such disputes have been listed for settlement by the Boundary Settlement Commission of the State. The attempts to resolve the disputes have not been very successful as shown by the fact that many of those before the Boundary Settlement Commission have been previously settled either administratively or even by the law courts. A major objective of this study is to examine the reasons why boundary disputes have been so prevalent in Western Nigeria.

A geographic study of boundary disputes necessarily emphasizes the spatial aspects of the problem. Consequently, the various chapters have focussed attention on the boundary as a line separating different zones of authority, Chapter I examines the processes by which boundary lines evolve whilst Chapter II discusses the factors which influenced the delimitation of boundaries in Western Nigeria during the twentieth century. Chapter III is on the nature of boundary disputes. Apart from illustrating a particular type of boundary dispute each of Chapters IV-VII also highlights another general aspect of boundary problems. Chapter IV illustrates the problems of administering disputed or formerly disputed territories whilst Chapter V discusses the problems arising from ambiguous boundary definition and shows the effect that lack of detailed knowledge could have on boundary claims. Chapter VI considers the principles that need be borne in mind when interpreting historical data in any attempt to settle boundary disputes and Chapter VII illustrates the problems that may arise if communal and administrative boundaries do not coincide. The last two chapters discuss the settlement of boundary disputes in Western Nigeria and the points that need be taken into account to make the settlement of boundary disputes more acceptable to the communities. A version of Chapter I and parts of Chapters V and VII have been previously published in learned journals. Chapter I under the title of "Evolution of Inter-Community Boundaries in Africa" in *Cahiers de Geographie de Quebec* Vol, 18 No. 43, 1974 pp. 83-105. The Ife-Ijesa boundary problem used as illustration in Chapter I in *Nigerian Geographical Journal* Vol. 13, 1970 pp. 23-38. The Ife-Ede boundary dispute discussed in Chapter VII as 'Local Boundary Disputes in Western Nigeria: The Example of Edunabon Enclave on the Ife-Ede Boundary' in *Odu*, University of Ife Journal of West African Studies, New Series No. 2, October 1969 pp. 78-101.

A study like this could not have been completed without the co-operation of many people. I should like to mention the assistance received from Government officials at Ibadan and in various Divisional Offices which I visited. In particular I wish to thank the Surveyor-General and officials of the Survey Division, Ministry of Lands and Housing, Ibadan for maps of disputed areas; the office of the Military Governor, Western State for letters of introduction to Divisional Offices; and the Boundary Commission for many frank and useful discussions on boundary problems. At the local level, I interviewed many Obas and Community heads. Particular mention should be made of Alaiyeluwa, the Ooni of Ife, Alaiyeluwa, the Owa of Ijesaland, and also the Onitaji of Itaji and the Bale of Akinlalu, all of whom threw much light on the territorial acquisition and boundary evolution among the Yoruba. The staff of the National Archives. Ibadan were most co-operative in the search for past records on boundary disputes.

The study was made possible by a research grant from the University of Ife, Ile-Ife. My colleagues in the Department of Geography and the Faculty of Law were most helpful in discussing with me my ideas and reading many drafts of the text. Special mention should be made of the comments and suggestions received from Dr Oladipo Adejuwon on Chapter I, Dr B. Ogundana on Chapter II, Dr P. A. Oluyede on Chapter IV and Dr I. O. Agbede on Chapters VIII and IX. Mr G. O. Kilanko assisted with the fieldwork for Chapters V and VII. Mr Ilesanmi Adeoti drew the diagrams and Messrs Z. Irejeunoh and S. A. Obafemi typed the manuscripts. To all these I express my profound thanks.

Finally I wish to thank Mrs E. Oluwasanmi, Executive Editor of the University of Ife Press and her assistants for their efforts in the final editing of the work and seeing to its publication.

I owe much to my father for his interest in this study and enlightment on boundary development and problems, and to my family for their encouragement generally.

ỌMỌLADE ADEJUYIGBE
Ile-Ifẹ

List of Maps and Diagrams

CHAPTER I

The Evolution of Boundaries

THE PRIMARY function of boundaries is to separate the areas of interest or jurisdiction of different parties (persons, communities or states). Therefore the most important factors in boundary development are the parties which are separated and whose authorities are limited by it. The need for the parties to define their areas of authority presumably developed because of a desire to avoid conflict over certain areas or resources. In considering the evolution of boundaries, it can, therefore, be assumed that:

    (i) each party has a distinct base or core area where it was first established;

   (ii) the different bases were initially separated by some territory which no one has claimed and which can be regarded as a frontier;

  (iii) expansion from the bases or cores into the frontier was for the purpose of exploiting its resources such as soil, vegetation (including fruit, grass and timber), minerals, water and animals (including fishes);

  (iv) the resources of the frontier are inelastic and therefore each side may, at a certain stage, want to have exclusive control over the resources in particular areas;

   (v) the parties will desire to avoid conflict or the resumption of conflict over resources and hence will seek agreement on the sections of the frontier to be exploited by each side.

Expansion from the base could be in two stages. First, there is exploration of parts of the frontier. The aim of exploration is to assess the resources of the area and to be conversant with the nature of the terrain. The second stage involves exploitation of the resources of the explored territory. During the initial stages it is possible for people, expanding from different bases, to explore and exploit the resources of the same general area without coming into contact

1

with each other. This is the more so if the exploration takes place at different periods. In that case two people might know the same area and each believes that he is the only one there. Ordinarily, knowledge of other party's existence or interest in the same area would come when each leaves behind evidence of his presence there. Such evidence could be the establishment of camps or marks indicating exploitation of the resources. However, evidence of resource exploitation will depend on the nature of the particular resource. Whereas people engaged in activities such as the felling of timber, mining or farming would leave behind evidence of their activities, there may be nothing to indicate the operations of those involved in the collection of fruit, hunting or fishing. In the latter case later explorers of the area of operation may think that they are the first people to visit the area and therefore that they are entitled to claim it.

Even when the people involved in exploration in a frontier area come into contact they may jointly exploit the resources of an area without any conflict whatever. This could be the case with resources such as water, fruit and game. More than one person could collect the fruit of a single plant, and game in a given area could be sought by two (or more) hunters who are aware of each other's presence. The essence of this argument is that at the early stages of contact between members of different communities there may be a great deal of intermingling among them in the area of contact. Therefore, at that stage there may be no exclusive claim to any part of the contact area or frontier.

It can be assumed that the first contact between two different communities takes place through two persons. Each of these may have enough for his own needs and may therefore not be opposed to sharing the resources of the contact area with the other party. However, in the course of time, the population of each community within the contact area will increase. Since there is no unoccupied space for expansion the increased population will be limited to the contact area. In order to satisfy their needs they will make more intensive exploitation of the resources. Intensive exploitation will involve more frequent visits to, for example, hunting grounds and eventually concentration by each person of his activity in a given area. Consequently each person will start to lay exclusive claims to his area of operation. In the course of time adjacent members of the two communities may agree on the limits of their areas of concentration and the course of the boundary between them. The type of situation which exists in frontier areas has been aptly described by Peattie:

When the world was less thickly populated there were waste spaces between settlements. The space between was only vaguely claimed if at all . . . . The hunting ground between one settlement and the next is a common. Such were also the forested areas between clearings in the feudal days of the early middle ages in northern Europe. As populations increased and the outer zones of the fiefs or groups of fiefs came to overlap each other the forests were designated as marks or marches, areas of defence. As the marches became populated, the fence markings or enclosure markers of the administrative units were moved outward until a common boundary line between the two expanding countries was established.[1]

Other scholars have also recognized the evolutionary nature of boundaries. Thus, Whebell identified the following stages: (i) establishment of a core—and *ipso facto*, (ii) existence of frontiers of separation between cores. Through expansion from the cores . . . these frontiers become (iii) frontiers of contact and the rationalisation of conflicting or overlapping jurisdiction requires (iv) establishment of formal boundaries.[2]

The essence of the foregoing is that the following stages can be recognized in the evolution of a boundary between two communities: (i) *Expansion stage* when both communities spread out from their bases or what Whebell styled core areas; (ii) *Contact Stage* when people from both communities come against hinderances to their expansion at various points within the frontier area; (iii) *Stabilisation Stage* when people from opposite communities lay claim to territory and attempt to prevent encroachment into that terrtiory by those from the other side; (iv) *Allocation Stage* when adjacent members of the two communities agree on a boundary between themselves; (v) *Delimitation Stage* at which there is a discussion, description and acceptance of the course of a boundary between the two communities; (vi) *Demarcation Stage* when the boundary is traced on the landscape, surveyed and marked with pillars or in other suitable manner; (vii) *Administration Stage* when the boundary is periodically supervised to ensure that it is not overgrown by vegetation and also that the boundary marks are not damaged or removed. The development of each of these stages is further explained below.

EXPANSION STAGE

It can be assumed that in the early stages of territorial partitioning each community is engaged in one of the primary occupations of gathering, hunting, herding or farming. In such a situation the zone immediately surrounding each base would be devoted to cultivation or intensive grazing and may be surrounded by a protective rampart. Such an inner zone would normally be divided amongst the major sub-groups or families of the community. Beyond the farming zone there would be the gathering zone where forest products are collected. Although some hunting may be done in the gathering zone the main hunting grounds would be beyond it, that is, in the outer zone (Fig.1).

As the population increases at each centre there would be need for more land for each of the major activities. Consequently, the farmland would extend into the initial gathering zone. In order to replace what has been lost to farming and also to satisfy the larger population, the gatherers would take up adjacent areas of the hunting zone. The overall population increase would lead to growth in the number of hunters who would have to go farther than before. In this way each community would continue expanding its areas of operation in all directions until its members are prevented from doing so by a physical impediment or contact with members of other communities. It would appear that it is this stage of boundary evolution that Brigham described as the tribal stage.[3]

In real life expansion from the base or settlement is influenced by knowledge of the position of other communities and the tendency is to expand more in the direction away from those other communities. The direction of expansion is usually that which the migrants believe to be unoccupied. As Goblet rightly notes:

People are attracted by and move towards regions of gentle relief and fertile soil or those in which the sparse and backward population will offer little resistance; and these people will advance until they encounter geographical or human forces which are too powerful to be overcome by their own force of expansion.[4]

It is difficult to find an example of on-going expansion which illustrates the above points. But the accounts of the foundation of many communities in Western Nigeria suggest that their expansion could not have been much different from that hypothesised in the

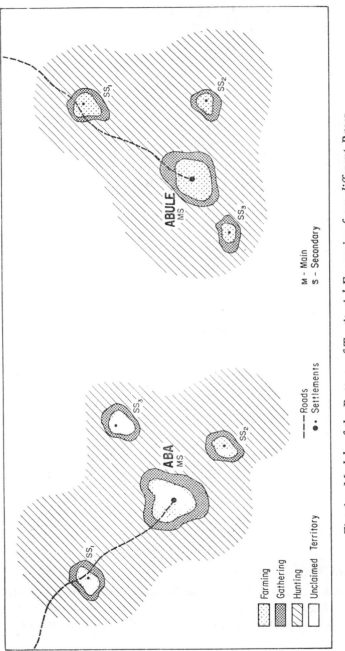

Fig. 1 Model of the Pattern of Territorial Expansion from different Bases

model. Also, there is evidence that groups of migrants tended to move away from each other. Thus in the case of the founders of Ilesa and Osogbo who started from the same base (probably at Ibokun) each side originally expanded in opposite directions. From Ibokun the group which founded Ilesa went to Ipole from where the final move to Ilesa was made.[5] The following account indicates the movement of the founders of Osogbo after they left Ibokun: '. . . they first settled at Ipole near Omu River, then at Apata Ere . . . then at Ohunto, a dry site on the meander loop of the River Osun'.[6] (Fig. 2).

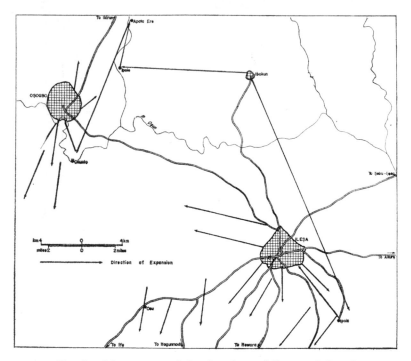

Fig. 2   Movements of the founders of Ilesa and Osogbo

CONTACT STAGE

In order to achieve maximum success, people (usually hunters) who form the vanguard of expansion would, at any stage, spread themselves out so that each of them would concentrate in one area which would be regarded as his hunting ground and in which others would not normally hunt. New arrivals would try as much as possible to avoid the hunting grounds of established hunters, and would go beyond such areas to land yet unclaimed. In this way the hunters from each community would go on expanding their areas of operation in various directions until they come in contact with physical impediments such as rivers or hills or people from another community.

When a person encounters a stream the tendency would be to avoid crossing it and move along its banks. However, later members of the same community may find it necessary to cross the stream and expand on the opposite side. Such expansion would continue until they meet members of another community. At that stage they would turn away from the advancing community to land yet unoccupied, that is the frontier, within which they would move in the same direction but roughly parallel to the major stream. This will continue until they encounter another stream, which can be called the diverting stream, at which point each side would turn towards its community along the bank of the stream. The party going towards the confluence of the major and the diverting streams would follow the bank to the confluence but the one going towards the source of the diverting stream may soon cross it and continue expanding on its opposite bank (Fig. 3).

The effect of hills is not much different from that of rivers. People would first attempt to go around a hill or cross it through cols or passes rather than ascend it. If, in the process of going around, they encounter members of another community they would turn to ascend the hill and eventually reach the crest at which place they may turn back, since they may not like to take the trouble of descending to the other side where members of the opposite community might be established already.

The hunter's contact may not lead to a boundary. In fact it would not lead to territorial claims in the first place. Its purpose is to make each side aware of the other's existence. For this reason it can be regarded as a primary contact, as distinct from those established later and which may lead to boundaries.

As the population of each community increases and the farming or intensive grazing zone encroaches more and more into the gathering and hunting zones, hunters in the frontier area may change their occupation and start farming or intensive grazing.

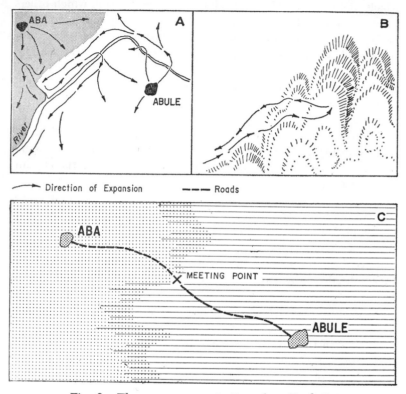

Fig. 3   *The contact stage in Boundary Evolution*

This will lead to the establishment of permanent settlements. A farmer needs less land than a hunter, hence the hunter-turned-farmer may not be able to control all the areas in which he used to hunt. Nevertheless, he will retain his knowledge of all areas known to him in his hunting days and pass this on to those from his own community who may follow him. Such knowledge will include information about hunters, from other communities, whom he has met. The latter might also have settled down and their bases may be linked with his own. The accounts given by the first arrival would make his followers believe that he controls the territory as far as the places he visited, and they may rely on him for guidance on how far they should move to settle. This will start another phase of expansion in the course of which farmers from both sides will meet. That meeting may be styled as secondary contact. So long as there is much uncultivated land for all there may be no conflict and farmers from different communities may intermix freely. This is the more so if the secondary contact occurs away from meeting points established during the primary expansion stage.

Although most communities do not have accounts of contacts with their neighbours, such contacts can be inferred from the territorial claims now being made by the various communities. The inference is possible because no community would claim an area not known to its members and in all probability none would claim less than the area actually visited by its members. Since the claims of neighbouring communities usually overlap the area of overlap can be regarded as the frontier within which they interacted and hence where they came in contact with each other. One good example of this is the contact zone between Akure and its northern neighbours (Fig. 4).

The expansion stage of the communities can be reconstructed from the territorial claims of each of them. In a definition of the boundaries of Akureland it was stated that:

> Akure is bounded on the west by the River Owena, on the south by the River Ofosu and Benin ... on the east by the River Ogbese and on the north by Igbara-Odo and Ikere.
> In the primitive age when lands were being partitioned out among the emigrants from Ile-Ife on the western side Akure had its boundary with the Owa of Ijesha, the northern side with the Ewi of Ado.[7]

From the first statement it would appear that Akures recognise Igbara-Odo and Ikere as their northern neighbours. Judging by the second paragraph it seems that in Akure's view, both towns are on land which belonged to Ado 'in the primitive age'. However, this interpretation is not supported by other definitions of the northern boundary of Akure, one of which runs as follows:

> Although there is no river to form the northern boundary of Akureland yet this is well defined. It was demarcated at two points: (a) by a rock between Igbara-Odo and Ilawe known as Ota Ekun and (b) by a large heap of stones at the market place at Ikere gathered for this purpose by the early settlers. From a point on the Oruo near its junction with the Owena in the vicinity of Ogotun and Igbara-Odo, a line drawn in a northeasterly direction through the pile of stones at Ikere referred to in (b) above to (the point where the Ikere-Ise road crosses) the Ogbese River.[8]

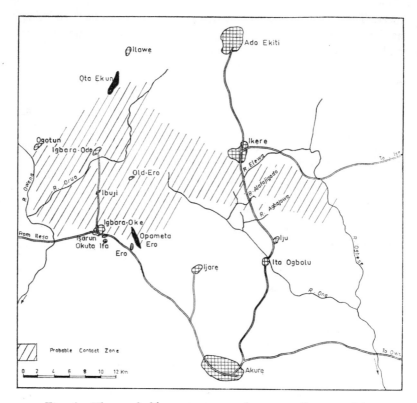

Fig. 4   *The probable contact zone between Akure and its Northern neighbours*

An alteration to this description was made when the Akures claimed that their boundary with Ogotun is at Oja-Elepo in that town.[9] One important feature of the description is that it brought Igbara-Odo within Akureland and hence it contradicted the first one which excluded Igbara-Odo from Akure's territory.

The main interest in the description is that it gives an idea of how far the Akures expanded in the early stages. Since no one would lay claim to a point he did not know, it is clear that the Akures had knowledge of the areas they claimed. Such knowledge was most probably gained from accounts given by some Akures who had been to the various places. Therefore it can be assumed that in the primary expansion stage members of the Akure community went as far as Oja-Elepo, Ota-Ekun, and the present site of Ikere. It can be further assumed that at that stage they came in contact with members of other communities to the north. Going by the statements cited above it would appear that Ado-Ekiti was the only community with whose members the Akures came in contact. If that be the case the primary expansion pre-dated the establishment, in their present locations, of some of the present towns, particularly Ikere and Igbara-Odo. This would explain the contention of the Akures that traditionally they had no boundaries with those towns. In fact it is claimed that Ikere was founded after a boundary had been established between Akure and Ado-Ekiti and on the latter's side of the boundary.[10]

According to Ogotun, their boundary with Akure is at Opa-Meta-Ero on the Akure-Ilesa road.[11] As in the case of Akure it can be assumed that the Ogotun claims indicate the farthest points reached by their members before they came in contact with the Akures during the primary expansion stage.

The Igbara-Odos claim that their boundary with Akure is at Okuta-Ifa between Isarun and Igbara-Oke.[12] Again this indicates that they went as far as that point before establishing contact with Akure.

The Ikeres have no definite claim as to their boundary with Akure. Nevertheless, they have occupied land between their town and Iju, Ita-Ogbolu and Ijare which are all in Akureland.

The claims indicate that there was an area known to the Akures as well as to their neighbours to the north. It cannot be doubted that the Akures interacted with members of those communities within the frontier zone. None of the communities claimed exclusive use of all areas known to it. Therefore they did not object to members of the opposite community settling on parts of the area. Thus Akure raised no objection to the founding of Igbara-Odo, south of Ota-Ekun and on part of the territory known to its members, and neither did they oppose the expansion of Ikere beyond the heap of stones as far as which they went. On their part Ogotun did not oppose Akure occupation and establishment of settlements (at Isarun, Ibuji and Old Ero) west of Opa-Meta-Ero as far as which the Ogotuns went. Similarly Igbara-Odo did not object to the establishment of Old Ero and Ibuji north of Okuta-Ifa. All this indicates that there was no established boundary between Akure and her northern neighbours within or outside the frontier area. Furthermore it shows that neither the Akures nor any of their northern neighbours attempted to claim specific territory in the early days. If they had done so they would have exercised ownership rights by demanding *isakole* (land rent) from later occupants of the territory so claimed.

The lack of any specific boundary within contact zones or frontier areas is not limited to the above example. It can be demonstrated in such zones between any two communities in Western Nigeria and possibly anywhere. However, as land, or any other resources, becomes scarcer there will be need for each side to lay exclusive rights over particular territories. Thus the stabilisation stage will be reached.

STABILISATION STAGE

As the number of people within the frontier increases, land for further expansion will become scarcer. Therefore, individuals will concentrate their activities on very small areas from which they will attempt to exclude others. Usually the boundaries of the areas so claimed are not defined, hence others may encroach on the outer edges. The attempts to exclude others from particular areas will lead to the diminution of the zone of interaction established in the contact stage. Sometimes the exclusion may be sought as a way of reserving exclusive rights over some natural resource (timber, minerals or fruit trees). More commonly, however, stabilisation takes place as a result of direct contact between farmers and the subsequent scramble over farmlands. When farmers from opposite communities first come into contact they do not make specific claims over territory because there is still enough land to satisfy everyone. But as land becomes scarce each side attempts to lay exclusive claim over parts of the farmlands and this leads to stabilisation. Very often the claims of one side are challenged by the other side which tries to prove that it, too, has rights over all or parts of the territory being claimed by the opponent. For this reason the stabilisation stage is characterised by disputes over territory. The stabilisation stage is the period during which the position of the boundary is being suggested and challenged. It is therefore similar to the transition stage of Brigham[13] and the outline or sketch stage of Lapredelle.[14]

A very good example of the stabilisation stage is that on the Aiyede/Orin boundary in Ekiti. Aiyede and Orin had known of each other's existence for a long time and had been expanding their farmlands in the frontier between them. However, they did not achieve secondary contact until after 1960 when the government acquired a part of Orin's farmlands for a Farm Settlement. All those previously farming on the acquired territory were evicted and had to seek new farmlands. They turned towards the greatly diminished frontier between them and their neighbours and in the process came in contact with Aiyede farmers. Because unfarmed spaces were scarce each tried to claim exclusive right of whatever space remained. The following account[15] gives an idea of the claims of both sides (Fig. 5).

The first plot, on part of which there were some old cocoa trees, was surrounded in the west and south by cocoa plots owned by Aiyede farmers. The Aiyede claimant said he cleared the area and planted cocoa there in about 1959 but did not take care of the cocoa until 1966, at which time he was challenged by Orin farmers. The Orin claimants stated that they cleared the plot and planted cocoa there in about 1960/61 and again in 1965 when they also planted another lot of cocoa, but that the latter were uprooted by Aiyede farmers. In reply the Aiyede claimant said it was the Orin farmers who uprooted his cocoa in order to plant their own.

The only evidence of cultivation on the second plot were some stands of plantain belonging to an Orin farmer. The Aiyede claimant owned the adjacent plot on which he had cocoa. He objected to the Orin people's attempt to clear land which he intended to use in the future.

The third plot carried some cocoa which both sides claimed to have planted at about the same time, in 1961. The plot lay between the established cocoa farms of the two claimants and each had witnesses from his community supporting his claim. The fourth plot carried some fairly old cocoa trees and also some younger ones in addition to plantains. It was stated that an Aiyede man planted cocoa on the plot in 1960, whilst an Orin man said that although he cleared the area in 1960 he did not plant plantain on it until about 1963 and cocoa in about 1963. These accounts would explain the presence of cocoa of different ages on the plot.

An Orin farmer uprooted cocoa trees on the fifth plot because, according to him, the land belonged to his ancestors and he had not given permission to anyone to plant cocoa there. The cocoa in question was planted by Aiyede farmers and formed part of a

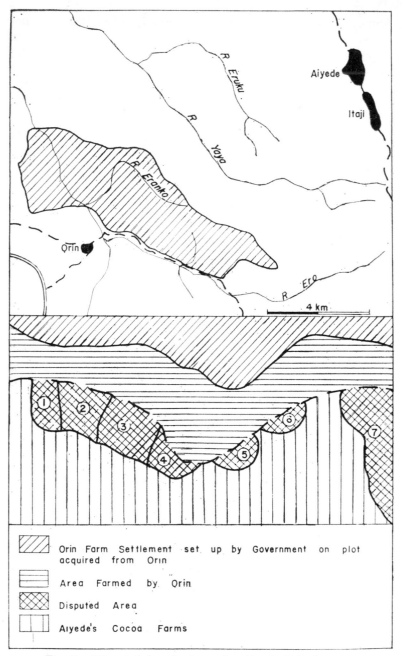

Fig. 5   Disputed farmlands on the Aiyede-Orin frontier

larger cocoa farm. When the cocoa was planted no one challenged their rights to the plot.

Complaints about the sixth plot arose when labourers, engaged by an Orin farmer to clear uncropped land, extended their work to a part of an existing cocoa plot belonging to an Aiyede farmer. The latter feared that the Orin man was planning to take over his cocoa and so protested. However, the Orin man explained that he had no intention of challenging anyone's right to the plot and that the clearing was done by mistake.

An Aiyede farmer with a cocoa plot nearby had previously cultivated the seventh plot, and left it fallow without planting any permanent crops on it. An Orin farmer then came there and established a farm on it.

This example shows very well the type of situation which develops when contact is established by those making intensive use of the land. Obviously the various claims and counter-claims represented an attempt to exclude others from the given territory and therefore to stabilise territorial claims. Evidently the only way of avoiding clashes as described above is to have a mutually agreed boundary. Such a step may lead to boundary agreement between individuals and the other later stages of boundary evolution.

ALLOCATION STAGE

In order to resolve disputes arising from conflicting claims to territory, adjacent farmers or villages may agree on boundaries between their respective farmlands. The agreements would be recognised only by the farmers or villages concerned. There will be no agreement on a boundary in places where farmers are not in contact or in those areas where there is still enough land for all to use. The boundary agreement may be made possible by the intervention of an arbitrator acceptable to both parties. In either case the main feature of the allocation stage is that it applies only to small sections of the boundary and the agreed sections are separated by others where no decision has been reached on the boundary. Indeed, sometimes allocation may be a simple statement as to the rights of each party to territory on either side of an agreed point, the details of the boundary being left to a later stage. The allocation and other stages of boundary evolution have been previously recognised by Jones.[16]

An example of the allocation stage is that of the Ibadans and the Ijebus on their common boundary. Ibadan did not develop into an important centre until the mid-nineteenth century. Up to that time it was part of the Oyo kingdom with which the Ijebus allegedly shared a common traditional boundary. The Ijebus claimed that their territory used to extend to parts of the present city of Ibadan.[17] However, since the latter became important in the nineteenth century its citizens had extended southwards and established settlements. By the close of that century they had founded Olubi on the Ijebu-Ode–Ibadan road and Araromi on the Ijebu-Igbo–Ibadan road and were extending south of Araromi towards Ijebu-Igbo.[18] The Ijebus had also expanded towards Ibadan and by the close of the nineteenth century had founded Abeku and, by 1906, Dagbolu and other settlements around the Ijebu-Igbo–Ibadan road[19] (Fig. 6).

The effect of this pattern of occupation was that the Ijebus could no longer insist on a boundary passing through Ibadan. Instead they accepted a suggestion, made in 1897, that the boundary should pass through River Mamu near Olubi.[20] The course of the boundary east of Mamu was left till a later date. Although attempts were made in 1908, 1911 and 1915 to determine its exact location the boundary was not satisfactorily delimited until after 1924.

The first attempt to determine the exact course of the boundary was made in 1908 when both communities agreed that Apata Olowe on the Ijebu-Igbo–Ibadan road should be on the boundary which was then defined as:

> Mamu to a point on the Ijebu-Igbo-Ibadan road 7° 11½'N marked by very large granite boulder (Apata-Olowe). From this point south east to the junction of the Osun and Alaguntan Rivers.[21]

This agreement was communicated to the Governor for ratification, but he did not approve it because of objections from the Ibadans who argued that the boundary was unfair to them in that it grouped Araromi, a recognised Ibadan settlement, with the Ijebus.[22] In addition they pointed out that Ibadan farms extended southwards for up to four miles (6.5 km) from Apata-Olowe to areas south of Araromi.

The non-approval of Apata-Olowe as a point on the boundary meant that the only agreed point was Mamu and the government assumed that the boundary should be along a straight line due directly east of Mamu. An attempt was made in 1911 to implement this by demarcating a boundary along the line.[23] The Ijebus objected to this on the grounds that some of their settlements, such as Dagbolu and those in the River Apasan area, were grouped with Ibadan; and also presumably because it gave more of the unoccupied land to Ibadan, thereby depriving the Ijebus of room for further expansion.

In an attempt to find a solution to the problem the Olubadan suggested in 1915 that the boundary should pass through Igikola instead of Apata-Olowe because 'the whole land from Olowe to Igikola was farmed wholly by people from Ibadan'.[24] It would appear that the proposal was made without adequate consultation with the Ibadan farmers in the area because the suggested boundary would have grouped Araromi and other Ibadan settlements with Ijebu. That such a grouping would have been unacceptable to the Ibadans is shown by the fact that when he realised its implications the Olubadan denied making the proposal.[25] Also the demand of the Ibadan farmers in the area differed considerably from that in the proposal—they suggested that the boundary should pass from Onija-Erin farm near River Osun to Esudeyi and Erikorodo.[26] They later claimed Budo-Epo near the Osun River. These latter suggestions were rejected by the Ijebus. The lack of agreement on the boundary led to serious disturbances in the area, with Ijebus attacking Ibadans, particularly between 1916 and 1923. In order to prevent further disturbances the Residents for the two areas met at Mamu in June 1924 and recommended that the boundary should run:

> From the survey pillar S.E.S. 208 on the Ijebu-Ode–Ibadan road south of Olubi in a straight line to its intersection with the River Omi. The Omi in a northerly direction as far as its confluence with Alafara and from that junction the Alafara to its source. From the source of Alafara straight line to River Osun at the point opposite to that at which the River Alaguntan flows into it.[27]

The Ijebus rejected this suggestion because it fell short of that of 1908 which they wanted. Because of that rejection the matter was referred to arbitration. The resulting recommendation, which both sides accepted, was that the boundary should be along a line,

> Commencing at a point on the Ijebu-Ode–Ibadan road half a mile north of Mamu due east to the intersection with the Omi

River. Thence along the left bank of the Omi in a northerly direction to its intersection with River Apasan. Thence along the left bank of the Apasan in an easterly direction to its intersection with the Alafara River. Thence along the left bank of the Alafara to its source, 1,400 ft northwest of Ajayi village. Thence by a line due east to the River Osun[28] (Fig. 6).

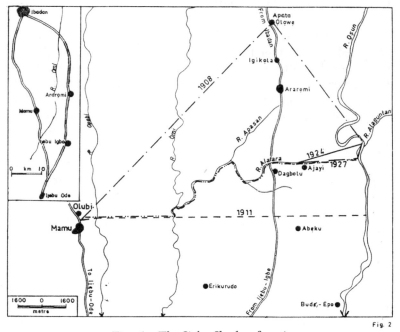

Fig. 6   The Ijebu-Ibadan frontier

The disputes over the course of the Ibadan/Ijebu boundary indicate the limitations of the allocation stage in boundary development. Although both sides accepted Mamu there was still disagreement as to where the boundary should be fixed.

The allocation stage is not always restricted to agreement on points. It could involve determination of long stretches of the boundary between adjacent settlements or members of the two communities.

DELIMITATION STAGE

One main difference between the allocation and delimitation stages is that the latter usually involves the full length of the boundary, as against sections of it, agreed upon during the allocation stage.

The aim during the delimitation stage is to reach agreement on the location of the boundary in areas where none was reached in the allocation stage and also in other areas. However, if delimitation is carried out by an arbitrator such as a government official, rather than by a meeting and agreement of the two communities, or if the communities fail to involve the people in the different sectors of the frontier area in discussions leading to boundary delimitation, it is quite possible for the delimited boundary to overlook agreements reached during the allocation stage. In that case the delimited boundary might be rejected by those who lose territory because of the oversight.

Boundary delimitation started in Western Nigeria when British colonial officials wanted to know the limits of each indigenous kingdom so that they could determine the areas of jurisdiction of District Officers and other functionaries of the colonial regime. The negotiations concerning the boundaries were conducted through the District Officers who usually delimited the boundaries.

An example of a boundary delimited in this way is that between the Ijebu and Ife Divisions. In 1927 the government defined this boundary as the intersection of the Isoya–Atikori road and River Sasa and 'thence northward along Isoya–Atikori road to its intersection with the Opa River, then in a southeasterly direction down the River Opa to its confluence with River Oni'[29] (Fig. 7A). This boundary was based on wrong information that the River Opa (or Olopa) is a tributary of the River Oni, while, in fact, that river flows into the Sasa. That mistake apart, the boundary was rejected by the Ifes on the grounds that it cut off to the Ijebu side some Ife villages, the most notable being Abeku, where the Oni, Ademiluyi, who was then on the Ife throne, claimed to have lived before he became *oba*.[30] On the other hand, the Ijebus claimed that their boundary with Ife was along 'the intersection of River Sasa and the Atikori–Isoya path northward along the path to its intersection with River Opa and up that river to its source and then in a straight line to a point called Ojuho on the River Oni'.[31] After many attempts a new boundary, to which both sides expressed no opposition, was defined in 1931 as:

> the intersection of the Ibadan/Ijebu boundary with the Sasa and thence along the Sasa to its confluence with Owena, thence along the Owena to its intersection with the Laoke–Oke-Igbo path at Aiyetoro, thence by this path in a south and easterly direction

passing through Abeku, Fowoseje, Obutu (or Jagun), Molafara and Olomo to its intersection with River Oni[32] (Fig. 7).

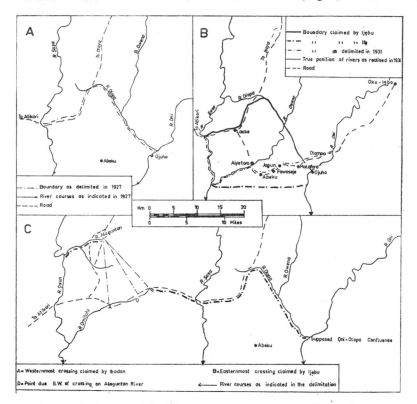

Fig. 7 Evolution of the Northeastern Boundary of Ijebu Province

Delimitation, in that it is the stage at which the course of the boundary is fixed, is a very important stage in boundary evolution. A good delimitation will resolve existing disputes over the boundary and ensure that others do not occur in the future. To achieve that objective the course of the delimited boundary must be discussed with, and agreed to, by the parties concerned. In addition both sides must have a clear idea of the location of the delimited boundary. This requires that prior to the final delimitation there should be a detailed survey of the borderlands through which the boundary is to pass so that the pattern of occupance by the parties concerned and the positions of the natural features there are accurately located.

DEMARCATION STAGE

After a boundary has been delimited it is necessary to trace it on the ground and fix suitable boundary marks. After this, members of the two communities should have no difficulty in identifying the boundary and in limiting their movements accordingly. It is the process of doing this that is called demarcation.

Very often the demarcating team may experience difficulty with the interpretation of the boundary definition. This may be due to ambiguity in the definition or the adoption of non-existent features as reference points. Such problems are referred to the communities so that they can clarify the situation and if necessary agree on a re-definition of that section of the boundary. When the boundary has been demarcated, a final definition of it will be prepared, incorporating any alterations to the delimitation agreement made during the demarcation stage as well as references to boundary marks and the direction of the boundary from them. The post-demarcation definition represents the final and binding version of the boundary.

In modern times boundary demarcation requires the use of sophisticated survey equipment for locating directions and measuring distances. For this reason the demarcation stage is usually left to surveyors. The types of alteration (to the delimited boundary) occurring during demarcation may be illustrated with the example of the northern boundaries of Ijebu Division east of River Osun. In 1927 it was defined as the intersection of the Ibadan/Ijebu boundary with River Osun and:

> Thence downstream along Osun River to its junction with Alaguntan River, to its intersection with Apomu–Atikori road, thence in a south-southeast direction to the Omitutu crossing on the Isoya–Atikori road, thence along this road in an easterly direction crossing the River Shasha [Sasa], thence northward along this road to its intersection with the Opa River, thence in a southeast direction down the Opa River to its confluence with Oni River[33] (Fig. 7C).

During the demarcation of the boundary in 1928 the following problems arose:[34]

(1) that there were new and old Apomu–Atikori roads;
(2) that the position of Omitutu crossing on the Isoya–Atikori road was not clear;
(3) that the confluence of the Rivers Opa and Oni does not exist anywhere.

The first of these problems was resolved by seeking clarification on which of the two roads was intended. It was explained that the boundary should follow the old Apomu–Atikori road. The second problem was not easily solved because the two communities concerned did not agree on Omitutu crossing on the Isoya–Atikori road. Actually the road crosses the river three times but none of these was exactly south-southeast from the intersection of the Alaguntan stream with the Apomu–Atikori road (Fig. 7C). The Ijebus claimed that the easternmost crossing, which gave them more land, was intended in the description, whilst the Ibadans insisted that the westernmost crossing was the one intended. During the demarcation of the boundary it became known that the River Opa was not a tributary of the River Oni, but of the River Sasa (Fig. 7B). This meant that the Opa-Oni confluence did not exist anywhere and made a new definition of that section of the boundary necessary.

ADMINISTRATION STAGE

In order to avoid trespass across the boundary by either side, it is necessary to keep it from being overgrown with vegetation. To this end arrangements are made for clearing it regularly and for ensuring that the boundary marks are in good order. This process of maintenance and supervision is termed the administration stage.

Most demarcated boundaries are not administered as such. Reliance is placed on the acceptance of the boundary by both sides and it is assumed that neither side would want to remove the boundary marks. In a few cases, however, the boundary is maintained and cleared every year. This is usually the case where demarcation followed fierce dispute, the recurrence of which both sides wish to avoid.

IMPLICATIONS OF THE MODEL

One important implication of the boundary evolution model described above is that disputes over boundaries will tend to occur at the stabilisation stage and also as a result of poor delimitation. The model implies that boundaries evolve over a period of time and are not usually fixed before there is effective occupation of the frontier areas.

The evolutionary approach is different from the conceptions of most Yoruba communities in Western Nigeria on how their boundaries emerged.[35] The common ideas on how boundaries were fixed and the way they have developed in recent times in Western Nigeria are considered in the next chapter.

Notes and References

1. R. Peattie, *Look to the Frontiers: A Geography for the Peace Table* (New York and London: Harper Brothers, 1944), pp. 57–8.
2. C. F. J. Whebell, 'Core Areas in Intrastate Political Organisation', *Canadian Geographer*, Vol. XII, (1968), pp. 99–112 (especially pp. 99–101).
3. A. P. Brigham, 'Principles in the Delimitation of Boundaries', *Geographical Review*, Vol. 7, (1919), pp. 201–19 (especially pp. 201–2).
4. Y. M. Goblet, *Political Geography and the World Map* (New York: Frederick A. Praeger, 1955), p. 165.
5. G. O. Ekemode, Lecturer in History, University of Ife, August 1968.
6. A. Oloyede, 'Rural-Urban Relationships of Odo Otin and Oshogbo', B. A. Essay, Geog. Dept., University of Ife, 1969, p. 6.
7. Deji of Akure to District Officer (D. O.), Ekiti, 5 April 1927.
8. L. Adegbola, Memorandum on Akure-Idanre Land Dispute, File AK. NA. 234/1, AKDIVCO 2, National Archives, Ibadan (further cited as N.A.I.).
9. Notes on Akure–Ogotun Boundary Reconciliation Meeting held in Ogotun on 11 January 1950, File LR 22/1, AKDIVCO 4, N.A.I.
10. Information collected at Akure, August 1969.
11. Notes on Akure–Ogotun Boundary Reconciliation Meeting held in Ogotun on 11 January 1950, File LR 22/1, AKDIVCO 4, N.A.I.
12. Information collected during fieldwork in July 1969.
13. A. P. Brigham, op. cit.
14. P. de Lapradelle, *La Frontiere* (Paris, 1928), cited by J.R.V. Prescott, *The Geography of Frontiers and Boundaries* (London: Hutchinson, 1965), p. 64.
15. Reports of investigation by Mr. S. A. Akerele of Aiyede and Mr. J. O. Ajibola of Orin into the clash between Aiyede and Orin Farmers at Egan, September 1966.
16. S. B. Jones, *Boundary-Making: A Handbook for Statesmen, Treaty Editors and Boundary Commissioners* (Washington: Carnegie Endowment for International Peace, 1945), p. 5.
17. Summary of Papers on the Ibadan-Ijebu Boundary, 4 August 1923, File 815 Vol. I, Oyo Prof. 3, N.A.I.
18. File 815 Vol. I, Oyo Prof. 3, N.A.I.
19. File 1725A Vol. I, Ijebu Prof. I, N.A.I.
20. Ibid.

21. File J 27/1923 Vol. II, Ijebu Prof. 6/6, N.A.I.
22. File 1725A Vol. I, Ijebu Prof. I, N.A.I.
23. File J 27/1923 Vol. II, Ijebu Prof. 6/6, N.A.I.
24. File J 51/1920, Ijebu Prof. 6/3, N.A.I.
25. File J 27/1923, Ijebu Prof. 6/5, N.A.I.
26. File 1725 Vol. I, Ijebu Prof. I, N.A.I.
27. File 815 Vol. I, Oyo Prof. 3, N.A.I.
28. Ibid.
29. Gazette Notice on the Northern Boundary of Ijebu Province, 3 March 1927.
30. Oni of Ife to D. O., Oyo, 2 February 1927, File 07839, Vol. I, Oyo Prof. 3, N.A.I.
31. Joint Report on Ife-Ijebu Boundary by Acting D. O., Ife, and D. O., Ijebu-Ode, May 1928, File 07839 Vol. I, Oyo Prof. 3, N.A.I.
32. Gazette Notice on the Northern Boundary of Ijebu Province, May 1931.
33. Gazette Notice on Northern Boundaries of Ijebu Province, 3 March 1927.
34. File 815 Vol. II, Oyo Prof. 3, N. A.I.
35. See, for example, the statement of Akure on how they arrived at the boundaries they now claim, cited above in Deji of Akure to District Officer, Ado Ekiti, 5 April 1927.

Chapter II

Development of Boundaries in Western Nigeria

ONE IMPORTANT feature of Western Nigeria is its organisation into political, landowning units each of which is under an *oba*. The indigenous political unit consisted of a metropolitan and many subordinate settlements. The usual account is that the metropolitan town and its settlements belong to one community, owing its origin to a single migration from Ile-Ife and under a leader, usually presumed to be a child of Oduduwa. What is important for the present topic is how the community acquired rights over the territory it now claims and the development of its boundaries.

Most communities claim that their territories were allocated to them by Oduduwa who also fixed the boundaries.[1] This implies that Oduduwa sent out his children or followers to specific areas of which he had previous knowledge. It seems highly improbable that Oduduwa knew the details of all parts of Yorubaland. Therefore he could not have allocated territories and fixed boundaries for those who left Ile-Ife. This view is supported by the fact that the history of each community makes it clear that the founding group came to the present location by chance rather than by design. For example, the founders of Ilesa were said to have wandered about before finally settling down at the present site,[2] so also did those of Akure,[3] Osogbo,[4] Apomu[5] and many other towns. Such wandering shows that the founding group had no prior knowledge of the places which they were to occupy. Moreover, if a specific territory had once been allocated to the founding group, details of its boundaries would have been passed down and therefore would be known by the present leaders or other people. However, information collected by the present writer shows that no one knows the details of the boundaries of each community. The *oba* himself relies on

25

information supplied by citizens living or farming in the various sectors and such people know only the details of their own particular areas.[6] This indicates that the boundaries were not clearly defined at any time in the past, and in any case, Oduduwa could not have fixed them when the areas were first occupied by migrants from Ile-Ife.

Accepting that each community was established by a group of migrants under one leader, it can be assumed that the members founded a main settlement, where the leader and the greater part of the group lived, and also some subsidiary settlements. The latter could have developed in one of three ways. First, subsidiary settlements could have arisen in places where the group stopped for some time in the course of its migration from the source region to the main settlement. If some members of the group chose to stay permanently at a stopping place then a settlement would develop and the whole group could claim it and the areas occupied by the people there. Second are those arising as a result of war. If the people in the main settlement were forced to flee from it during a war and they stayed temporarily in another place the community would claim the new place and other places near it which might have been occupied by those left there at the end of the emergency when the main body of the group returned to the main base. Third are settlements established by individuals leaving the main settlement either in search of better game or better farmland. The territory of the community would therefore consist of areas occupied by its members in their various settlements. At the early stages the main and the subsidiary settlements would be close to one another in order to facilitate contact between them.

BOUNDARY DEVELOPMENT

At the early stages the various centres of a community would be separated by some unoccupied areas whilst the operating zones of neighbouring communities would be separated by vast expanses of territory unclaimed by anyone. As the population increases each centre and the whole community would need more land and would therefore expand into the unoccupied areas between their settlements. The effect of the general expansion is that the unoccupied areas between the various centres of a community would come under effective use and the only room for expansion would be the frontier between neighbouring communities. Expansion into the frontier would lead to its diminution so that people from neighbouring communities would come into contact and eventually each side would attempt to lay exclusive claim to particular areas. When contact has been established, common meeting points between the nearest members of the different communities would become recognised. Such points could be places where hunters meet, riversides from which both sides draw water, hilltops at which each side usually returns to its base. The points could also be those at which each ends the maintenance of the path or road linking the two sides. The recognised meeting points may be marked by the planting there of special trees such as *peregun* (*Dracaena manii*) or akoko (*Newbouldia laevis*). The series of such points would be cited as the limits of their territories by the communities.

Until the end of the nineteenth century the population of most communities in Western Nigeria was not large and it was concentrated within a few kilometres of the headquarters in which the *oba* resided. Therefore there were still extensive frontier areas within which hunters interacted without making exclusive claim to territory. In other words, boundary evolution was still at the contact stage at the time colonial administration started in the late nineteenth century.

The activities of the colonial government and other British interests encouraged the early onset of the stabilisation stage of boundary development in the region. The most important of these was the attempt to exploit the natural resources, particularly timber. This made it necessary to determine the community to which royalties on the resources should be paid. The community which granted rights for the exploitation of resources in an area usually asserted that it had exclusive claims on the territory and that it should retain all the royalties. Very often the claims were challenged by the other side which would also assert its own rights over the same territory. In attempting to settle such disputes government officials made enquiries about the position of the traditional boundaries. On the basis of information collected, they allocated territories between adjacent communities and later on delimited or demarcated the boundaries. Another factor which encouraged the onset of the stabilisation stage in the evolution of boundaries in Western Nigeria was the introduction of the system of Indirect Rule by the colonial government. The system made it necessary to delimit the area under each *oba*. This area was then constituted into a Native Authority.

The delimitation involved inquiries about the boundaries, an exercise which made many communities challenge the claims of their neighbours to exclusive rights over parts or the whole of their common frontier. The boundaries established as a result of such inquiries were sometimes defined in written agreements, signed by both sides, and later demarcated.

The foregoing discussion shows that formal boundaries in the form of continuous lines bounding a territory did not develop until the establishment of the colonial administration in Western Nigeria. Many factors influenced the analysis of the information collected by colonial officials on boundary development in pre-colonial times and also the boundaries subsequently fixed by them. Notable among these factors were:

  (i) the policy of the government to keep people owing allegiance to a kingdom or an *oba* within the same local administrative unit or Native Authority area;
 (ii) the insistence of each comunity on the maintenance of alleged traditional boundaries;
(iii) the characteristics of traditional territorial limits;
(iv) the decision of government officials to use easily identifiable features such as rivers, footpaths and hills as boundaries;
 (v) the lack of good maps and detailed surveys.

KEEPING OLD LOYALTIES

One of the basic government policies in the delimitation of local administrative units in Western Nigeria was the keeping in one unit of people owing allegiance to a kingdom or an *oba*. This was stated in 1913 during discussions of the boundaries of Ilesa District:

> All District boundaries should be made as far as possible to include all the people in each District irrespective of the fact that they might be in occupation of land which in some former time might have belonged to some other District.[7]

Because of this policy many local administrative units or Native Authorities were based on the pre-colonial political units. Throughout the colonial period the government upheld the rights of the suzerain power over any settlement. For example, it decided in 1923 not to transfer Ifewara from Ijesa to Ife and later to keep Araromi with Ijesa rather than Ife. In both cases the reason was that the area concerned was under Ijesa just prior to the arrival of the British. The same principle was applied much earlier on in grouping the present Osun Divisions with Ibadan rather than with the areas from which the founders of the various settlements originated.

INSISTENCE ON PRE-COLONIAL TERRITORIAL CLAIMS

The policy of the government mentioned above coincided with the wishes of most people except in those cases where there was disagreement as to the limits of a district. As shown above there were no boundaries as now conceived in pre-colonial days, hence the attempt by the colonial administration to fix boundaries in a given place often conflicted with the declared interests of one or both of the parties to the boundary. The causes of the conflict were twofold:

(a) disagreement as to the actual point being claimed,

(b) the course of the boundary between the claimed points.

Very frequently the two sides to a boundary did not agree on the points between them which used to mark the limit of their authority. Thus on their northern boundary the Akures claim Oja-Elepo and Ota-Ekun while the Ogotuns, one of the communities to the north of Akure, claim Opa-Meta-Ero on the Akure–Ilesa[9] road and Igbara-Odo claims Okuta-Ifa near Igbara-Oke [10] (Fig.4). There is also disagreement on the points claimed by both sides on the Akure/Idanre boundary, the Ife/Ijebu boundary, the Oyo/Ogbomoso boundary and the Iwo/Ejigbo boundary, to name only a few.

These differences affected boundary evolution in that following complaints about any boundary delimited by the administration, there were re-considerations leading to long negotiations as to the location of a satisfactory boundary. Even after such negotiations, the eventual boundary may be rejected by one or both sides. Thus the Ife/Ijesa boundary, which was first demarcated in 1901, had to be changed in 1913 because of objections from Ilesa, and the one delimited in 1913 had to be changed in 1932 after long negotiations following objections by Ife. Although the agreement setting out details of the 1932 boundary was signed by both parties, the Ijesas have since rejected that boundary.[11] The Akure/Idanre boundary was discussed over many years, starting in 1912. After the District Officers had failed to set an acceptable boundary, the matter was taken to court in 1939 and a judgment rendered in 1943. In spite

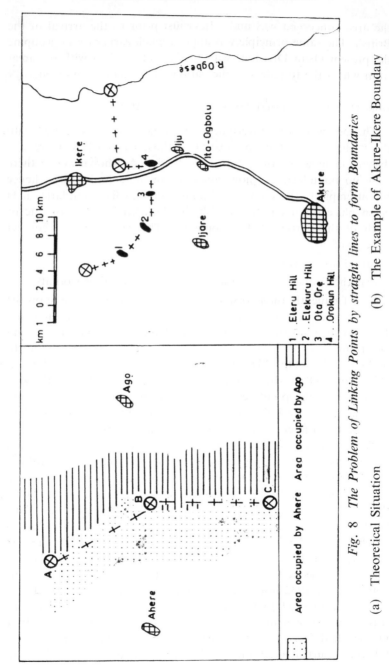

Fig. 8 *The Problem of Linking Points by straight lines to form Boundaries*

(a) Theoretical Situation   (b) The Example of Akure-Ikere Boundary

of that, it has been impossible to clearly demarcate the boundary between the two communities.[12] All these cases and many others like them suggest that the long negotiations preceding boundary delimitation were due to the claims, or at least the perceptions, by both sides with regard to the pre-colonial territorial limits.

THE CHARACTERISTICS OF PRE-COLONIAL TERRITORIAL LIMITS

Quite apart from the insistence of communities on particular points, the evolution of political boundaries has been affected by the characteristics of the pre-colonial 'boundaries'. The most notable of these is the difficulty of linking the points claimed. This may be illustrated graphically as in Fig. 8A where points A,B and C may be generally agreed upon by both Ahere and Ago. As explained earlier there is no agreement on the course of the boundary between the various points. However, the interpretation normally given, since the attempt to delimit formal boundaries, is that the boundary should be straight lines joining the agreed points. While this interpretation may accord well with the definition of a boundary as a line joining known points, it could also lead to dispute in that it is possible for people in the intervening area, between, for example, points B and C, not to be aware of designated points some distance away from them and they may therefore cross over from their own side of the straight line BC and settle on the other side without meeting any opposition. With the introduction of a formal boundary, people from Ago who had crossed to the Ahere side of line BC would be accused of trespass and asked to withdraw or pay *isakole*. Such people would refuse and demand that the boundary be drawn in such a way as to include not only the areas they effectively occupy, but also other areas on the Ago side. Such conflicting claims would make it difficult to determine a boundary between the two sides. A good example of this is the development of the Akure/Ikere boundary. Following arbitration, both sides agreed to accept a boundary linking a number of points: (i) on Eleru hill, (ii) on Elekuru hill, (iii) on Ota-Ore, (iv) on Iju-Ikere road, (v) on Orokun hill[13] (Fig.8B). After the boundary was demarcated it was found that it did not prevent disputes between the two communities but that Akure complained that the members of their community on the Ikere side were being molested. Consequently the agreed boundary was rejected.[14]

USE OF EASILY IDENTIFIABLE FEATURES

Arising partly out of lack of definite traditional boundaries and partly out of age-old practice the world over, government sought, wherever possible, to use any easily identifiable feature as the boundary. The two most frequently used were rivers and roads and sometimes these were used in direct contradiction of the principle that people who owe loyalty to a district should be kept together. An example of this was the decision to retain the River Sasa as a boundary between Ede and Edunabon after it was known that the latter had farmed on the northern (Ede's) side of the river , and after the District Officers had taken great pains to demarcate a boundary between Ede and Edunabon in that area[15] (Fig.23). There was also the decision to use the Irele–Oniserere road (Fig.9) as a boundary between Ikale and Ondo in 1928 even though it was known that the Ikales were on the northern side of that road, which side would be under Ondo if the road were made the boundary.[16] Roads were also used in the delimitation of the Ijebu/Ibadan boundary and the Ife/Ijebu boundary (Fig.7).

The idea behind the use of roads or rivers is that both can be easily recognised by officials as well as the local people. Unfortunately, however, the use of roads could lead to confusion for two reasons. In the first place the traditional practice was to use points on roads and not the roads themselves. Each community constructed and maintained the road inside its territory and hence a road could not have been a boundary. Therefore boundaries based on roads tend to be rejected. The Ife/Ijebu boundary has not been fully accepted as there are frequent disputes as to the correct area with which the settlements along the road are to be grouped. There was a dispute in 1968 as to the Local Authority which should collect taxes at Abeku, one of the villages along the path adopted as the boundary[17] (Fig. 7B). The adoption of roads as boundaries could also create problems because there may be more than one route between two stated places, as is the case between Osu and Ede which has led to problems on the Ife/Ijesa boundary[18] (Fig. 16). Roads could also be changed in part or in whole and this would create difficulties in the interpretation of the boundary definition.

LACK OF GOOD MAPS AND DETAILED SURVEYS

Another major factor in the evolution of the present political boundaries in Western Nigeria was the lack of good maps and detailed surveys of the area through which the boundaries being delimited were to pass. Very often the officials had to depend on descriptions by the local people or by casual visitors to the area concerned who often did not know the details about every section through which the boundary passed. For instance in the delimitation of the Ife/Ijebu boundary the River Olopa was thought to join the River Oni[19] whereas the former flows into the River Sasa (Fig. 7). Of the same type is the judgment on the Akure/Idanre boundary which was defined as follows by the presiding judge:

> I have already accepted that the cairn at Alade market was set up by Major Reeve-Tucker as a boundary between the Akure and the Idanre. It is indisputable that a boundary line running through the extent of the land marked was not made and I can therefore understand the difficulty which both parties might have had if called upon to show the boundary lines, but it cannot, in my view, be disputed that an imaginary line through Alade market running west and east was intended by Major Reeve-Tucker. It appears to me that he would have stated the starting point of the boundary and where it ends if he had intended anything different.
> I hold that the northern boundary of Idanre runs from Aiyede through Alade market to where the eastern boundary of Idanre, if any, intersects the line[20] [Fig. 12].

Although it was generally agreed that the judgment was meant to uphold the Reeve-Tucker boundary there was some dispute as to the location of the one allocated by the court. Following the judge's interpretation, the Reeve-Tucker boundary ran east and west of Alade market. But the last sentence gave another line which was found, during demarcation, to be quite different from the one running east and west of Alade (Fig.13). Hence it was difficult to agree on the correct location of the boundary. It is quite obvious that such problems would have been avoided if there had been detailed maps of the area on the standard of, say, the first edition of the topographical sheets on scale 1:50,000 which are now in use. The absence of such maps delayed finalisation of many other boundaries and could therefore be regarded as an important factor in the evolution of boundaries in Western Nigeria.

THE EXAMPLE OF ONDO/IKALE BOUNDARY

To illustrate the model discussed in Chapter I and some of the problems enumerated above, the rest of this chapter will lay emphasis on the Ondo/Ikale boundary. Particular attention will be paid to the reasons given to support boundary claims by the two communities and those used to justify boundary decisions by government officials. In each case there will be an assessment of the reasons in the light of the model and other relevant facts on territorial rights and boundary development among the people of Western Nigeria.

Ikale and Ondo are two adjacent communities in the southern part of Ondo Province. The former are in Okitipupa Division whilst the latter consitute Ondo Division. The head of the Ikales is the Abodi of Ikoya, but it appears that unlike most other Yoruba dialectal groups the various Ikale settlements exercise a great deal of independence. These other towns include Akotogbo, Aye, Idepe, Igbotako and Irele[21] (Fig.9). Okitipupa was founded near Idepe which it has now absorbed. Ilutitun was established in about 1920 by some villagers of the Osoro section who decided to come together.[22] The head of the Ondos is the Osemawe, resident at Ode-Ondo (more commonly called Ondo) and their other main settlements include Ile-Oluji in the northwest and Oro, Odigbo, Imorun and Araromi on the Ondo/Ikale borderlands.

EXPANSION STAGE

Accounts of the founding of each community vary, but there is agreement on the fact that the Ondos came from the north (probably Ile-Ife) by way of Ile-Oluji. They stopped at Ile-Oluji where some of them remained whilst the others went on to found Ondo.[23] From Ondo they expanded southwards and established settlements in many places including Oro and Odigbo. The expansion was still continuing by the late nineteenth century when they founded Imorun, Araromi, Agbabu, Otugbembo and Taibo (Fig. 9).

The Ikales came from Benin [24] by way of Igbobini and founded their various settlements listed above. From there they expanded northwards and founded many other settlements among which were Mobaro, Mulekangbo, Gbelejuloda, Kinmeha and Luere (Fig. 9).

CONTACT STAGE

From various accounts it appears indisputable that hunters led the expansion from the main settlements. The first inhabitants in the Ifon area were hunters. The Ikales claim that Pele, an Ikale elephant hunter, had a cave in the Oniserere area where he used to

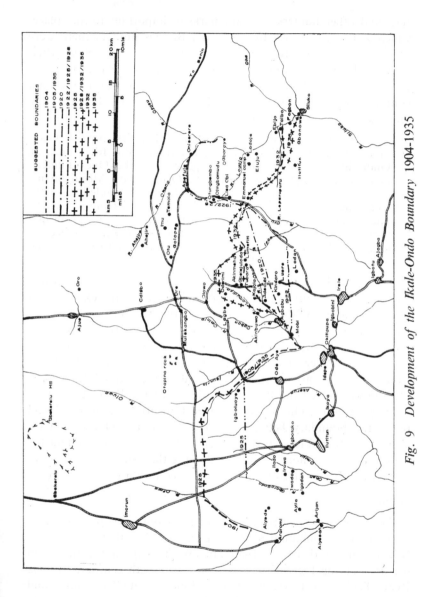

Fig. 9   Development of the Ikale-Ondo Boundary 1904-1935

rest, and other hunters had landmarks or important resting places which were well known to the Ikales. Besides hunters there were other visitors to the frontier. For example, the Ikales claim their route to Ife passed through the area and they once established a resting place at Gbekelu north of Imorun. However, the first contact between the Ondos and Ikales was established through hunters as shown by the following account:

> ... We had never heard of the Ondos. The first time we heard of them was when Monikenyin, a hunter from Idepe, met an Ondo hunter at Otakpina (a large rock). The Ondo hunter's name was Orunja. When they came Orunja gave Monikenyin a piece of meat. Monikenyin took some salt, sprinkled it on the meat and gave some of it to Orunja who asked from whence he had obtained the salt and was informed that it came from that part of the country in which he dwelt. From thence they became friends. Orunja making a path from Otakpina to Odigbo and Monikenyin one from Otakpina to Aye and on to Idepe.[25]

This primary contact took place long ago; there were also other contacts in other areas. For example, in the area of the Oluwa River the two sides established contact between the River Ore and the River Oluwa. The Ikales carried on roadworks as far as Iota's kola trees on the Ondo side of the River Oluwa whilst the Ondos had a village between the River Oluwa and the kola trees. In the east hunters from both sides interacted. For example, in the area of Otugbembo the Ondos allowed the Ikales to settle whilst the Ikales claim they gave land to those Ondos who founded Imu. River Ahejire was said to be the boundary between the Ikales and the Ondos at Oro. There was therefore a period when both communities interacted within their common frontier without either side attempting to restrict the other's use of the land or exploitation of its resources.

STABILISATION

The desire for exclusive control of the frontier or parts of it by either of the communities was not expressed until the arrival of British officials there and their attempts to exploit the timber in the area during the earlier part of the twentieth century. In 1902 Reeve-Tucker, a travelling commissioner, visited the area and remarked on the quantity and quality of its timber. Subsequently he arranged with Irele[26] for a timber concession for one Mr McNeil on 17 October 1902. The Ayes, in 1904, granted a timber concession to Mr Robert Brown on the Oluwa and Isunrin rivers.[27] Messrs

Renwick and McIver got concessions from Ondo in the area of the Ofara River.[28] Each timber exploiter paid royalties to the side from which it got the concession. These timber royalties provoked attempts by each side to exercise exclusive control over the frontier area. To that end each challenged the rights of the other to collect royalties from timber in the area.

In the area of the River Ofara in the west the Ikales challenged the rights of the Ondos to grant concessions and collect royalties. They based their challenge on the ground that the traditional boundary was at Gbekelu, a rocky outcrop north of Imorun. They claimed that the boundary was determined as a result of their previous occupation there. The occupation was made when an Abodi who was returning from Ile-Ife fell sick and he and his chiefs had to stay at Gbekelu. The Abodi died in Gbekelu and the Ikales later deserted the village they established on the spot.[29] When the Ondos got to the area[30] and founded Imorun (about 1897) and Araromi (about 1892) there was no evidence of Ikale's earlier occupation and, as earlier noted, the Ikales did not object to the Ondo settlements. The Ondos maintained that it was within their rights to grant concessions in the Ofara area on the grounds that they owned the land beyond the Ofara and it was only after some persuasion that they allowed the Ikales to claim as far as Ofara River. They disagreed with the claim that the Ikales constructed the Imorun–Igbotako road and stated that the road was made by the Ondos.[31]

The Ondos objected to the payment of royalties on timber from the area around the Oluwa, Akerun and Isunrin Rivers to the Ikales of Aye.[32] But the Ayes claimed that their boundary with Ondo was at Iota's kola trees on the Ondo side of the River Oluwa, and that they used to carry on road works as far as that point.[33] Against the claim was the fact that the Ondos had a village between the Oluwa River and the kola trees claimed as boundary by Aye.

Further east the Ondos challenged the right of the Ikales to grant timber concessions in the area of River Otu. But the Ikales of Irele maintained that they had such rights because the boundary was at the place where the Irele–Oniserere road crosses the Otu.[34] They claimed to have given permission to an Ondo man to settle at Imu and that the man paid timber royalties to the Ikales of Irele. The Irele claim over Imu was not accepted by the Ondos who contended that their *oba* gave permission for the establishment of a settlement at Imu.[35]

It is clear from the foregoing that due to the increased economic importance of the frontier area, which resulted from the exploitation of its timber, each side wanted to lay exclusive claims to certain parts of it. This contrasted with the situation in the contact stage when there was a great deal of mixing without any attempt to claim definite territory. One result of the conflicting claims was the realisation that a boundary had to be agreed upon so that each side would know the limits of its rights.

ALLOCATION

The allocation stage involved agreements on the boundary in three areas, namely, the Ofara River, the Oluwa River and the Otu River areas. In each case the determination of the boundary was undertaken by government officials who were anxious to ensure that timber exploitation was not disturbed by the dispute over territory and who also used it as a means of preventing disorders. The first attempt to fix a boundary in each of the various sections took place after each side raised objections to the granting of timber concessions to the other.

The Ofara River Area: In the west an inquiry was held in 1904 by Mr Cummins, a District Commissioner. According to the Ondos he set the boundary at the River Ofara, but the Ikales claimed that it was at Imorun. Whatever the case the River Ofara was regarded as the boundary by government officials. The Ikales objected to this on the grounds that it deprived them of their land between the river and Imorun, as far as which they agreed Ondo could have the land. They argued that they had always maintained the Igbotako–Imorun road.[36]

By accepting Imorun as the boundary the Ikales waived their claims to land as far as Gbekelu. It was easy for them to do that because they had no settlements beyond Imorun and Gbekelu. Much more important to the section of the boundary was the Ikale acceptance of Ondo settlements in areas south of Imorun, particularly in the Araromi area. The construction of the Igbotako–Imorun road, which the Ikales claimed they had undertaken, was 'for the purpose of selling yams to those who were tapping at Imorun'.[37] If the rubber tappers at Imorun had been Ikales they would have constructed a road which yam sellers could use. That the latter had to construct the road suggests that the rubber tappers did not leave from Igbotako and were most probably from Ondo. The inference is supported by the Ikale claim that Imorun was first set up as a provision store for those Ondos working on the road to Araromi. The statement indicates that the Ondos were the first to settle in the Imorun/Araromi area in any permanent way and that they were welcomed by the Ikales who even traded with them happily.

The Ondos claimed that they constructed the Imorun–Igbotako road. This seems plausible on first consideration, but on closer examination it does not carry much conviction. For one thing, the main Ondo concern was a road from their chief town, Ode-Ondo, to a navigable river. The road passed through Imorun to Araromi which was their port. It is therefore difficult to see the reason why the Ondos should have constructed a road to Igbotako. In view of this one would accept the Ikale claim as to the construction of that road. If that be the case it can be argued that the Ikales could not have constructed a road in foreign territory. The conclusion would imply that the Ikales have a claim over the territory between Igbotako and Imorun.

Since the adoption of the River Ofara as boundary did not reflect Ikale's territorial claims, that community demanded a new boundary. In an attempt to investigate their claims an inquiry was held in 1917 by the Acting District Officer, Ondo District, Mr Findlay. After taking evidence from both sides he observed that the area being claimed by the Ikales of Igbotako included:

1. Imorun, an Ondo town with an Ondo *bale*, established about twenty years before the investigation (i.e. *c*.1897);
2. Araromi, an Ondo settlement established about 1892 by Ipame who settled at Ajebandele with the consent of the Osemawe;
3. timber concessions granted by the Ondos and on which the Osemawe collected royalties without any dispute. The concessions included those granted to Brown in 1906 and to Lomofe in 1908;
4. the only Ikales in the area were those around Owode who paid rent to the Osemawe.

In view of all this he decided the Ofara River should remain the boundary between Ondo and Ikale.[38]

Since this decision was later cited to support the retention of the Ofara as boundary it might be well to note that the main points in its favour were that the Ikales did not dispute the payment of royalties to Ondo and that the Ikales in Owode paid rent to the Osemawe. It is to be noted that the concessions cited were granted after the Cummins decision of 1904. According to the Ikales that decision was to the effect that no Ondos should go south of Imorun. If that were so one would expect them to dispute the payment of royalties to Ondo and also to object to the payment of *isakole* to the Osemawe by their farmers at Owode. That they did not do either indicates that they were either accepting that they had no right on the land or they were complying with a government order. They themselves state that the latter was the case. That being so, the order would be to the effect that the Ofara should be the boundary. Their objection to the Ofara would appear to be based on their need for farmlands and the desire to share the timber royalties.

Oluwa River Area: In the area of the River Oluwa an inquiry was held in 1905 by Mr Pinkett, a travelling commissioner. After hearing evidence from both sides he accepted that the Ikale of Aye used to maintain the road as far as Iota's kola trees, but concluded that it was no proof of territorial ownership. According to him such road maintenance was 'often done when one town has a very long stretch to clean. It is used by both.'[39] On account of that view he fixed the boundary between the two communities as:

> The Oluwa (River) left bank adjudged to be the boundary between the Ondo and Lapoki of Aye from the point where the Aye–Odigbo road crosses it to the village of Agbabu. Leaving thus the Ondos the left bank and Lapoki the right. From the point where the Aye–Odigbo road crosses the said River Oluwa to the village of Agbabu situated on the left bank being therefore in Ondo territory[40] [Fig. 9].

It has been mentioned earlier that the point at which roadworks stop is often used as boundary between adjacent communities. On the strength of this it seems likely that the Aye claims to territory as far as Iota's kola trees on the Ondo side of the Oluwa River were correct. Unfortunately the investigating officer did not see things that way. Three reasons could be adduced for this: first, the District Commissioner believed that rivers are the boundary between peoples. This is shown by his remark of 21 December 1904 '. . . water is nearly always a boundary mark with natives and when they want to dodge round trees, farms, etc., it is suspicious to say least of it.'[41] Second, the Commissioner appears to have made up his mind not to believe the Ikales because three days before his formal inquiry and decision he remarked '. . . saw the point up to which Lapoki wishes to claim on the left hand side of River Oluwa. The more I look at it the more preposterous I consider the claim. He wants me to believe that there is an invisible boundary between him and the Ondos from a clump of young kola trees to an invisible point on the Ondo-Agbabu road.'[42] Third, this preconceived idea was somehow confirmed by the Ondo settlement between the Oluwa River and the point claimed by the Ikales. However, the grouping of the village with Ondo could have been achieved if it had been realised that the boundary need not be the straight line claimed by the Ikales, but one drawn in a way to include the village on the Ondo side. All this appears to have affected the boundary fixed in 1905 along the Oluwa River.

Further developments took place in 1912 and 1916. In the former year there was a dispute as to the ownership of Mobi,[43] south of Agbabu, which was then only a landing place on the Oluwa River. Ondo's claim to the place was based on the contention that Pinkett awarded the land north of the Oghan (Owan) to the Ondos and therefore Mobi and all the land up to Agbabu belonged to the Ondos (Fig. 9). The investigating officer, S. M. Wood, observed that the nearest settlements to the landing point, Mobi, were a small Ijo village in the north and Mobaro, an Ikale village then said to be about sixty years old. He also noted that the farms around Mobaro 'belonging to its inhabitants extended past Mobi Wharf and past Ijo village and the cultivation is up to the river bank.'[44] He then decided that 'Mobi does not belong to the Osemawe.'[45] Commenting on the basis of the Ondo claim he was of the opinion that Pinkett did not know of the existence of Mobaro and since the Ondos did not claim Mobaro they could not 'claim land to the south of it and Mobi which is practically its wharf.'[46] He concluded his report on the inquiry with a suggestion:

> should it become necessary to fix the southern boundary of Ondo it might be either:
> (1) the marshland south of Agbabu as far as the Irele–Agbabu junction with the Oghan River;
> (2) a line due east from the Agbabu marshland to the Irele–Onishere road.[47]

Later on, in 1913, one Mr Tabor investigated the boundary claims and suggested that some land north of the Oluwa River should be given to the Ikales. The District Commissioner opposed this and added that if the Ikales wanted land in the area they could apply to the Osemawe and then pay the customary rent.[48] No doubt the District Commissioner was anxious to retain the Pinkett decision of 1904 which has been discussed above.

The real problem about the 1904 decision did not arise until 1916 when the Osemawe demanded the withdrawal of the Ikales who were farming on the Ondo side of the Oluwa river. At an inquiry (in August 1916) held to resolve the problem, the Osemawe stated that the Ayes did not cross the river until about 1910 when 'they began crossing the river and farming my land without any reference to me.' When the Oloja of Aye was asked to order a withdrawal of his people he replied:

> My people are farming on a land which they have always posse-
> ssed. I do not know anything about the boundary between my land
> and Ondo land. I own the land on the left and on the right of
> the Oluwa River. I have had the farms on the left bank for
> four years. The land belong to our forefathers. . . . I did not
> know the Oluwa River was made the boundary. I will not now
> tell my people to leave this land because the land belongs to me
> and my people have farmed it for four years.[49]

In his ruling the investigating officer remarked that Pinkett's decision shows that the land belongs to the Osemawe and, 'As the Lapoki of Aye is not willing to withdraw his people from the land, I have no alternative other than to report the whole matter to the Government and to request that I be given authority to fine the Lapoki of Aye £100 for contempt of court for permitting his people to cross over and farm on land belonging to the Ondo people without the consent of the Osemawe and against his wish.' The authority to impose the fine was given in a letter of 12 September 1916.

As may be observed the decision was based on the idea that the Pinkett ruling of 1904 was right or that it should be maintained.

Otu River Area: Following the opposition by Ondo to the granting of timber concessions in the Otu River area by the Ikale of Irele, an inquiry was held in 1904 by Mr Pinkett as to the location of the boundary in that area. In his diary of December 1904 he reported thus '. . . saw Oloja of Irele re concessions and boundaries. He seems the straightforwardest of the lot and admits he doesn't know where his boundary on the Owena is with Ondo.' Later he also reported '. . . the Otu, according to the Oloja of Irele, is the Ondo-Irele boundary on the Onisere–Odigbo road. The reason he gives, because he cleans the road up to it on that road, does not altogether convince me that his limit is a correct one.'[50]

One substantial reason for Ikale's claim to territory between Odigbo and Oniserere was that a District Officer asked them, in 1903, to maintain the Odigbo–Oniserere road.[51] If the claim is correct one can deduce three reasons for it: (1) Oniserere, being an Idanre settlement, could not be asked to construct a road through foreign country; (2) the Odigbos, being Ondos with a north–south orientation, had not expanded towards Oniserere and did not wish to be saddled with the road works in territory which they did not claim; (3) the Ikales, being the people between the two settlements and possibly with hunters in the area, were therefore asked to finish up from the point where the Odigbos left off.

These explanations would justify Irele's claims to all lands east of the junction of Otu with the Irele–Onishere road. But then it does not indicate the northern limits of Ireleland and secondly, it leaves Imu on the Ikale side. Seen from the Ikale side these two points do not create any problem because they claimed that the northern boundary is the River Ahejire and that the founder of Imu got permission from Irele. The main problem with the last explanation is that the Ondos also claimed that the Ondo founder of Imu got permission from the Osemawe.[52] Furthermore, if the first explanation were right, one would expect the Ikales to insist on retaining all the royalty from timber south of Ahejire. Instead of doing this the Ikales agreed that the Ondos should have the greater part of the timber royalties in that area.[53] This suggests that the Ikales were not quite convinced of the truth of their claims. This interpretation is reinforced by the statement of their *oba*, reported by Pinkett, that he was not certain of the location of the boundary on the Owena.[54]

In 1920 another inquiry was held with a view to resolving disagreements over the boundary fixed in 1905. At the end of the inquiry the District Officer suggested that the boundary should be from Mobi by a straight line northeasterly to the junction of the River Otu and the Irele–Oniserere road, then by the Otu as far as Emmanuel Gbembo's camp and then southeasterly to Eyansan.[55] This suggestion was rejected by both sides.

After the rejection both sides agreed to submit the dispute to arbitration. Mr Sayle was appointed arbitrator in 1922. Evidence was collected from both parties as well as their neighbours—the Idanres and the Binis. The Ondo witnesses stated that Iguon, on the left side of the Irele–Oniserere road between the Ifon and Otu Rivers, was founded by them as also were Larabusin—forty minutes walk to Omi—and Agbede. They further claimed that an old house at Olugbomudu was inhabited by an Ondo. An Ibadan man stated that he obtained permission from the Osemawe to settle at Agbede and one Osodi said he got permission from Ondo to settle on the other side of Owena from Oniserere. One Lisa Obi said his people got permission from Ondo to settle at Emmanuel's camp.[56] The Idanres, who were invited by the officer conducting the inquiry, stated thus:

> When the Governor first came to our country he advised us to build roads as we had no means of transport by water. We then started a road from Idanre to Oniserere. We then wanted a road to the waterside so the Owa asked the Ikales, who were our neighbours near Oniserere to build a road. There were no Ondos there then, . . . There had been no dispute as to who owned the land before and we thought of it as Ikale country to the south of the road. The Owa of Idanre considers that the Oniserere-Igbobini road is the dividing line between the Ondos and the Ikales; the Ondos on the North and the Ikales on the South.[57]

At the end of the inquiry the arbitrator decided that:

> The Oniserere–Irele road be the boundary between Ondo and Ikale from Oniserere to that spot on the road where it meets the line joining the Oluwa and Ifon Rivers through Mobi. All land lying to the north and west of this boundary line to be Ondo land and all land to the south and east to be Ikale land [58] [Fig. 9].

He also ordered that:

(1) The Oniserere–Irele road shall continue to be cleared by Ikale people as has been done before.
(2) Any Ondos at present residing on land which has been declared to be Ikale be permitted to remain without let or hindrance.
(3) Any Ikales residing on land which has been declared Ondo be permitted to remain without let or hindrance.
(4) The proportion of timber royalties which accrue from the land in dispute to the aforesaid parties and on which a boundary has now been fixed be decided by the conservator of forests . . . . [59]

The decision would appear to have been based almost exclusively on the evidence of Idanre quoted above. This is because it took no account of the pattern of occupation of the land and neither did it take into account evidence adduced by the Ondos to their right over Emmanuel's camp or Agbede. This raises two fundamental issues: the first concerns the degree of reliance to be placed on knowledge claimed by any community about the boundary between two of its neighbours (as in the case of the Idanre claim); the second issue concerns the advisability of adopting a road as a boundary.

The ability of a community to know details of a boundary to which it is not a party must be highly doubted because of the nature of the boundaries and the lack of any records. It has been said earlier that even where a community is a party to a boundary it may not know the details. Idanre is no exception to this as is shown by its dispute with Akure over boundaries.[60] If Idanre is not certain of its own boundaries very little weight must be attached to its evidence on boundaries to which it is not a party as is the case with the Ondo/Irele boundary. If anything at all, the Idanre evidence only means that the Ondos are to be found somewhere to the north of the road and the Ikales somewhere to the south. The only valuable point, therefore, is the historical one about the construction of the Irele–Oniserere road. If the Ikales constructed and maintained the road without being challenged by the Ondos then the title of the latter to the area must be questioned. However, the fact that the Ikales had earlier suggested the sharing of the timber royalties in the area and went on to accept forty per cent, as against the Ondos sixty per cent, also indicates that the Ikales were not quite convinced that they were right.

The arbitrator would have realised the unreliability of Idanre's evidence had he known that a road could not possibly be a boundary between two communities, even though a point on the road may be chosen. The reason for this is clear from the general model of boundary development discussed earlier. A community is likely to utilise both sides of a road it constructed from its own settlement and go on doing so until it reaches an impediment or comes in contact with its neighbours. It is therefore difficult to accept that, having constructed the Irele–Onisere road, the Ikales would keep only to the southern part of it, particularly when there were no Ondos in the neighbourhood of the road. The chances are that the Ikales would have settled on both sides of the road and hence it would be wrong to adopt that road (or any other) as a boundary.

One other important point about the settlement is the subsidiary decisions of the arbitrator, particularly the second and the third, which stipulated that members of either community having land on the opposite side should not be hindered. Two issues arise from these decisions: first, those two clauses indicate an acceptance of the failure of the arbitrator to set the boundary between the two sides because one purpose that a boundary serves is the separation of members of two communities. Secondly, the failure to separate the communities raises the question: what was the *raison d'être* of the decision and would it have prevented the recurrence of boundary disputes in the area? Since the areas occupied by each community on the other side of its boundary was not clearly marked it is likely that the conditions would not prevent future boundary disputes in the area.

Delimitation

Although there is no evidence that the arbitration decision on the Otu River section of the boundary was acceptable to any side, the Ondos were the first to reject it and went on to institute an action in the High Court in order to set it aside. In 1923 the Supreme Court gave judgment that the decision of the arbitrator be set aside.[61]

Following the decision of the High Court the Ondos instituted proceedings in the Provincial Court and laid claim to the land occupied by the Ikale people. The evidence adduced by both sides was substantially the same as for the previous inquiries on the boundary discussed above; hence they need not be repeated again. At the end of the hearing the court stated that the Ondos did not prove conclusively that the land rightly belonged to them. Therefore judgment was given in favour of the Ikales. In addition the court decided the boundary between the two communities as follows:

> From the Owena at Oniserere by the now existing bush path from Oniserere to Irele as far as the point at which a line drawn due east and west through the village of Mobi (south of Agbabu) crosses it. Thence by the latter line to the village of Mobi. Thence the left bank of Ominla to its junction with River Oluwa at Sheba. Thence by the right bank of River Oluwa to the point at which the Aye–Odigbo road crosses it. Thence by a line drawn west to the River Gbaragada on Ijebu boundary[62] (Fig. 9).

The Ondos appealed against the 1925 judgment on the ground that the court was not asked to delimit a boundary. The Supreme Court upheld the appeal and ordered that the Provincial Court should re-hear the case. At such a re–hearing evidence should be taken from all sources and judgment should be limited to the claims of Ondo, that is no boundary should be fixed.[63] The case was re-heard in 1927 and the 1925 judgment was confirmed.[64] Following the second judgment the Ondos expressed satisfaction with the boundary delimited at the first judgment, but the Ikales did not.[65]

In 1928 the Waterside area, of which Ikale is a part, was separated from Ondo Division with which it had hitherto been administered and constituted into a separate Okitipupa Division. The Ikales were in the northern part of the latter Division and hence the administrative boundary between Okitipupa and Ondo became closely associated with the Ondo/Ikale communal boundary. The Divisional boundary was defined as follows:

> The Ofara River from the point where it meets the [Ondo/Ijebu] provincial boundary to the point at which this river meets the Imorun–Igbotako road, thence by the southern boundary of the Oluwa River, thence downstream by the Oluwa River to its confluence with the Ominla River at Sheba, thence upstream by the Ominla River to Mobi thence in a straight line due east to the Irele–Oniserere road, thence by the Irele-Oniserere road to the Owena River to its confluence with the Ohoshu [Ofosu] River[66] [Fig. 9].

This was almost exactly the boundary suggested in 1925 and against which Ondo appealed before indicating, in 1927, that they accepted. Since the Ondo acceptance was not agreed to by Ikale it was necessary to explain whether the government intended the divisional boundary as the communal one. This was done in April 1928 when the government stated that the administrative boundary had nothing to do with the ownership of land and that it was meant to separate the jurisdiction of two commissioners of the Provincial Court.[67]

The Ondos accepted the government suggestion but the Ikales rejected it. Among the reasons why Ikale did not accept the boundary as suggested by the government was the grouping of Ikale settlements in the area north of the Irele–Oniserere road in Ondo. The road itself was made by Ikale and was not intended as a boundary. Notable among the settlements cut off from the Ikales were: Kinbode

Basola, Ogunti, Abetu and Luere in the west, as well as Oderimi, Kinbi, Tubara, Lametiti, Lijoka and Kinmeha in the east (Fig. 9). Some Ondo settlements were grouped with Ikale, among these being Bajare and Taribo.[68]

Although the government intended that the boundary fixed in 1928 was only for administrative purposes they attempted to adopt it as a communal boundary between the Ondos and Ikales. This is well shown in the appeal of the Lieutenant Governor, Southern Nigeria, to both sides.

> ... For many years government had waited for both parties to come to an agreement as to the boundary. At last in February 1928 an administrative boundary was gazetted, thereby creating the Waterside a Division. This boundary had nothing to do with the ownership of land but with the jurisdiction of two commissioners of the Provincial Court, though in every case government tried to make tribal or communal boundary coincide with the administrative one. The practical effect of the gazetted boundary is that everyone living or found north of the boundary will pay tax to the Ondo Native Administration and everyone south, to the Waterside Native Administration. If now the Ondo Native Administration agrees to accept the gazetted boundary as the communal one, strangers taking up land north of the boundary will pay rent to the Ondo Native Administration and the same procedure in the case of the Waterside Native Administration if the latter accepts the gazetted boundary.
>
> If one or the other of both parties accept the gazetted boundary, such acceptance, interdependent the one of the other, should be embodied in two formal documents which the commissioner of lands should be requested to draw .... [69]

The implication of the explanation was that if only one party accepted the boundary as the communal one the government would not listen to complaints by the other. It indicates that the government was attempting to force a boundary on the area. This was unfortunate in that the boundary did not separate members of the two communities as is well shown by the provisions on tax collection. The tax provision overlooked the fact that people normally wish to pay to the community to which they owe allegiance. Thus the Ikale areas would prefer to pay to Ikale while the Ondos would prefer Ondo.

The intention of the explanation was to reverse this trend and hence there was opposition to it from the people, particularly those on the Ikale side. As a result of such opposition the Resident ruled in 1929 that the Ikales farming north of the administrative boundary could continue to pay their taxes to the town to which they belonged (i.e. Ikale towns). Following further discussion of the problem the Resident also instructed that people farming on the side which does not belong to their own community should pay a rent of ten shillings to the Native Administration on their side of the boundary. However, the decision was not implemented, due to instructions given by the Secretary to the Southern Provinces. The effect of all this was that the 1928 boundary was not effective as an administrative boundary and it only delimited the areas of authority of the District Officers.

In the Ikale Assessment Report of 1932, B. J. Matthews remarked that 'there is evidence to show that the Ikales have occupied land north of the [1928] boundary from olden times.'[70] On the strength of that report the Resident appointed N. C. Weir, an Assistant District Officer, to collect evidence on the boundary problem. He did this in 1932 and 1933.

During his investigations he suggested to the Ondos that they accept the alteration to the 1928 boundary in the area of Mobi so that it runs as follows:

> ... the Confluence of the Ominla and Ohun Rivers and along Owun Eleja River to the point where it crosses Mulekangbo–Oniserere Road along that road to the point where it meets the northern boundary of the Irele Reserve along that boundary to Emmanuel's Camp and from Emmanuel's Camp to the existing tract to Taibo[71] [Fig. 9B].

He explained that the suggested alteration would mean that fifty-one square miles (131km^2) would be transferred from Ondo Division to Okitipupa Division and forty-four square miles (113km^2) from the latter to the former. 'Furthermore it would mean that all the Ondo villages now in the Okitipupa Division would return to the Ondo Division and all the Irele settlements with the exception of Oderimi, Kinmeha, Kimbe, Tubara and Lametiti would be in the Okitipupa Division....'[72]

The Ondos did not accept the alteration but went on to repeat their intention to recognise the 1928 boundary as the communal boundary and requested the government to take steps to make the Ikales do the same.

After Weir had submitted his report Captain Foulkes-Roberts was appointed to undertake a review of the boundary and to recommend a new one. Foulkes-Roberts relied on earlier records and decisions, including the Weir report, and also undertook a tour of the disputed area during which he visited many places, particularly in the eastern parts.

In his report, submitted in 1935, Foulkes-Roberts observed that no boundary existed in really ancient times when there was a wide no-mans-land between the two sides. He also noted that 'the Ikale claim is as it has been whenever in the past the question has arisen and in every part except Gbekelu the boundary claimed by the Ikale appears to be the reputed limit of Ikale hunters' activities in the past.'[73]

He remarked that there was no indication that the Ikale villages on the Ondo side of the River Ofara were founded before 23 April 1917, the date when the river was first made the boundary between the two sides. Also, that although he found an Ikale village called Lowo on the Ondo side of the Oluwa River, he saw no reason, after examining past records, to recommend an alteration of the boundary in those areas. On the eastern side he found evidence to believe that the Ondos had rights over Gbonowe, Logbe, Deyeye, Olugbomudu, Emmanuel's camp, Osodi and Oniserere west of Owena, Eluju and Taibo, while the Ikales had rights over Akinbuwa, Adedubi, Ayadi, Olotin, Oloda, Kinbi and Kinmeha (Fig. 9). Finally he recommended that the boundary should be:

> The middle of the main channel of the Ofara River from the point where it meets the Ondo/Ijebu Provincial boundary to the point at which that river meets the Imorun–Igbotako road, thence the southern boundary of the Oluwa Forest Reserve to the Oluwa River, thence the left bank of the Oluwa River to its confluence with Ominla River, thence the middle of the main channel of the Ominla and Owun-Eleja River to the confluence of the Owun-Lamudifa River with the Owun-Eleja River, thence two straight lines (not yet demarcated) to the Ifon River, one line to be made in a northerly direction from the confluence of the Owun-Lamudifa and Owun-Eleja such that it places the village of Oloda in Ikale and the village of Logbe in Ondo land and the second line to be made in a westerly direction from the northernmost point of the Irele Forest Reserve such that it places the villages of Kinmeha, Oderimi and Kindoro in Ikale land and the village of Deyeye in Ondo land, thence the middle of the main channel of the Ifon River to the Irele Forest Reserve, thence the northern and eastern boundaries of the Irele Forest Reserve to Emmanuel's camp (thus placing the Irele Forest Reserve in Ikaleland and the whole of Otu Forest Reserve in Ondoland),

thence the bush parth to the Omi Lepurupuru River near Taibo village, thence a line (not yet demarcated) to the Ondo/Benin Provincial boundary, this line to be as straight as possible and to reach the Siluko River immediately south of Gbonowe village, but such that it places the village of Taibo, Fagbon and Gbonowe together with their farms in Ondoland[74] (Fig. 9B).

He also recommended that where the Otu river forms the eastern boundary of the Irele Forest Reserve the middle of the main channel of that river shall be the intercommunal boundary.

The Ikales objected to the settlement on the ground that Foulkes-Roberts did not visit all the places where they wanted to show him evidence of their earlier occupation. They also said that they had never accepted the decision about the Ofara and Oluwa Rivers and were not a party to the establishment of the boundaries of the forest reserves which were adopted by Foulkes-Roberts.[75] Because of these complaints the Resident ordered that evidence be taken from the Ikales, and the Foulkes-Roberts decision be reviewed in the light of any new information they might give. This was done by the District Officers of Okitipupa and Ondo in April 1936. The former officer, who took evidence about the eastern section of the boundary,[76] was told that the Ikales were the first settlers at Imu and Golope and that an Ikale had a shrine at the akoko tree in front of the house of Ojon, the founder of Imu, and that the man hunted and farmed up to Ahejire River which formed the boundary between him and the Ondo people at Ajue, Ibuowo and Oro (Fig 9). The Ikales also claimed that Pele, who was an elephant hunter, was a member of their group and had a cave in the Oniserere area. However, the Ikales admitted that at the time of the inquiry they had no settlements in the area. In view of the last item of information the District Officer did not visit the places mentioned but suggested that the recommendations of Foulkes-Roberts should be confirmed. The District Officer for Ondo, was asked to visit Otapina and see the evidence the Ikales wanted to produce to support their claim to that area. On the day arranged the Ikales did not turn up. After the inquiries the Resident decided, in 1936, that the Ikales had not produced any further evidence to justify their objection to the Foulkes-Roberts boundary, and on 18 July 1936 he confirmed it. Subsequently the boundary was demarcated.[77]

Since no record of Ondo objection to the Foulkes-Roberts decision has been traced it can be taken that they were in general agreement with it; therefore only the Ikale objections need be examined. The bases of the objections can be identified as:

(1) that some Ikale settlements west of the Ofara River were left in Ondo;

(2) that areas in which they had hunted or farmed in the Oluwa and Otu Rivers areas were left in Ondo.

The first decision was made because the Ikales could not produce evidence that the settlements were established before 1917 when River Ofara was first made the boundary. In other words the administration was of the view that the Ikales should have kept within the limits fixed in 1917. However, the Ikales and the Ondos do not agree on their accounts of the Cummins decision of 1904 on which the 1917 decision was partly based. Moreover, Pinkett noted in 1905 that there was a map showing that the Ikales had some land west of River Ofara. One would therefore have expected the 1935 review to take account of all the earlier comments before refusing to alter the boundary to include all areas in which the Ikales had established settlements.

The Ikale claims in the east are less easy to defend because it would appear that the area they claimed was the old frontier within which their hunters intermixed with those from Ondo. The fact that the Ondos had settled in the area is evidence that they visited the place before and the most likely purpose would be for hunting. Since the Ondos were the first to found permanent settlements within that part of the frontier it is only right that they should be allowed to have the land. The only basis on which the Ikale claims could have been defended is that they maintained the Irele–Oniserere road. But then the road was not made until the late nineteenth century, and one cannot therefore justify their claim on that basis. The fact that the Oloja of Irele stated in 1904 that he did not know where his boundary with Ondo lies on the Owena indicates that Irele did not have detailed knowledge of the country in that section before the advent of the British.

On the whole, therefore, the dispute[78] which has arisen about the 1935 boundary can probably be best resolved by transferring the Ikale settlements and their farmlands west of the Ofara River to the Okitipupa Division, and retaining the approved boundary in other places where it does not join Ikale settlements or farmlands to the Ondo Division.

IMPLICATIONS

Three main conclusions can be drawn from the development of the Ondo/Ikale boundary. First, people in one sector of a boundary know nothing about the position of the boundary in other areas. This is shown by the fact that separate negotiations were conducted with Igbotako, Aye and Irele, which were the main Ikale settlements interacting with the Ondos. In each case no reference was made to the boundary in the other sectors. Secondly, the boundaries claimed by each community are ill-defined. In most cases the claims are restricted to a number of points rather than lines. Thus the Ikales claim Gbekelu, Otapina, Iota's kola trees, the junction of the Oniserere–Odigbo road with the Otu River and then River Ahejire. The points are located far apart, a feature which at one time made some think that the people had no idea of boundaries before boundary delimitation in the present century. Even if the points claimed by the Ikales were not disputed by the Ondos other problems could have arisen during delimitation, mainly because of the insistence that the boundary was formed by straight lines joining the stated points. The source of the problem would be as follows: since only the points were agreed upon and people in one sector were not informed of the location of the agreed points elsewhere it was possible for those from one side to have gone beyond their side of the straight line being claimed as the boundary. For example, the Ondos could have gone beyond their side of the straight line linking Gbekelu and Otapina or the one linking Iota's kola trees with the junction of River Otu and the Oniserere–Odigbo road. When such crossing was being made, possibly during the contact stage, the Ikales would not realise it and may have raised no objection. Therefore, the Ondos would have opposed any attempt by the Ikales to claim the areas so occupied.

Another example of an ill-defined boundary claim is that of the Ondos to all territory occupied by the Ikales. There was no definition of the exact boundaries of the land being claimed; therefore, even if the Ondos had got judgment in their favour there would still remain the definition of the boundaries of Ikaleland with other communities.

The third important point is that the government distinguished between administrative and communal boundaries and, in some cases, as in the Ondo/Ikale one, the two do not coincide. It is necessary for anyone dealing with boundary matters and who may wish to adopt existing administrative units for purposes other than that for which they were originally created to realise this point. In particular the point should be constantly borne in mind in any dispute that may arise over inter-state boundaries, since they are based on administrative boundaries decided in the same way as that of Ondo and Ikale.

Of immediate relevance to the present study is that the problems discussed above are not limited to the Ondo/Ikale boundary. They are of general application and have contributed in one way or the other to delays in the evolution of boundaries in Western Nigeria. However, the main source of delay in boundary development in the area are the various boundary disputes, the nature and examples of which will be examined in the following chapters.

Notes and References

1. For example, by Akure as stated in a letter from Deji of Akure to District Officer, Ekiti Division, 5 April 1927.
2. G. O. Ekemode, Lecturer in History, University of Ife, 1968.
3. P. A. Oluyede, 'A Comparative Study of Selected Problems Relating to Nigerian Land Law with Particular Reference to Yorubaland', Ph.D. Thesis, Queens University, Belfast, 1969, p. 27.
4. A. Oloyede, 'Rural-Urban Relationships of Odo–Otin and Oshogbo', B.A. Dissertation, Geog. Dept., University of Ife, 1969.
5. O. O. Oyetunji, 'Ikire/Apomu/Ikoyi Conurbation', B.A. essay, Geography Dept., University of Ife, 1969.
6. At Ile-Ife, Ilesa, Akure, Odigbo, Irele and Itaji during 1969 and 1970.
7. Minutes of a meeting at the Residency, Ibadan, 28 October 1913, to decide the boundaries of Ilesa.
8. See below, Chapter V.
9. 'Notes on Akure/Ogotun Boundary Reconciliation Meeting held in Ogotun on 11 January 1950', File LR 22/1, AKDIVCO 4, N.A.I.
10. Information collected during fieldwork in July 1969.
11. See Chapter V.
12. See Chapter IV.
13. Inquiry held by Mr C. H. Richardson, District Officer, to decide the boundary between Akure District and Ikere District, 14–24 July 1954.
14. Deji of Akure to Ogoga of Ikere, 26 August 1954, File LR. 22/3, AKDIVCO 4, N.A.I.
15. See Chapter VII.

16. See below.
17. Omolade Adejuyigbe, 'The Evolution and Structure of Ife Division' in S.A. Agboola and G.J.A. Ojo, eds., *The Ife Region.*
18. Omolade Adejuyigbe, 'Ife/Ijesa Boundary Problem', *Nigeria Geographical Journal* 13, (1970), pp. 23–38.
19. Description of the northern boundary of Ijebu Province, *Gazette* of 10 March 1927.
20. Suit No. W/40 1939, Supreme Court, Benin City. Judgment on 30 June 1943.
21. Bale of Igbotako in evidence in Ondo/Ikale boundary dispute case, Ondo Provincial Court, March 1925.
22. B. J. Matthews, 'Assessment Report on the Ikale District, Okitipupa Division', File O/C. 143/1914, Ministry of Local Government, Okitipupa, pp. 50 ff.
23. Sasere of Ondo in evidence in Ondo/Ikale boundary case, Ondo Provincial Court, March 1925.
24. Bale of Idepe in evidence in Ondo/Ikale boundary dispute case, Ondo Provincial Court, April 1927.
25. Ibid.
26. Official Diary of Major Reeve–Tucker, Travelling Commissioner, 20 April 1902 and 17 October 1902. See File C.15/1921, Ministry of Local Government, Ondo.
27. B. J. Matthews, op. cit., p. 224.
28. See entries for 7 November and 13 and 14 December 1904 in 'Travelling and District Commissioner's Office Journal and Diary, 1903–12', Ondo Div. 8/1, N.A.I.
29. P. R. Foulkes-Roberts, 'Report on the Ondo/Ikale Boundary Dispute 1935, File 31615, C.S.O. 26, N.A.I.
30. D.O.'s 'Review on Evidence at Meeting held at Araromi on 23 April 1917'. See File C.15/1921, Ministry of Local Government, Ondo.
31. Chief Lomafe of Ondo in evidence at meeting held at Araromi on 23 April 1917. See File C.15/1921, Ministry of Local Government, Ondo.
32. B. J. Matthews, op. cit., p. 224.
33. Lapoki, Bale of Aye, to District Commissioner, 2 February 1905, File C.15/1921, Ministry of Local Government, Ondo.
34. Entries for 21 and 29 December 1904 in 'Travelling and District Commissioner's Office Journal and Diary, 1903–12', Ondo Div. 8/1, N.A.I.
35. For the views of both sides see 'Records of the Ondo/Ikale Boundary Case', Ondo Provincial Court, 1925 and 1927.
36. 'Meeting held at Araromi on Monday, 23 April 1917', File C.15/1921, Ministry of Local Government, Ondo.
37. Bale of Igbotako and 14 chiefs to District Commissioner, 5 September 1912.
38. Meeting held at Araromi on Monday, 23 April 1917, to consider the claim of Nigwo (Bale of Igbotako) to boundary beyond Ofara River. Those present included Nigwo, Bale of Igbotako; Chief Lomafe and Chief Losere (Logbosere), both of Ondo.
39. Pinkett to Colonial Secretary, 10 February 1905, in File C.15/1921, Ministry of Local Government, Ondo.

40. B. J. Matthews, op. cit., p. 224.
41. 'Travelling and District Commissioner's Office Journal and Diary, 1903–12', Ondo Div. 8/1, entry for 21 December 1904.
42. Ibid., entry for 7 February 1905.
43. Inquiry into ownership of Mobi, 23, 24 and 26 August 1912, File C.15/1921, Ministry of Local Government, Ondo.
44. Ibid.
45. Ibid.
46. Ibid.
47. Ibid.
48. District Commissioner, Ondo, to Colonial Secretary, Lagos, 29 September 1913, File C.15/1921, Ministry of Local Government, Ondo.
49. Meeting at Ondo between Resident, Ondo Province; the Acting D.O., Ondo, Osemawe and Patako, the Bale and Lapoki of Aye, 25 August 1916; extracts in File C.15/1921, Ministry of Local Government, Ondo.
50. Ibid.
51. Entries for 21 and 29 December 1904 in 'Travelling and District Commissioner's Office Journal and Diary, 1903–12', Ondo Div. 8/1, N.A.I.
52. Inquiry into Ondo/Ikale Boundary, 1905. See Extracts of Records in File C.15/1921, Ministry of Local Government, Ondo.
53. Ibid.
54. Sasere of Ondo in evidence in Ondo/Ikale boundary case, Ondo Provincial Court, April 1927.
55. Meeting held at Lisa-Obi's farm in the presence of the A.D.O., 1 October 1920. Those present included Chief Genetu and Emmanuel Gbembo, representing the Osemawe and Adaja, Ogunsakin and Kunude Agbede, representing the Odogbo of Omi and the Ikales.
56. For records of the hearings at the arbitration see File C.15/1921, Ministry of Local Government, Ondo.
57. Statement by Chief Alidu of Ondo before A.D.O., Ondo, 1 June 1922, File C.15/1921, Ministry of Local Government, Ondo.
58. Ibid.
59. Ibid.
60. See Chapter IV.
61. B. J. Matthews, op. cit., p. 224–5.
62. *The Osemawe of Ondo* v. *The Bodi and Chiefs of Ikale*, Ondo Provincial Court, 20–27 March 1925.
63. *Aladekolurejo, the Osemawe and the Chiefs of Ondo* v. *Itiolu, Abodi and Chiefs of Ikale*, Suit No. 1 of 1926, Supreme Court of Nigeria.
64. *The Osemawe of Ondo* v. *The Abodi of Ikale*, Ondo Provincial Court, 11 March–14 April 1927.
65. B. J. Matthews, op. cit., pp. 224–5.
66. Ibid., p. 225.
67. Ibid., p. 226.
68. N. C. Weir, 'Report of Inquiry into the Ondo/Ikale Boundary Dispute, 1933', File G.406, Ministry of Local Government, Ondo.
69. B. J. Matthews, op. cit., pp. 226–7.

70. Ibid., p. 229.
71. N. C. Weir, op. cit.
72. Ibid.
73. P. R. Foulkes-Roberts, 'Report on the Ondo/Ikale Boundary Dispute, 1935', File 31615, C.S.O. 26, N.A.I.
74. Ibid.
75. H. P. James, 'Review of Captain P. R. Foulkes-Roberts' Report on Ondo/Ikale Boundary, September 1935'.
76. K. Robinson, 'Review of Ondo/Ikale Boundary, 1936'. File 31615, C.S.O. 26, N.A.I.
77. File 31615, C.S.O. 26, N.A.I.
78. For more recent information on the dispute see File 372, Ministry of Local Government, Divisional Office, Ondo.

CHAPTER III

The Nature of Boundary Disputes

IN A DISCUSSION of boundary disputes, it is necessary to distinguish between two related but different concepts: the need or demand for a boundary and a boundary dispute. The need for a boundary arises when it becomes necessary to have a record of the extent of territory of each community. Since the territory of a community is represented by the areas claimed by all its members, and since every citizen should know the limits of his own territorial rights, each community ought to have a clear idea of its territory and its boundaries. Ideally the boundaries as conceived by both sides should be the same. Therefore when the two sides meet to discuss the boundary the only development ought to be a recording of the boundary and not an argument as to where it should be.

A boundary dispute exists when one of the parties separated by its objects to the boundary being suggested or desired by the other. The suggestion may be aimed at fixing a boundary where none was in existence before or at replacing an existing one which is unsatisfactory to the party making the suggestion. An objection to a suggested boundary could be made because the objecting community feels that the suggestion does not accord with its conception of its own territorial rights or, in the case of a previously fixed boundary, it is dissatisfied with the existing or demarcated boundary.

Boundary disputes which have been common in Western Nigeria during the twentieth century were almost unknown in the area until the end of the nineteenth century. The disputes began when government officials and communities started to delimit boundaries in the late nineteenth and during the twentieth centuries. The aim in this chapter is to examine, first, the common explanations of the incidence of boundary disputes, secondly, the justification given by various communities for their territorial claims, and, thirdly, the causes of boundary disputes. There will also be a discussion of

58

the bases of classifying boundary disputes and the various types identified in Western Nigeria.

COMMON EXPLANATIONS OF BOUNDARY DISPUTES

Although the kingdoms and communities in Western Nigeria had been established for hundreds of years they did not quarrel over boundaries until after the inter-state wars of the nineteenth century had stopped and a single government had been established for all the kingdoms. The period was also one of increased economic activity in the frontier areas, particularly in the form of the exploitation of forest resources of which timber and wild rubber were the most important. The increased forest exploitation and the introduction of new crops, such as cocoa, caused people to move out from the towns and community headquarters to the rural areas to occupy land previously under forest and frequented by hunters only. The rate of agricultural expansion increased after 1920 when the cultivation of cocoa was intensified and people had to go to the unoccupied frontier areas to establish farms. Also during this period, the government wanted to know the exact limits of each kingdom or community so as to determine the areas of jurisdiction of each local administrative authority. To that end government officials made enquiries as to boundaries and embarked on delimitation and some demarcation. Each of these developments is generally considered to have contributed to the incidence of boundary disputes in Western Nigeria. The bases of the considerations in each case are examined in detail in the following paragraphs.

EXPLOITATION OF FOREST RESOURCES

After the colonial administration had been established, British citizens started to take interest in the extraction of timber and wild rubber from the forests. Such forest produce was more abundant in areas not under agriculture and these were usually in the frontiers between the communities.

Before the exploitation started it was necessary to get clearance from the landowners, that is, one of the communities separated by the frontier and which was believed to exercise jurisdiction over the area. Since, as earlier noted, there was interaction between neighbouring communities within the common frontier, each one believed it exercised suzerainty over the frontier, or at least over large parts of it. For this reason it was often difficult to determine the community which should be approached for concessions in the frontier area. This is well shown by the example of the Ikale/Ondo boundary discussed earlier. One effect of the situation was that any community which was approached first felt it within its power to give the concession and hence collect timber royalties from the timber merchant. Knowledge of royalty agreements and payments usually made the other community challenge the rights of the grantor over the affected territory. The second community would claim that it owned part of the territory or all of it and should therefore collect part or all the timber royalty from the area.

A good example of disputes which arose in the way described above is the beginning of the dispute between Ondo and Ikale over their boundary. It started early in the present century when timber merchants sought and got timber concessions from both Ondo and Ikale on their frontier. Each side challenged the right of the other to grant the concessions. The Ikales, for example, were to collect ten shillings on each tree felled on the Oluwa River. When the Ondos heard of this they claimed that the land there belonged to them and not to the Ikales. The Ikales were furious and they attacked the Ondos in their midst.[1]

Another good example of a dispute which arose over timber exploitation is that between Akure and Idanre over their common boundary. It started after timber concessions had been granted to Miller Brothers on the Akure/Idanre frontier. Disputes arose as to which side was to collect the royalty on timber felled by the timber merchant. A temporary truce was achieved in 1912 when both sides agreed that the royalties should be shared equally between them.[2]

The examples cited in the foregoing paragraphs illustrate the fact that some boundary disputes arose when exploitation of the resources of the frontier started. The question, of course, is why should exploitation of resources cause disputes? Among the obvious answers to the questions would be that each side wanted a share of the benefits accruing from the frontier area and the larger the area controlled the bigger the benefits. To ensure this, each side wanted to prevent the other from occupying a large area, thus it would be better placed to establish some claim to the area.

INCREASES IN RURAL POPULATION

One of the main developments of the present century is an increase in the number of people in rural areas. The increase is due both to natural increase of the rural population and to migration from the urban areas by urban-based farmers. The increase in rural population led to the expansion of the agricultural zone of each community into land previously used exclusively for gathering and hunting. In the process there was more contact between members of neighbouring communities. Furthermore each side realised that unless it laid exclusive claims to sections of the frontier the other side might expand and occupy every bit of it. The claims and the direct contact between the communities led to conflicts over boundaries.

The beginning of many boundary disputes can be traced to direct contact by farmers from neighbouring communities. The Aiyede/ Orin dispute, discussed in Chapter I, is, of course, a classic example. The boundary dispute between Akure and Ikere started when farmers from both communities came into contact with each other. Ijare farmers (on the Akure side) were reported to have uprooted crops planted by Ikere farmers.[3] This led to boundary claims and a dispute arose.

Sometimes the contact may not be as direct as those cited above. In the Ife/Ijebu dispute there was no competition for particular plots but for a much wider area which was being peopled by both sides.[4] In such cases the desire is to restrict the expansion of the other side and thereby ensure that the unoccupied land is made available to citizens of the claimant community.

These examples show that disputes arose when people from neighbouring communities came into direct contact with each other. Since the expansion which brought the contact about was caused by population growth, that factor might be held responsible for the boundary disputes.

GOVERNMENT POLICIES

Some boundary disputes arose soon after the implementation of a government policy. Two aspects of the situation may be considered: first is the acquisition or reservation of some territory for specific use and evacuation of farmers from or restriction of farming activities in those areas. For example, when government acquires a piece of land for a farm settlement or an institution the previous occupants are usually evacuated and have to look for farmland elsewhere. When an area is declared a forest reserve, people are prevented from expanding their farmlands there and newcomers are completely barred. The newcomers or any increase in the population of farmers within a forest reserve must therefore look for farmlands outside the forest reserve. In both these cases the affected communities may be forced to expand within the frontier area between them and their neighbours. The expansion could bring them into direct contact with people from the opposite community and a dispute could develop. The arguments in this case are similar to those advanced in the preceding section and need not be repeated.

The second aspect of government policy to be considered is the delimitation of boundaries between neighbouring communities. Many boundary disputes started after the government delimited boundaries between neighbouring communities. For example. the dispute on the Ife/Ede boundary started after the River Sasa was adopted as the boundary between the two communities (Fig. 22). After the decision it became clear that there were some Ifes on the northern or Ede's side of the boundary. The Edes asked the Ifes on their side to leave the place which they regarded as part of Ede's territory. The Ifes refused on the ground that they owned the land they used. The refusal led to a dispute.[5]

Similarly, the dispute between Oyo and Ibadan over their boundary in the area of Iware and Ikereku started after its delimitation. As a result of the boundary delimitation Ikereku was under Ibadan while Iware was under Oyo. But Iware claimed land on the Ibadan side and continued to claim tribute from settlers there.[6] The collection of tribute was opposed by Ibadan and this resulted in a boundary dispute.[7]

The evidence above is that boundary disputes arose after the delimitation of boundaries by government officials. It might therefore be concluded that such boundary disputes would not have developed if boundary delimitation had not taken place.

. . .

Although the situations described above appear to be different from each other, they do have some common bases. In each of them a community is refusing to give up the rights it has acquired (over the ages or since a government decision) over a particular territory. In the case of exploitation of forest resources the dispute is usually over that part of the frontier where there has been interaction between the communities. Since, in every case, all adjacent communities operated within a frontier, each thought it could establish exclusive claims over parts or the whole of it. But the establishment of exclusive claims meant that the other side was being denied the rights it had enjoyed in the area. The losing side wanted to obtain an acknowledgment of its interests in the area. Sometimes the acknowledgment came in the sharing of the revenue or other benefits from the disputed area. Thus in the Akure/Idanre[8] and Ondo/Ikale[9] disputes the parties once agreed to share the royalty paid on timber in the disputed areas. In each of the cases the disputes were revived only when one side wanted to upset the agreement and claim all the revenue. In other words exploitation of the resources in a frontier area will cause a boundary dispute only when the rights of both communities to share in the revenue are not acknowledged. Where the rights are acknowledged or where there is no conflict regarding ownership of territory, exploitation of resources will not lead to boundary disputes. For example, exploitation of forest resources on the Akure/Ijesa frontier has not led to a boundary dispute because both communities accept River Owena as the boundary.

Contact by farmers arising from increase in rural population leads to boundary disputes only when the interests of one side are being challenged by the other. The essential point in conflicts arising from contact is not always that one side is farming on land being claimed by the other, it can also be that the farmer does not accept that he has no rights over the land and that he is only a tenant. Thus the disputes between Idanre and Akure,[10] Ijebu and Ife[11] and Ibadan and Ijebu[12] arose because the members of the first named community would not accept that they were tenants on the land in dispute. In each case the claimant community is not in need of the disputed land, but would want its rights in it acknowledged. The occupants of the land always claim that their ancestors owned the land and did not pay *isakole* (land rent) to anyone. The claim has some justification in that during the contact stages no community demanded *isakole* from another with which it intermixed in the frontier area. The reason is that, at the time, no community laid exclusive claim to any section of the frontier area.

In frontier areas where the occupants acknowledge the rights of the claimants on the land, contact between farmers has not led to boundary disputes. For example, since Owo farmers in the area west of the River Ogbese acknowledged Akure's rights over the land no boundary dispute has arisen even though the Owo farmers still occupy the land.[13] In other words, contacts between farmers cause boundary disputes when the interests of one community in the land is being disregarded by the other.

The delimitation of boundaries causes boundary disputes only when it involves superimposition and the community which benefits refuses to allow a change or to acknowledge the previous rights of its neighbour on the land. Where the rights or interests are acknowledged no dispute arises even if the government refuses to alter the boundary. For instance, since Ede acknowledged the rights of Edunabon in the Edunabon enclave that boundary dispute has abated even though the government has not altered the boundary.[14]

JUSTIFICATION FOR TERRITORIAL CLAIMS

The preceding discussion shows that boundary disputes arise because each side wants to maintain past or present interests in the territory enclosed by the different boundaries being suggested by the disputants. It is therefore necessary to understand: (a) the bases of the claims of each side over the disputed territory; and (b) the implications of claiming the territory.

THE BASES OF TERRITORIAL CLAIMS

The model in Chapter I shows that boundaries are, in the first place, established between individuals. Examples such as Ibadan/Ijebu,[15] Akure/Ikere[16] and Aiyede/Orin illustrate[17] the fact that many boundary suggestions are rejected because they do not respect the claims of individuals in the boundary area. It follows, therefore, that an understanding of territorial claims by communities must be based on that of individuals.

Among individuals, rights to territory are based on primo-occupation, meaning that the first person to occupy a territory can lay claim to it. A community protects its members and their property, hence territory acquired by an individual comes under the protection of his community. The territory is generally regarded as belonging to the community; therefore the main basis of territorial claims by a community is the fact that its members were the first to settle in the particular area. This is well shown by the type of arguments advanced by the Ikales to support the claims they made regarding their boundary with Ondo. The claim to the Otu River area was justified on the grounds that the Ikales were the first to hunt there.[18] Similarly the claim of Ogbomoso over the Ikoyi area was supported by the rights in the area, of individuals absorbed into the Ogbomoso community during the nineteenth century.[19]

Many problems have arisen over the identification of the first occupants of some areas. As explained in Chapter I, the first people in frontier areas were usually hunters or other migratory groups. Although the movements of the migrants gave each community a knowldge of wide areas it did not lead to the establishment of permanent settlements. The main problem here is that there was no visible evidence of earlier visitors to an area, therefore each set of visitors might have felt that it was the first in an area and had a right to claim it. The problem was caused by the nature of hunters-movements. A hunter would normally concentrate his activities in a locality. Such practice had two effects on subsequent territorial claims. First, only the resting place or hut of the hunter would be fixed. At the extreme edges of his area of concentration each hunter would interact with some of his neighbours. In the area of interaction it would be difficult to decide which hunter was the first to arrive because none would leave behind evidence of his visit. Secondly, not all the territory known to the hunters of each community would be effectively exploited. The reason for this is that when some hunters ceased to operate in their hunting grounds other hunters from their community might not have gone there immediately. Instead, the hunting grounds might remain unvisited for some time. In the period when it was unoccupied members of another community might have occupied it. When members of the first community returned to the grounds they would challenge the new occupants and accuse them of trespass.

Another difficulty in identifying occupants of a territory would have been caused by the fact that each set of hunters did not settle permanently, with the result that the first people to establish permanent settlements felt that their claims should take precedence over those of earlier visitors or hunters. Such claims have been supported by the courts which usually hold that the first people to establish permanent occupation should have priority in claims over a territory. For example, in the Emure/Supare boundary case the court rejected the claims of Emure because that community failed to prove that it established effective occupation in the disputed area, even though its citizens used to hunt there. At the same time the court upheld Supare's rights over the territory because its members had farms of cocoa, kola and palm trees as well as schools and churches in the disputed territory.[20] This practice has worked satisfactorily where a community can give evidence of permanent occupation. However, it has failed to satisfy everyone where there is no agreement as to which community established the first permanent settlement. As a general rule each community claims that it gave permission to its members to settle in the frontier area. But, in many cases, a community may claim that it granted permission to a member of an adjacent community to settle in the frontier area. Thus on the Ife/Ijesa boundary Ife claimed that it granted permission to an Ijesa to settle at Alakowe on the Ife/Ijesa frontier.[21] Similarly, in the matter of the Ondo/Ikale boundary, the Ikales claimed that they granted permission to an Ondo to settle at Imu.[22] In each of these cases the claims were challenged by the other community.

Sometimes the dispute is not over a particular territory but over one or more settlements which each community wants to have grouped with it. In general, the principle is that the settlements founded by members of a community are grouped with it. The only exception is where the founder acknowledges the suzerainty of another community over the land. The policy creates problems in two situations: (1) where the founder settles on the frontier being claimed by another community, and (2) where a frontier settlement was captured by an adjacent community to which the captured settlement paid homage or tribute.

IMPLICATIONS OF TERRITORIAL CLAIMS

The implications of territorial claims can be considered from the point of view of individuals within disputed territories and also from that of the community as a whole. Since, as was mentioned earlier, the rights of a community over a territory were acquired through its members there, it is advisable to consider how boundary claims affect the rights of individuals in the disputed area. The particular rights to be considered are those over land and those affecting the choice of the people on the land as to which community they are to be administered by.

The rights of a person over land may be affected by a boundary dispute in two ways: first, his land may be in the disputed area and if his community loses the case he may lose his rights to the land and be expected to pay *isakole* on his farmlands; secondly, his farmland may be split by the boundary being advocated by the opposite community and his plans for expansion could be frustrated. Neither of these situations is welcomed by people in the frontier area.

Indeed, in almost all cases, the boundary disputes which have been most difficult to settle are those where the suggested boundary groups part or the whole of land effectively occupied by some members of a community with the territory of its neighbour. The people who are adversely affected raise objections to the boundary and consequently their community rejects it.

Although the above argument is true there is reason to doubt its applicability to all boundary disputes. The reason is that some boundary proposals are rejected before their detailed location is examined. Thus the Akures rejected proposals by District Officers on the Akure/Idanre boundary without examining its exact locations.[23] Similarly, the Ikales rejected many proposals on their boundary with Ondo without knowing the detailed location of the suggested boundary.[24]   It would therefore appear that the rejections were not caused by the fact that the suggested boundaries grouped members of the objecting community on the opposite side. However, a detailed examination of these disputes will reveal that the suggested boundaries did not in fact include a settlement or the site of a deserted settlement claimed by the party which rejected them. Thus the boundary proposals rejected by Akure did not group with it either the site of settlements destroyed during the wars with Benin in the nineteenth century or Alade and Atosin, claimed to have been founded by the Akures. Similarly the Ikales rejected all proposals which excluded some settlements or areas effectively occupied by them. Ibadan and Ijebu also wanted all territory occupied by their citizens.

From the foregoing it can be concluded that an implication of territorial claims is a desire by each community to have on its own side of the boundary all the territory once or presently occupied by its own members.

There are many reasons why each community wants its members together in the same political unit. The first is that each community used to be a distinct and independent political unit. As a political unit the larger the population the stronger it was and the more influence it could exert. In addition any of its members in another community would be considered foreigners there and might be expected to pay *isakole* for using the land or discriminated against in the provision of amenities. Furthermore, such people could be subjected to customs and traditions which are different from those of their own community. For these reasons the people grouped on the side of the boundary opposite to that of their own community do not want to stay, and their community does not want to lose them. For example, the Idanres, in the area formerly disputed with Akure and which was grouped with Akure District Council, complained of discrimination against them in the distribution of amenities and of being subjected to customary laws to which they were not used.[25] Consequently they demanded transfer to Idanre District Council.

Of equal importance is the relationship between people in the rural areas and their community headquarters. A man in the rural area attempts to build a house in his community headquarters where he sends his children to school. He prefers to go to hospital and make use of services in his community headquarters. He is therefore socially and emotionally attached to the community headquarters. For this reason he prefers to contribute to the development of the headquarters. Since, on the whole, the rural areas contribute more to than they receive from the headquarters the latter does not want to lose their support. It is therefore in the interest of the headquarters to ensure that it does not lose any rural population to its neighbours.

CAUSES OF BOUNDARY DISPUTES

The preceding discussion suggests that boundary disputes are caused by a combination of factors. The type of combinations of the factors discussed in the earlier section of the chapter may be illustrated as follows:

SCHEMATIC REPRESENTATION OF SOME CAUSES
OF BOUNDARY DISPUTES

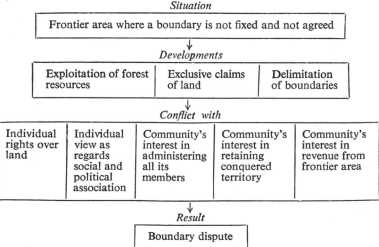

Situation

Frontier area where a boundary is not fixed and not agreed

↓

Developments

Exploitation of forest resources	Exclusive claims of land	Delimitation of boundaries

↓

Conflict with

Individual rights over land	Individual view as regards social and political association	Community's interest in administering all its members	Community's interest in retaining conquered territory	Community's interest in revenue from frontier area

↓

Result

Boundary dispute

The implication of the diagram is that boundary disputes arise when one community attempts to deny its neighbour the rights which the latter has, or had (enjoyed freely) within the frontier within which they intermixed during the contact stage of boundary evolution. Such attempts are most common during the stabilisation stage of boundary development. The reason is that with expansion and closer contact in the frontier areas each side tries to lay exclusive claim over some territory. The claims are based on each community's conception of its territory. The attempt at stabilisation caused each side to realise the intention or conception of its neighbour. Where the conceptions conflict, disputes arise. Therefore there is insistence on boundaries which accord with the present or past pattern of occupance. The claimant community may not even realise that the boundary it is suggesting would group some members of its neighbour with itself. On the other hand, an exaggerated claim may be made in the hope that after bargaining the claimant will be left with a fair share of the contact zone or area in dispute.

TYPES OF BOUNDARY DISPUTES

The purpose of a classification is to group together units having similar features and thereby reduce the complexity of phenomenona, thus bringing some order into the study of the units under consideration. It should be possible, as a result of classification, to make some generalisation about each of the groups. The type of generalisation made will depend on the objectives of the study and hence that of the classification itself. The study of boundary problems may aim at an understanding of the processes of boundary evolution or, alternatively, at the solution of the problems. The two objectives are interrelated. The completion of the processes of boundary evolution implies that the boundary problems (if any) have been solved and the boundary has been demarcated and is being administered. Therefore one cannot study the processes of boundary evolution without considering the solution of boundary problems. Hence it can be concluded that the study and classification of boundary problems is directed towards their solution. Each of the classes arrived at should comprise disputes which can be solved in similar ways.

If boundary disputes are to be satisfactorily settled it will be necessary to know the conditions which make it difficult to fix acceptable boundaries between communities. It would appear that disputes arising from the same or similar difficulties can be settled in the same way. Thus, the bases of classification adopted here are the situations and conditions which make it difficult to arrive at an acceptable boundary between adjacent communities. The different situations are as follows:

(1) where each side claims different points in the frontier as its boundary;

(2) where there is one agreed boundary point but no indication as to the direction of the boundary from that point;

(3) where there is desire by one side to claim back the part of its territory occupied by another (victorious) side in a past conflict;

(4) where there is opposition to the alteration of a superimposed boundary by the side which gains from it.

Disputes arising from the first situation may be described as *territorial disputes* in that they involve claims over some territory. Disputes of the second type are concerned with the location of the boundary and the interpretation of the boundary agreement. They may therefore be called *positional disputes*. The third situation arises from the military occupation of some areas and hence will involve what may be called *annexation disputes*. The fourth situation owes its origin to the superimposition of the boundary on the cultural landscape and disputes of this type may be called *superimposition disputes*.

It should be noted that the classes are not mutually exclusive. It is possible for disputes pertaining to different sections of a boundary to come under different classes. In general the class to which a particular boundary dispute belongs should be decided by the principal cause. If disputes over the various sectors differ considerably as to their causes each should be considered separately. In the following chapters each type will be examined in detail and illustrated with one example.

Notes and References

1. B. J. Matthews, 'Assessment Report on the Ikale District . . .' Part VIII, File O/C 143/1914, Ministry of Local Government, Okitipupa, p. 224.
2. Minutes of meeting held at Alade market between District Commissioner, Ondo and Akure, and Idanre representatives on 19 September 1912 to discuss forest concessions to Miller Brothers.
3. Ogoga of Ikere to Deji of Akure, 18 May 1953, File LR 22/2, AKDIVCO 4, N.A.I.
4. For example, see Resident, Ijebu Province, to Secretary, Southern Provinces, 6 April 1930, File 815 Vol. I, Oyo Prof. 3, N.A.I.
5. District Officer, Ife, to Commissioner, Oyo Province, 18 May 1916.
6. Oniware to D.O., Ibadan, 16 February 1932, File 72/1927, Oyo Div., N.A.I.
7. Jimo Osuntebo to D.O., Ibadan, 11 November 1930; and Bale of Ibadan to D.O., Ibadan, 24 November 1930, File 72/1927, Oyo Div. 2/14, N.A.I.
8. Minutes of Meeting held at Alade market, op. cit.
9. Sasere of Ondo in evidence in Ondo/Ikale boundary case, Ondo Provincial Court, April 1927.
10. See the Statements of Claim in Akure/Idanre boundary case, Suit No. W/40/ 1939, Supreme Court, Benin.
11. See D.O., Ife, to Senior Resident, Oyo Province, 18 March 1927; and Resident, Ijebu Province, to Resident, Oyo Province, 16 November 1927, File 07839 Vol. I, Oyo Prof. 3, N.A.I.
12. See the reasons given by Ijebu for rejecting the awards of 1924 and report by D.O., Ijebu-Ode and Ibadan, in April 1924 on the Ijebu/Ibadan boundary, File J51/1920, Ijebu Prof. 6/3, N.A.I.
13. The Owo farmers in an area formerly disputed between Akure and Owo now accept tenant status and pay *isakole* to Akure. For details of the boundary dispute, see Akure/Owo boundary case in *Deji of Akure* v. *Sasere of Owo*, Suit No. W/20/1939, High Court, Warri Judicial Division.
14. Officials of Ede District Council informed the writer in 1968 that the taxes in the formerly disputed area were collected by Edunabon. For further details, see Chapter VII.
15. Motaso, Bale of Araromi, opposed any boundary which cut across the territory he claimed, see File 1725A Vol. I, Ijebu Prof. 1, N.A.I.
16. The problems arising from non-compliance with individual claims made Akure reject the 1954 boundary agreement with Ikere: Deji to Ogoga, 26 August 1954, File LR 22/2, AKDIVCO 4, N.A.I.
17. The Aiyede/Orin boundary dispute is, in fact, a series of disputes between individual farmers who are in direct contact, see Chapter I for further details.
18. K. Robinson, 'Review of Ondo/Ikale Boundary Settlement', File 31615, C.S.O. 26, N.A.I.
19. Western Nigeria Boundary Commission, *Findings of the Ogundare Commission of Enquiry into the Boundary Dispute between Oyo and Ogbomoso given on the 29th Day of January*, 1971.

20. Judgment in Emure/Supare boundary case: *T. A. Adewumi* v. *Chief Omotosho Ojade*, Suit No. AK/27/63, High Court, Ado-Ekiti, 24 June 1970.
21. Oral information by Oni of Ife, 17 September 1968.
22. K. Robinson, op. cit.
23. See Chapter IV.
24. See Chapter II.
25. Idanre community, on the Idanre/Akure disputed area, to Ministry of Local Government, 1955, File LR19, AKDIVCO 4, N.A.I.

Territorial Boundary Disputes

COMMUNITIES IN Western Nigeria usually state that they have boundaries with their neighbours. In many cases there is no agreement on the location of the boundaries. In such situations each side will support the boundary it claims by reference to some factors which could be one or more of the following: (1) historical occupation, as evidenced by the establishment of settlements within the area enclosed by the boundary; (2) the point as far as which a link road was maintained; (3) alleged agreement by ancestors on boundary points on hills, along rivers or at specially decided places where trees or mounds were erected; (4) the boundary marks placed by government officials in the late nineteenth or the early twentieth centuries. In some cases there may be much territory between the different boundaries being claimed by the two sides. For this reason such disputes are described as territorial boundary disputes. The aim in this chapter is to examine the validity of the factors used to support boundary claims and to illustrate the nature of territorial boundary disputes by discussing one in detail.

HISTORY OF OCCUPATION

The first person to occupy an area effectively is regarded as the owner of the territory. But there is some disagreement over the interpretation of effective occupation. Some communities have laid claim to territory on the ground that they used to hunt there. This is the case with the Ikale claim to parts of the Otu River area now in Ondo Division.[1] As against such claims others have justified their rights over certain territory by the fact that they were the first to occupy it permanently by farming or establishing a settlement there. As explained in the previous chapter the latter view has been upheld by the courts. It is also generally agreed that a community's territory includes all unoccupied land between the farms and settle-

73

ments of its members. Despite these generally accepted principles disputes still arise for two reasons: first, some settlements were destroyed and their territory reverted to forest; and secondly, there may be disagreement over the community to which the founder of a settlement belongs.

Many settlements were destroyed during the interstate wars of the nineteenth century. Some of the settlements were never rebuilt and their sites have reverted to forest. In some cases the inhabitants of the settlements have either built new ones on another site or taken up residence in an existing neighbouring settlement. Where the inhabitants did not return to the land they occupied in the destroyed settlement there may be disputes over ownership of such territory at later time. The disputes would arise between any two of the possible claimants of the now forested site of the destroyed settlement. The claimants are: (1) the community which owned the destroyed settlement, (2) the community which overran the destroyed settlement, (3) a third community which later entered the forest which it regarded as virgin forest and in which its members were the first to make effective occupation. The arguments used when the first and second situations occur together will be examined under annexation disputes in Chapter VI. Where the first and third conditions occur each side will try to justify its claims by reference to the history of its occupation of the area.

Even where there has been no destruction of settlements there may be disputes, particularly over the allegiance of the founders and of the inhabitants. Traditionally, a settlement belongs to the community of the founder. In the case of settlements founded in a frontier area by someone who is not a member of either of the communities bordering on the frontier a settlement is regarded as that of the side which gave its founder permission to settle. Nevertheless, disputes may arise in two ways: over the origin of the founder, and over his allegiance.

The Yoruba are a patrilinear group, hence a person is presumed to belong to the community of his father. If a man founds a settlement it will normally be regarded as belonging to his father's community. Even then complications could arise in allocating settlements to either of two communities; for example, in the situation where a man leaves his father's community and first stayed in a neighbouring community before founding a settlement between his natal and his residential (or adopted) communities. The latter

could claim that it permitted such a person to occupy the area and
found the settlement, whilst the natal community could also lay
claim to the settlement. This is exactly the case with Alakowe,
between Ife and Ilesa. The founder was Ijesa, but he migrated to
Ile-Ife where he became the secretary to the Oni. Later he founded
Alakowe, eight kilometres from Ile-Ife and twenty-four kilometres
from Ilesa. The Oni of Ife claimed that he gave land to the founder.[2]
During discussions leading to the delimitation of the Ife-Ijesa boundary the latter claimed Alakowe on the ground that the founder
was Ijesa (Fig. 10).

Claim over a settlement could also be established through allegiance owed to a particular community. Everyone leaving a community still regards himself as part of that community. This was
especially so in the case of the hunters and farmers who occupied
the frontier areas and established settlements there. The allegiance
is usually expressed in the form of tribute paid to the *oba* of the
community from whom sanction is sought for the appointment of
chiefs in the rural areas. Therefore one way of determining the
allegiance of a settlement is to find out the community which appoints
its chiefs and to which the majority of the people are socially attached.
In some cases the main group of people in a settlement may be from
a different community from that of the founders, and the appointment of chiefs may be undertaken by the community of the majority
of the inhabitants. Among settlements in this category are those
between the Rivers Sasa and Osun which were founded by Ife and
which originally owed allegiance to that community. During the
nineteenth century refugees from the Oyo kingdom, under siege of
Fulani armies,[3] flocked into them and became the dominant element
in their population. Consequently those people started electing the
chiefs and allegiance of the settlements to Ife was broken. Examples
of settlements in this group are Gbongan and Apomu. Of a similar
nature is that of Alade which was founded by Akure elements but
where Idanres settled and became dominant, thus changing the
allegiance of the settlement.[4]

Each of these situations may lead to conflicts involving the
affected settlements and hence to disputes as to the extent of territory
claimed. In other words the territorial claims will not be mutually
exclusive as would have been the case if such situations did not arise.

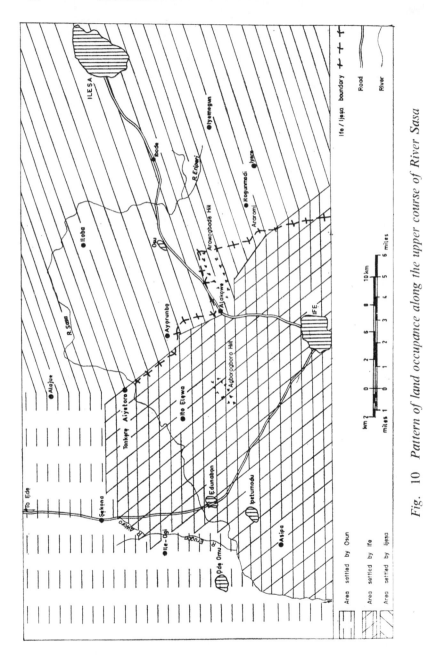

Fig. 10   *Pattern of land occupance along the upper course of River Sasa*

POINT TO WHICH ROAD WORK IS EXTENDED

The maintenance of the road between any two settlements is undertaken by both and the point at which they meet is generally regarded as their boundary. For this reason each community ensures that its neighbour does not extend roadworks beyond the boundary. For example the Ife community protested when Edes wanted to extend roadworks beyond River Aworo which was the boundary being claimed by Ife[5] (Fig. 23). Unfortunately this practice was misunderstood by government officials who were delimiting boundaries early in the twentieth century—they started adopting the roads themselves rather than points along them as boundaries. The problems created by such interpretation were discussed in Chapter II. Even without such misinterpretation of the practice, disputes arose as to which point on the road each side stopped road works. Thus Idanre's claim regarding its boundary with Akure (which was not accepted by Akure) was based on the extent to which it carried on roadworks.[6] The same is true of the claims of Ikale, Igbotako and Aye regarding their boundary with Ondo, which claims the latter disputes.[7]

RIVERS AND HILLS

There is abundant evidence that important features such as rivers and hills were adopted as boundaries between communities and nearly all large rivers have certain sections of their courses used as boundaries. Nevertheless, even here there are disputes deriving their sources from disagreement over hills and rivers as boundaries. In the case of hills, the problem is mainly one of identification: first, of the name of the hill and secondly, of the location.

It is possible for two communities to agree that the boundary lies on a range of hills but they may disagree on which of the peaks to use. Each side will recognise a different peak and the difference between the two may be considerable. In other cases there may be no agreement on the range of hills and the distances between the hills being cited could be considerable. For example the hills cited as boundaries by Akure and their northern neighbours (Ota-Ekun by Akure, and Opa-Meta-Ero by Ogotun)[8] are located many kilometres apart (Fig. 4).

The most probable explanation for the first situation is that the names were given to hill ranges rather than to individual peaks in them. Therefore there could be differences as to which peak is the most important and to which the name should apply. Evidence that names are attached to hill ranges rather than individual peaks can be found in many areas. For example Ota-Ekun, between Igbara-Odo and Ilawe, is the name of a range of hills stretching for a distance of about six kilometres (Fig. 4). The same is true of Orokun hill, between Iju and Ikere (Fig. 8B), and also of Arowogbade hill near Ile-Ife (Fig. 10).

The second situation is probably due to the fact that each side is claiming the farthest extent to which its people went before meeting members of the opposite community. There were no permanent settlements at such points which were visited only occasionally. For that reason most communities do not consider it vital that they should now have rights as far as the hills claimed. Thus the Akures themselves described their claim to Ota-Ekun as 'fantastic'[9] and Ijesas have not insisted that their boundary with Ife should be made to pass through Agborogboro hill which they once claimed marked the boundary.[10] In these and other cases the communities have settled for less than they originally claimed.

There are two problems in the case of rivers. In the case of large rivers there may be disagreement on the point at which the boundaries start. The reason for disagreement is that although the point at which a river starts to be the boundary is either a crossing point or a confluence there could be more than one crossing point and there could also be differences as to the confluence at which the boundary starts. Large rivers can be crossed near their sources and the communities occupying the area in which they take their sources would make such crossings at many points until they reach the area where the return journey to their base is not easy (Fig. 3). Downstream of such a point there would be other crossing points. It is therefore possible for one community to name one point whilst the other claims another one. An example of this is found along the River Sasa which is the boundary between Ife and Osun Divisions to the west (Fig. 10). The river takes its source near Iyere in Ijesaland where it is known as Eriperi. It flows generally westwards before turning north, in which direction it flows for about three kilometres before turning eastwards. In the upper course both sides are farmed by Ijesas. Downstream both sides are farmed by Ifes and the Ifes founded settlements such as Ogi on the opposite side. Ifes, at Edunabon, have crossed it to farm on the opposite side. Further downstream, about the latitude of Asipa, Ife had no farms on the opposite side and the only ones there are those of people in Osun. In the early twentieth century the River Sasa was made the boundary between Ife and the western neighbours now in Osun Division. However, there was no statement as to the point from which the boundary starts on the river. Ede, one of the communities in Osun, claimed it starts at the point where the Ijesa/Ife boundary reaches the Osun. That interpretation meant that Ife would have no claim to land on the opposite side of the river. Ife pointed out that it had occupied land on the other side before the river was adopted as the boundary. It therefore suggested that the Ife/Ede boundary should start at the confluence of the Rivers Sasa and Erugba, about thirteen kilometres downstream of the area claimed by Ede.[11]

Apart from disagreement on points on a river there may be disagreement on the rivers named as the boundary. An example of this type of dispute is that between Ifon and Ilobu. Ifon once claimed that the boundary is at the River Erinle (or Enle) and that the Ilobus were trespassers on the land they occupied. At the same time Ilobu claimed that the boundary is at River Elentere[12] (Fig. 11). The cause of such disputes is possibly the failure by both sides to specify the points at which the boundaries being claimed started and ended on the rivers. It is possible that each had rights as far as the river named. Thus in the Ifon/Ilobu example the two communities could be right as to their having the rivers as boundaries. However, the fact that Ifon may have claims to the upper courses of River Erinle does not mean that it has rights over other sections. Similarly, the fact that Ilobu may have claims to the lower course of River Elentere does not mean that it had any rights in the upper course. But so long as the communities do not specify the points at which boundaries start and end on rivers, it may be difficult to avoid disputes of this nature.

A third problem that could arise on rivers is dispute as to which rivers were intended in boundary agreements. The dispute could be due to either the wrong naming of streams on the map accompanying the agreement or to disagreement as to which river bears a particular name. An example of the first situation is that of the map accompanying the boundary agreement between Ife and Ijesa in 1932 (Fig. 16). The agreement was to the effect that the boundary should be along River Amuta, but the accompanying map placed it along River Opa, which was mistakenly named River Amuta.[13]

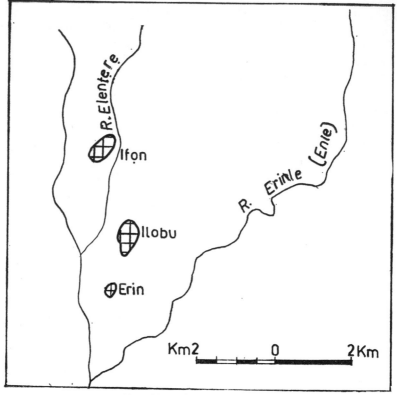

Fig. 11   *Ifon-Ilobu frontier*

BOUNDARY MARKS PLACED BY GOVERNMENT OFFICIALS

Many communities support their boundary claims by reference to boundary marks placed by government officials in the late nineteenth or the early twentieth centuries. There are many reasons why this is done. In the first place, many communities point out that the government officials made enquiries as to the location of the boundary before fixing the marks. It is argued that the truth was told then and later denials of the points admitted were afterthoughts. Quite often the community seeking a change argues that it had no idea of what was happening or that the government officials did not explain that they were fixing boundary marks.

An examination of the records kept by some of the officers shows that they always enquired about boundaries. However, in some cases there was strong opposition to the boundary they delimited.

A good example was that between Ondo and Ikale, where the boundary was imposed against apparent opposition from the Ikales.[14] There is also the fact that government officials overruled objections from both sides on the boundary they fixed between Ife and Ijesa in 1913.[15] The foregoing, and the admission by government officials of the fallibility of earlier decisions, indicate that not much reliance can be placed on the boundary marks they fixed. The admission of fallibility is shown by the attempts to reconsider earlier decisions and, where necessary, establish new boundaries. The various attempts made to delimit the Ondo/Ikale boundary, the Ife/Ijesa boundary and the northern boundaries of Ijebu Province all illustrate the point that government officials realised that earlier decisions could be wrong.

Among the reasons why wrong decisions were taken were impatience and lack of understanding of indigenous boundaries. For example, note the remark, by the official enquiring about the Ikale/Ondo boundary, that the end of road works is not indicative of territorial rights.[16] There was also the practice of adopting roads as boundaries, and lack of understanding of the full implications of marks adopted by the local people. On the one hand they did not always realise that it implied a straight line passing through the point, and even where lines were adopted the directions were not clear to them. The lack of understanding is shown by the complaint of the Owa of Ilesa thus:

> In the Major Tucker's description (1901) and in the subsequent boundary agreements of 1913 and 1932 geographical description which where foreign to the parties concerned and could not be intelligently assimilated by them where employed. There were no explanations for their introduction and neither side knew, exactly, the position of the imaginary lines 'North-West, North-East' and so on; hence the [not] infrequent cases of trespassing and the incessant feuds in their trail.[17]

AKURE/IDANRE BOUNDARY DISPUTE

There is scarcely any boundary dispute where all the reasons listed above are cited by one or even by both sides. Ideally it would have been better to give detailed descriptions of a number of boundary disputes to illustrate all the references. But such an approach would lead to unnecessary repetition and make no major contribution to the understanding of boundary problems. Nevertheless it is considered advisable that one example of territorial boundary disputes be discussed to illustrate as many of the points as possible and at the same time show the characteristics of this type of dispute. The Akure/Idanre boundary dispute is chosen because it illustrates three of the four factors discussed above: history of occupation as shown by the establishment of settlements; point fixed by government officials in the late nineteenth and the early twentieth centuries; and reference to points fixing the extent of road maintenance. Besides, this was one of the most serious disputes in Western Nigeria.

Akure and Idanre are about twenty-three kilometres apart in the eastern section of Western Nigeria (Fig. 12). Idanre used to be situated on a rocky hill to which access was very difficult. Although the Idanre people themselves claim that they came to the hill at the time other communities were founded by migrants from Ile-Ife[18], it seems more likely that they sought refuge there during the wars before the twentieth century, but long after the migrations from Ile-Ife. Whatever the time of its foundation Idanre grew to be an independent kingdom and there was need for a boundary between it and neighbouring kingdoms. One of the latter was Akure which lies on the plains to the north of the Idanre hills and had a path to Benin along the eastern edge of the hills. As with many other kingdoms in Yorubaland the boundary between Akure and Idanre was not clearly established before the twentieth century, and in any case nobody attempted to locate it.

The first enquiry about the boundary between the two communities appears to have been made by one Captain Scott in 1897 when he asked the Owa (oba) of Idanre the location of his boundary with Akure. The Owa was reported as saying that the boundary was at Alade market,[19] about three kilometres from the scarp of the hills on which Idanre was then located. This last point was confirmed in 1902 when Major Reeve-Tucker, Travelling Commissioner, reached the area. It is claimed that he was told by the Owa that the boundary was at Alade market, whereupon he set a stone cairn to mark it.[20]

DEVELOPMENT OF THE DISPUTE

The first reported disagreement took place in 1912 when a forest concession was to be granted to Miller Brothers and it became necessary to determine how royalties from timber in the area should be divided between the two communities. It would appear that Akure first claimed that Idanre should not have any share in royalties. However, at a meeting held at Alade and attended by the District Commissioner for Ondo, Akure and Idanre as well as the representatives of both Akure and Idanre on 12 September 1912, the contention on both sides was that there was no boundary between them. Akure people stated that members of their community had farms as far as Idanreland, while the Idanres cultivated plots on the east side of the Idanre–Akure road as far as Ofosu River in Akureland. The Akures said that they would prefer not to have a boundary between themselves and Idanre, and that royalties from the forest should be shared equally between the two communities. The Idanres confirmed that there was never a boundary between them and agreed that revenue from the forest should be shared equally between them and Akure.[21]

The first real complaint was made in 1918 when Idanre reported that an Akure man was farming on Idanreland without the permission of Idanre chiefs. The man was reported to have claimed that the Deji (*oba* of Akure) gave him permission to farm in the area.[22] On receiving the complaint the Resident, Ondo Province, requested the Deji of Akure to tell the man to leave the land in question. This was done, although the Deji protested that the land belonged to the Akure people and that the Idanres only occupied it with Akure's permission. The Deji also complained that the Idanres were trespassing on Akure land.[23]

The first major complaint by Akure was made in 1926 when the Deji protested[24] against Idanre occupation of land belonging to some Akure villages destroyed by Benin during the nineteenth century. These villages were Oto, Ao, Idesi, Iriji, Odo, Aso and Amu. That protest was followed by another in January 1927 when Akure complained that the Idanres were extending their farms on Akureland.[25] Later that year the Akures declared that their territory was bounded on the west by the River Owena, on the south by the River Ofosu and Benin Province, on the east by the River Ogbese and on the north by Igbara-Odo and Ikere. They argued that they were claiming the land on the left bank of the River Owena extending eastwards to their boundaries with Owo and Benin. This was justified as follows:

> In the primitive age when lands were being partitioned among the emigrants from Ile-Ife, on the Western side Akure had

its boundary with Owa of Ijesha and the Osemawe of Ondo, on the Southern side with the Oba of Benin on the eastern side with the Owa of Owo and the Arinjale of Ise and on the northern side with the Ewi of Ado.[26]

They also stated that the Idanres migrated from another location to settle on Akureland and were allowed to stay because it was the custom to welcome strangers. Finally they requested that the Idanres should maintain their status as strangers and acknowledge Akure ownership of the land in dispute.[27]

ATTEMPTS AT RECONCILIATION

Because of the petitions, two Assistant District Officers were appointed by the government to visit the disputed area in November 1926. They reported that the Idanres made three different claims as to the location of their boundary with Akure. These points were at Iloro (about two kilometres from Akure), Adofure (about five kilometres from Akure) and Akinoro's farm (about ten kilometres from Akure) (Fig. 12). These claims were justified on the ground that the Idanres used to maintain the roads to the points named. For their part, the Akures claimed that the boundary crossed the Idanre–Akure road at Alade which was founded by one Deji and an influential woman named Olokoju.[28]

In assessing these claims the investigators observed that villages to the south of Akinoro's farm were inhabited by Idanre farmers who attended Idanre Native Court, while villages to the north were inhabited by Akures who attended Akure Native Court. They noted that construction work on the new road from Alade to Akure had been carried out as far as Akinoro's farm by the Idanres and that the road ceased abruptly there. The Idanres explained that the Akures were responsible for labour beyond Akinoro's farm. In view of these findings they recommended that:

> . . . the boundary be fixed from the Owena River to the Ogbese River running due east and west and crossing the Idanre–Akure road in the vicinity of Kinoro's [Akinoro's] farm[29] (Fig. 12).

The recommendations were rejected by Akure,[30] hence there was further discussion of a possible solution. During such discussion the District Officer, Ondo, apparently in support of the above recommendation, stated in 1928 that there was an almost direct route from Idanre to Owo which was made by the Idanres in 1924.

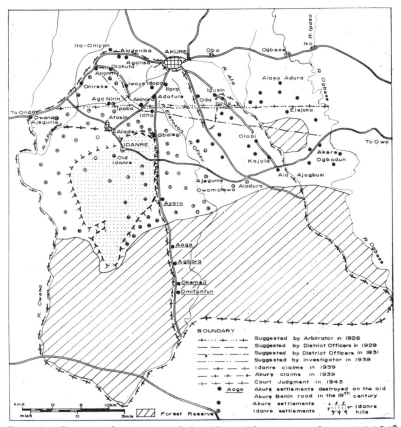

Fig. 12   *Suggested positions of the Akure-Idanre Boundary* 1926-1943

He was of the opinion that a large area of land to the north of the road was undoubtedly cultivated by the Idanres. He explained that the Idanres claimed that all land as far as Adofure belonged to them and that the road to Akure was made to Akinoro's farm with the intention of continuing it to Adofure. They stopped at Akinoro's farm because the Akures were not prepared to make the portion between Akure and Adofure. He then observed that the Idanres wanted a boundary drawn from the Aponmu River on the Ondo–Akure road, passing through Akinoro's farm and terminating at the point where the Idanre–Owo trade route crosses the Ogbese River.[31]

There was further discussion of the whole problem at the governmental level and this led to a decision to recommend a boundary defined as follows:

> The main road from the Owena River to the Aponmu on the Ondo–Akure road, thence from the River Aponmu on the Ondo–Akure road by a line passing through Kinoro's [Akinoro's] farm and terminating at the point where the Idanre–Owo trade route crosses the Ogbese River[32] (Fig. 12).

In sending this recommendation to the Deji of Akure the District Officer, Ado Ekiti, remarked as follows: 'if you are unwilling to accept this boundary then you must take your case to court and before a hearing can be given you must provide a detailed survey of the area in dispute at your own expense.'[33] The Deji replied that he was not prepared to accept the boundary and that he would engage a 'surveyor who will survey all the land around my town which belong to my fathers. I will then put the matter to court.'[34]

Following Akure's rejection of the recommendation, further attempts were made to settle the dispute. These led to a suggestion by the District Officers that Idanre should relinquish claims to the area between the Ala and Ogbese Rivers and the boundary should pass along a line from Aponmu, through Akinoro's farm to the Ala River. The suggestion was accepted by the Idanres[35] and the Owa signed an agreement to that effect in 1931. However, Akure did not accept the compromise, but insisted that the boundary should run from the intersection of the Ondo–Akure road and the River Owena to Alade and then eastwards to the Ofosu River. On account of this and the unsettled situation in the disputed area another investigation was ordered in 1938. Although the Akures first agreed to co-operate with the investigator, they withdrew their representatives and labourers when it appeared to them that too much attention was being paid to the boundary suggested in 1931 and that the new investigator might also recommend that boundary. Despite their withdrawal a new boundary was suggested as:

> From the village of Aponmu on the Akure–Ondo road by the bush path which goes in an easterly direction to Kinoro's farm, thence in a straight line east-west to the Ala River. The farm hamlet of Kinoro to be on the Akure side of the boundary[36] (Fig. 12).

This last suggestion was not accepted by the Akures who went on to institute a court action against the Idanres.

THE COURT CASE

The case was based on the statement of claim (quoted in full to show the arguments adduced,)[37] made by the Deji of Akure and which ran as follows:

1. The Plaintiff is the Deji of Akure and sues for himself and on behalf of the people of Akure.
2. The Defendant is sued as the Owa of Idanre for himself and on behalf of the Idanre people.
3. The Plaintiff is the owner of all that piece or parcel of land situate on the East of the Owena River in the Akure District in the Ondo province of Nigeria and bounded on the North by the Akure–Ondo Road, on the South by the Ondo/Benin provincial Boundary, on the West by the Owena River as shown in the plea filed in this action.
4. From time immemorial the Owena River has been the natural and recognised boundary between the Plaintiff and (a) the Ondo people towards the Southern section of the River and (b) the Ilesha people towards the Northern section of the River, while the Ofosu River towards its Southern section was the recognised boundary between the Plaintiff and the Benin people.
5. The Idanre people are strangers on the Eastern side of the Owena River; their original homes were known as 'Ikadun' and 'Itaja' on the Western side of the Owena River in the Ikale District.
6. The Idanre District dialect, salutations, facial marks, dress and customs are akin to those of the Ikale and Ondo tribes on the Western side of the Owena River and very much unlike those of the Akure and other Ekiti tribes on the Eastern side of the Owena River.
7. The Idanre people were driven from their original homes in the Ikale District by inter-tribal wars and incessant raids and a portion of them having crossed the Owena River settled on Akure land at a place known as Abababubu then under the supervision of the Olofin priest of Akure on the Eastern bank of the Owena River, but finding that they were open to constant raids by their enemies from the Western side of the Owena during the dry season they removed with the consent of the said Olofin priest and the approval of the then Deji of Akure to the hills and high rocks of Orosun where the Olofin priest was then residing, that being a place which was quite im-pregnable in the olden days, the high hills, caves, deep valleys and the rugged nature of the locality affording them protection on every approach except on the Akure side.
8. These Idanre settlers were allowed by the Deji of Akure to cultivate freely on the adjoining lands as long as they acknow-

ledge the Akure ownership of the lands which at that time was not at all disputed. As time went on the population of the Idanre settlers increased and the area occupied by them was being gradually extended, but at that time not beyond a radius of about four miles around the hills on which they settled.

9. After the last Akure/Benin war towards the close of the nineteenth century in which the Benins destroyed the entire villages and towns belonging to Akure in the Ofosu Forest and the neighbourhood thereof, the Idanre people had free access to some parts of the area devastated by the said war and extended towards Ofosu Forest, but as they did not then dispute the Akure ownership of the said lands no objection was raised by the Akure people.

10. After the advent of the British rule, and in 1902 Major William Reeve-Tucker, a Travelling Commissioner, who was then in charge of the District including Akure and Ondo discussed with the Deji and his chiefs the question of land boundaries between Akure and her immediate neighbours with particular reference to the Idanre people who were then occupying a large tract of Akure land. The Deji at first was unwilling to have any land boundary with the Idanres who were his strangers but on the advice of the Commissioner, the said Major Tucker, the Deji agreed to a demarcation of the land to be occupied by the Idanres. The Commissioner, with the representatives of the Deji of Akure and the Owa of Idanre, met together and fixed the boundary at Alade Market.

11. The limits of the said boundaries were observed until about twenty years ago when the Idanre people began to extend beyond the said boundaries and to make farms on the area now in dispute and also began to claim the said lands as their own and from that time the dispute began and continued and as a result the present action was instituted.

12. The Plaintiff has from time immemorial been the owner of the said area in dispute and has been in undisturbed and peaceful possession thereof.

13. The Defendant has exceeded the area allowed by the Plaintiff for the occupation of himself and his people and has trespassed on the land in dispute and in spite of repeated warnings, the Defendant, his servants and Agents have not desisted from committing acts of trespass on the said land of the Plaintiff.

In defence, the Idanres argued that their town was founded long before Akure. Further, they had long owned and occupied the land in dispute and where the Akures had settled in the area they were trespassers except where they occupied by leave and licence of the Idanres.

Judgment in the case was given in 1943 and in his summary the judge remarked that a witness pointed out that up to 1900 Idanre farms did not extend beyond a mile (1.6 km) radius of their hill settlement. Also that in all previous settlements Akure had rejected any boundary which gave part of the area claimed to Idanre. He accepted the claim of Akure that Major Reeve-Tucker set a cairn at Alade in 1902 to mark the boundary. He thought the intention of that cairn was that the boundary should run east and west of Alade market. He concluded as follows:[37]

> I hold that the Northern boundary of Idanre runs from Aiyede through Alade Market to where the eastern boundary of Idanreland, if any, intersects the line.

Also that:

> I am unable to accept defendant's claim that his territory extended beyond the Akure–Ofosu–Usehin road which has for many years been recognised as Akure road.
>
> The Northern boundary of Idanreland would therefore end at Badegi [Gbalegi] market where the Northern boundary line intersects the Akure–Ofosu–Usehin road [Fig. 13].

POST-JUDGMENT DEVELOPMENTS

Following the judgment the Akures made the following demands:

(i) All villages and farmsteads in the area should be administered by the Akure Native Authority.
(ii) Taxes collected from Akure villages in the area (Oke Meji, Ofosu and Aogo) by the Idanre Native Authority from 1934 onwards should be paid back to the Akure Native Authority.
(iii) Atosin village should be considered an Akure village from the date of judgment and taxes paid by the inhabitants to the Idanre N.A. should be paid back to the Akure N.A.
(iv) All royalties on timber from the area paid erroneously to the Idanre N.A. since 1914 should be refunded to the Akure N.A.
(v) Akure should take up the upkeep of the road from Alade to Owena with effect from the date of judgment.
(vi) All existing and new Idanre villages on the Ofosu road or within a quarter of a mile to the west should be administered by the Akure N.A.
(vii) The Deji's interest on the area lying to the west of Ofosu road which was granted to the Idanres as a concession for farming purposes and for occupation be maintained and that the position prior to 1914 be restored from 30 June 1943: i.e. that the royalties accruing on timber from that area

be shared fifty-fifty between Akure and Idanre, Akure claims in this respect during the interim between 1914 and the date of judgment being waived.

(viii) All Idanre farmers in the area should not extend their existing farms or clear new sites for farming purposes without written permission of the Deji and Council.[39]

The government did not agree to merge the area with Akure because 'the fact that a certain area of land has been awarded to a particular party or parties is no guarantee that the administrative boundary will be altered accordingly'.[40] Following the decision Akure requested that if people in the area would not pay their taxes to Akure they should pay *isakole*. Upon this, the people of Alade agreed to pay tax to Akure if the government directed them to do so.[41] The Alades were rebuked for their decision by the Idanres who pointed out that Alade people left Oke Idanre with the permission of the Owa in 1928. The Idanres also decided not to pay either *isakole* or to have the area transferred to Akure. In order to have their action certified they took Akure to court in 1948 on the following grounds:[42]

(i) That the people of Idanre are entitled to remain in peaceful possession of all those portions of land already occupied by them within the area adjudged to belong to Akure in 1943;

(ii) that the demand of Akure for the payment of *isakole* in respect of their said occupation of the land in dispute is illegal, oppressive and contrary to equity and good conscience.

Judgment in this case was delivered against the Idanres because, according to the judge:

It is an incontrovertible fact that the owner of a piece of land who has not lost title thereto is entitled to derive some benefit from his right of ownerships unless he willingly foregoes it. It is therefore natural for the Akure people to wish to derive some benefit from their ownership of the land in question.

The defendant has acted ... within his legal rights and the plantiff has failed to make a case to justify the declaration and the injunction asked for.[43]

The Idanres appealed against the judgment but lost the appeal. Following the decision of Idanre's appeal the government decided that the area be transferred to Akure District so that the administrative boundary follows that declared by the court and that:

... steps be taken to have the limits of the land awarded to the people of Akure in the judgment ascertained and demarcated as soon as administrative and survey officers can be found for this purpose in order that in due course the areas of jurisdiction of the two Native Authorities should be adjusted accordingly.[44]

The decision was not acceptable to the Idanres who decided to prevent the demarcation when it was started in 1952. When the demarcation was to be started, on 2 January 1952, some armed men from Idanre appeared on the scene. When they attempted to obstruct the work, policemen accompanying the surveyors were ordered to shoot. In the ensuing encounter some police officers were wounded and some Idanres killed. After that the surveyors carried on their work without molestation.

The surveyors encountered many technical difficulties during the demarcation. The most notable of these was that the boundary passed through cocoa farms such that it was difficult to be surveyed and demarcated without destroying a number of cocoa and other trees of economic value. The Idanres[45] were opposed to any destruction of their crops in order that the boundary should be demarcated. In the end compromise was reached as shown in Fig. 13.

ADMINISTRATION OF THE AREA

For purposes of administration the area was transferred to Akure District. The transfer was criticised by Idanre people in the disputed area who in 1955 appealed to the government to separate them from Akure District for the following reasons.[46]

1. Idanres constitute the entire population of the area and are quite different from the Akures with whom they were grouped for administrative purposes.
2. Some Idanres in the disputed area were forced to pay tax to both Akure and Idanre.
3. Customary court judges in Akure do not understand the native law and custom of Idanre settlers, but as a result of administrative grouping Idanres were forced to take their cases to Akure.
4. They were not well catered for by Akure District Council—their markets were neglected and they were discriminated against in the distribution of scholarships, health facilities and road development.
5. Their ability to produce more crops was hindered by the by-

law which required them to get permission from Akure before they could expand their farms and debarred anyone with up to thirty acres from cultivating more.

As against the above they based their demand to join Idanre on better communications between them and that town, historical association and their desire to pay their tax to Idanre District Council which had become less viable since they were required to pay to Akure District.

Their request was granted in 1961 when the area was transferred to Idanre District.[47] Following the transfer Akure decided to collect *isakole* from all Idanre farmers in the area but this was opposed by Alade people who claimed that they did not pay *isakole* before and prayed 'Idanre District Council not to pay any penny of our money as *isakole* to Akure people.'[48] Akure District Council replied that 'all privileges previously enjoyed by Alade people under the Akure District Council were automatically forfeited immediately they decided to become part of Idanre District Council.'[49]

Although Akure had the right to collect *isakole* in the area it appears they were not pleased with its merger with Idanre District Council. They revealed this in June 1969 when they said:

> Another request of very great importance to us is the restoration of Akureland being administered by the Idanre District Council to the administration of Akure District Council. Such an anomaly has not made for peace and good government in our area. For Akure to own the land on the one hand, and Idanre District Council to be made to administer it on the other hand poses a big problem for this or any other generation.[50]

AN APPRAISAL OF THE DISPUTE

The foregoing account illustrates many of the features of territorial boundary disputes in Western Nigeria and these may be examined under the following heads: (i) causes of the dispute, (ii) the role of administrators in reconciliation, (iii) the problems of boundary delimitation and demarcation, (iv) coincidence of administrative and communal boundaries.

CAUSES OF THE DISPUTE

The dispute started when the two communities were requested to indicate their boundaries in order to determine the amount of timber royalties to be paid to each by Miller Brothers. One of the most surprising aspects of the dispute is the fact that both communities stated at that time that there was no boundary between them and rather than agree on one they decided that the royalties should be divided equally between them. In spite of such agreement a boundary dispute started in 1918. This therefore raises the question: why did accusation of trespass start in 1918—six years after the two communities declared that there was no boundary between them? Among possible answers to the question are the following: first, that although there was no fixed boundary between the two communities each recognised its own area of influence and complaints began when the other side started to enter such recognised area. In support of this is the frequent use by both sides of the terms 'Akureland' and 'Idanreland' during the discussions in 1912. If the sphere of influence of each was not known at that time the distinction indicated by those terms could possibly not have been drawn.

A second possible answer is that there were agreements on specific points, particularly along the roads, but the location of a boundary between the points was not agreed upon. This can be supported by the fact that Idanre was reported as saying in 1897 and 1902 that the boundary was at Alade market. If that was true then it can be assumed that complaints began when Idanre started to cross the agreed points. Such crossing possibly started when, after the establishment of colonial administration, the Idanres began to come down from their hill location and occupy land on the plains. The resulting expansion led them to cross the meeting point with Akure. It may be suggested that in the case of such expansion the Idanres would have gone southwards where there was more land. That was not done for two reasons. The first is that in all likelihood people would have moved towards the main towns and major roads at the time. The main towns nearby were Akure and Ondo and the nearest market was Alade on the way to both towns. It seems quite natural, therefore, that people would expand in the direction of those towns. The main road was that from Akure to Benin, passing east of the Idanre hills and it would have been natural for them to move along that road. In other words there were adequate reasons why they should settle to the north and the east of the hills and hence occupy land which the Akures regarded as their own.

Secondly, there is the fact that the government declared most of the unoccupied land to the south of the Idanre hills a forest reserve in 1918.[51] People were thus prohibited from farming on it even though some land was set apart for the use of villages already established in the area. The effect was that the Idanres had no alternative to moving northeast and north of their hill location.

However, it should not be forgotten that if Idanre had accepted Alade as a boundary point and the rights of Akure to areas north of Alade, all that would have been needed was for Idanres to seek permission of Akure to use the land. That did not happen, instead Idanre claimed that the agreed point was much further north than Alade. It was the conflicting claims that gave rise to the dispute in the first instance.

THE ROLE OF ADMINISTRATORS

Once the dispute started it was not quickly settled because of the lack of detailed knowledge about the area by those who were to settle it. The point is illustrated by the suggestion which assumed that Idanreland extended as far as the River Ogbese, while at a later date, in 1931, the Idanres readily gave up claim to all areas between the River Ogbese and the River Ala. Again there was the assumption that because the Idanres were found south of Akinoro's farm on the Akure–Alade road they were in all areas south of a line drawn from Akinoro to the Ogbese River. In fact such a line would have given undisputed Akure land and villages to Idanre, the most notable of these being Oda. In any case fieldwork in the area during 1969 showed that the Idanres do not occupy all areas to the south of such a line (Fig. 12). There was also the apparent failure of the administrators to investigate and refute or confirm the Akure claim that some of its villages on the Akure–Benin road were destroyed by Benin before the advent of the British.

Part of the reason why the administrators failed in the instances mentioned above was that they had no good maps of the area and in any case no detailed survey was ordered until that of 1938 when the suggested boundary near Akinoro was to have been established. The administrative officers, with all their good intentions, could not suggest a boundary acceptable to both communities. The main point to note is that in spite of the long negotiations they did not enforce (although they suggested) an arbitrary boundary.

The Problems of Boundary Delimitation and Demarcation

One of the reasons why the administrators suggested an arbitrary boundary was lack of a detailed survey of the area showing the pattern of human occupation. But much more important is the fact that they were guided by only one point in fixing a boundary with a length of more than thirty kilometres The dependence on points also affected the court judgment which was based on two widely separated points at Alade and Aiyede. The court decision that the boundary should be a straight line joining Alade and Aiyede did not take into consideration the fact that the shortest distance need not be the boundary. Such a decision has the disadvantage that the straight line may pass through farms and even split hamlets and buildings. The latter creates problems during demarcation and the side adversely affected is likely not to co-operate in finding a solution. This was the case with the judgment boundary: when it was found to cut through farms, Idanre opposed the destruction of their crops so that the demarcation could be carried on. In the end the straight line was abandoned and a sinuous line substituted. The point being made here is that anyone concerned with the settlement of boundary disputes must realise that the straight line between any two fixed points does not necessarily make a good boundary.

Because of the problems discussed above, the demarcated boundary was different from that delimited in the court judgment of 1943, and hence the Idanres rejected it. The demarcated boundary followed footpaths to Idanre farms and in two instances it split settlements (Ayo village in the west and Alade itself) (Fig. 13). The practice of using footpaths as boundaries is objectionable because roads and footpaths are not divisive but unifying features. Members of the same community use land on both sides of a footpath or a road and their settlements are not confined to only one side of the road—buildings are erected on both sides. Hence roads have not served as good boundaries in those places where they have been so adopted. It is therefore not surprising that the Idanres have not accepted the demarcated boundary.

The problem created by the use of straight lines and footpaths can be avoided if those involved in boundary delimitation state that the boundary shall not divide a farm or a village between the two sides. In other words each individual would have his own farm on one side and all the buildings in a settlement would be grouped

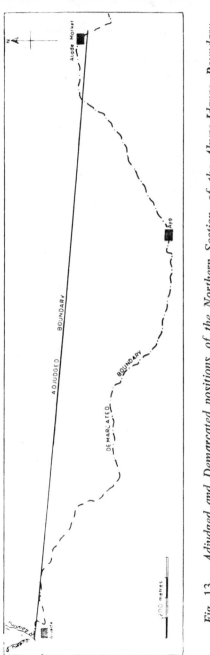

Fig. 13   Adjudged and Demarcated positions of the Northern Section of the Akure-Idanre Boundary

on only one side. If this had been adopted in the demarcation of the Akure/Idanre boundary the final outcome would probably have been acceptable to both sides.

SUGGESTED SOLUTION

In view of the foregoing it would be advisable for a solution of this problem to take the following lines:

(i) The boundary should be properly demarcated in a way that will be acceptable to both communities. In such demarcation no one's farm should be split by the boundary and no settlement should be divided between the two sides.

(ii) All Idanre farmers on Akureland, whether or not in the formerly disputed area, should pay *isakole* to Akure on bases agreed between the two communities.

(iii) Areas predominantly inhabited by Idanre in Akureland and adjacent to Idanreland should be administered as part of Idanre and all Idanre settlers there should pay their taxes to Idanre District Council.

(iv) Other settlers in areas transferred to Idanre under (iii) who desire to pay their taxes to Akure District should not be prevented from doing so by Idanre District Council. But a list of such farmers should be known to both councils in order that any misunderstanding shall be avoided.

(v) In spite of provision (iv) the Idanre District Council should provide all social amenities within the area transferred to them under provision (iii).

(vi) If, on account of provision (iv), Idanre District Council feels it cannot continue to provide amenities in any village or settlement, such feeling should be made known to Akure which should take over such obligations for the settlement or village. In such a situation Idanre farmers in the village should be made to pay taxes to Akure District Council in addition to *isakole*.

The advantage of these suggestions is that Akure will continue to exercise rights of ownership over the land while Idanre farmers will have the satisfaction of being administered as part of their own area. Therefore, there will be no basis for disagreement or bitterness between the two communities.

It is possible that the suggestions will be criticised on the ground that they make Idanre farmers perpetual tenants. The answer to this is that the only alternative to Idanre being tenants is for Akure to forego her rights over the land and allow Idanre to claim it. The long insistence of Akure on having her rights declared over the area, and the existing system of land ownership whereby citizens of one community cannot have free use of land in another make it seem unlikely that Akure will forego her rights. Akure people are likely to hold on to their rights to the land in order that future generations of Akures can have land for farming and other purposes. It is because of this consideration that the Akures want to control the expansion of farms by Idanres as that ensures that unoccupied areas are not totally taken over by Idanre farmers. Therefore one can say that the best solution under existing practices is that which allows Idanre farmers to continue to use the land but on terms agreed between them as tenants and Akure as landlords.

Notes and References

1. 'Review of Foulkes/Roberts decision on the Ondo/Ikale Boundary' by K. Robinson, File 31615, C.S.O. 26, N.A.I.
2. Minutes of second meeting of Ife and Ilesa representatives on Ife/Ilesa boundary dispute held at Obokungbusi Hall, Ilesa, 27 April 1949.
3. S. Johnson, *History of the Yorubas* (Lagos: C.M.S. Bookshops, 1921), p. 232.
4. 'Akure/Idanre Boundary Case 1939-49', Suit W/40/1939 (hereafter referred to as *Deji* v. *Owa*, 1939).
5. Oni of Ife to Resident, Oyo, 18 December 1929, File 1171, Simple List of Oyo Provincial Papers (Numerical Series S.O.P.P. 1171), N.A.I.
6. Evidence in *Deji* v. *Owa*, op. cit.
7. Lapoki, Bale of Aye, to District Commissioner, 2 February 1905, File C.15/1921, Ministry of Local Government, Ondo.
8. 'Notes on Akure/Ogotun Boundary Reconciliation Meeting held in Ogotun on 11 January 1950', File LR 22/1, AKDIVCO 4, N.A.I.
9. Ibid.
10. Minutes of a meeting at the Residency, Ibadan, to discuss Ilesa boundaries, 28 October 1913.
11. Oni of Ife to Resident, Oyo, 20 August 1920, S.O.P.P., 1171 N.A.I.
12. Resident, Oyo, to D.O. Ibadan, 25 October 1917, File 4309, Oyo Prof. 1/1, N.A.I.
13. See Chapter V.
14. Meeting at Ondo between Resident, Ondo Province, the Acting D.O., Ondo, the Osemawe and Bale of Aye, 25 August 1916, File C.15/1921, Ministry of Local Government, Ondo.

15. Omolade Adejuyigbe, Ife/Ijesa Boundary Problem', *Nigerian Geog. Jnl.* 13 (1970), pp. 23–38.
16. 'Travelling and District Commissioner's Office Journal and Diary, 1903–12', Ondo Div. 8/1, N.A.I. Entry for 7 February 1905.
17. Owa of Ilesa to D.O., Ife and Ilesa, 14 April 1949.
18. Evidence in *Deji* v. *Owa*, op. cit.
19. Ibid.
20. Ibid.
21. Minutes of meeting held at Alade market between District Commissioner, Ondo and Akure, and Idanre representatives on 19 September 1912 to discuss forest concessions to Miller Brothers.
22. D.O., Ondo, to Resident, Ondo Province, 20 October 1918, File 843, Ondo Prof. 1/1, N.A.I.
23. Resident, Ondo Province, to D.O. Ondo, 22 October 1918, File 843, Ondo/ Prof. 1/1, N.A.I.
24. Deji to D.O., Ado-Ekiti, 11 November 1926, File 843 ,Ondo Prof. 1/1, N.A.I.
25. Deji to D.O., Ado-Ekiti, 3 January 1927, File 843, Ondo Prof. 1/1, N.A.I.
26. Deji to D.O., Ado-Ekiti, 5 April 1927, File 843, Ondo Prof. 1/1, N.A.I.
27. Ibid.
28. Assistant District Officers, Ado-Ekiti and Ondo, to District Officers, Ondo and Ado-Ekiti, 27 November 1926, File 843, Ondo Prof. 1/1, N.A.I.
29. Ibid.
30. A. F. Abell, 'Inquiry into the Akure/Idanre Boundary Dispute, 1938'. Paragraph 11.
31. D.O., Ondo, to D.O., Ekiti, 19 December 1928, File 843, Ondo Prof. 1/1, N.A.I.
32. D.O., Ekiti, to Deji, 20 February 1929.
33. Ibid.
34. Deji to D.O., Ekiti, 8 March 1929.
35. A. F. Abell, op. cit., paragraphs 14, 15 and 16.
36. See paragraph 6 of the Statement of Defence by Idanre in *Deji* v. *Owa*, op. cit.
37. *Adesida, Deji of Akure* v. *Adegbule, Owa of Idanre*, Suit No. W/40/1939, Supreme Court, Benin.
38. Ibid., Judgment, 30 June 1943.
39. Deji to Resident, Ondo Province, 19 April 1945, File 318 Vol. II, Ondo Prof. 1/1, N.A.I.
40. Resident, Ondo Province, to Secretary, Western Provinces, 26 October 1946, File 318 Vol. II, Ondo Prof. 1/1, N.A.I.
41. Alade People to Deji of Akure, 26 November 1946.
42. Report of a meeting held in Idanre Council Hall on 24 January 1947 to discuss the behaviour of the Alade people in sending a petition dated 8 January 1947 direct to the Deji of Akure.
43. *Owa of Idanre* v. *Deji of Akure*, File ANA. 234 N.A.L. Suit WO B/36/1948, Supreme Court, Benin Judicial Division; AKDIVCO 2, N.A.I.
44. Ibid., Judgment.
45. Government decision in the Akure/Idanre land dispute, 26 October 1951, File A.N.A. 234, AKDIVCO 2, N.A.I.
46. Provincial Surveyor, Ondo Province, to D.O., Ondo, 13 April 1955.

47. Idanre Community, on the Idanre/Akure disputed area, to Ministry of Local Government, 1955, File LR 19, AKDIVCO 4, N.A.I.
48. Notice No. 464, *Western Nigeria Gazette*, 6 April 1961.
49. Chief Ijomu of Alade and five others to Secretary, Idanre District Council, 4 March 1964.
50. Secretary, Akure District Council, to Local Government Adviser, Ondo, 29 April 1964.
51. Akure Communal Land Trust in an address to the Commissioner for Lands and Housing, 20 June 1969.
52. The agreement on the reserve was first made with the Owa on 22 October 1918. Obviously the terms of the agreement would have been settled before that date, so that people would avoid the area of the forest reserve.

CHAPTER V

Positional Boundary Disputes

SOME BOUNDARY disputes concern the location of the boundary away from one or more agreed points or sectors. The agreed points may be one of the following: (1) a hill or a river, (2) a point fixed during delimitation of the boundary by government officials or as a result of arbitration by a third party (the third party may be a court of law or an agreed arbitrator), (3) the point at which both sides used to stop road works, (4) any other specially marked point. The lack of agreement on the boundary away from the points is due largely to the length of the boundary and the obvious impracticability of people at some distance from it being able to relate their position to the point or even to have knowledge of its existence as an agreed boundary point. Furthermore there is the problem of interpreting a boundary agreement based on only one or two points.

All communities would probably say that a boundary should consist of straight lines passing through an agreed point or points. The interpretation is in conformity with the conception that a boundary is made up of straight lines joining some fixed points. If the fixed points are close together the whole boundary may not be a straight line but the farther apart they are the longer the stretches of straight lines. Therefore if there are only two fixed points, the boundary will be a single straight line passing through the points. The adoption of the principle leads to conflict in Western Nigeria because of two reasons. The first concerns the definition of the straight line. The second reason is constituted by the pre-conditions laid down by the communities for drawing the line.

DEFINITION OF THE LINE

In some cases only one point is agreed upon. The idea is that the boundary is a straight line passing through that point. But a straight line is defined by two points not just one. Therefore it is impossible to fix an acceptable straight line on the basis of only one point. The difficulties involved and the conflicts that may arise are well illustrated on the boundary between Are and Afao.[1] In 1920 the Ewi (*oba* of Ado Ekiti) and the District Officer, Ekiti, fixed the boundary between the two at a point on the Are–Afao road (Fig. 14). No other point was specified. Both sides accepted that the boundary was a straight line passing through the point fixed by the Ewi. But there was disagreement on how to draw the straight line. Each side gave its own interpretation and farmed accordingly (Fig. 14). This led to a dispute and in 1953 Are took Afao to court on the grounds that Afao people caused disturbances by farming on the Are side of the land. The court was requested to order Afao to refrain from farming on the Are side of the line. On the other hand Afao claimed that the people of Are had been trying to cross the boundary to the Afao side. The court decided that 'an imaginary line cut at right angles from the [site of the] peregun tree on the [Are–Afao] footpath extending to the end of the land on the south and to its end in the north should be the correct course of the boundary decided in 1922.'[2]

One way of resolving the problem is to interpret the agreement on a point as meaning that the line passes through the point until it intersects with the boundaries with other communities. For example the Akures suggested a definition of their boundary with Ogotun as:

> ...the course of Oruo River from its confluence with River Owenna upwards to the point where Alatere stream joins it; and from there following the Alatere upwards its course to the terminus of Ogotun's land *on their eastern boundary with Igbara-Odo* [Ado District][3] [Fig. 15B].

The only agreed point here is the confluence of the Oruo and Owena Rivers. But the proposal was that the boundary should end at the eastern boundary of Ogotun with Igbara-Odo. The suggestion is based on the assumption that the Igbara-Odo/Ogotun boundary is fixed and that it lies in the area suggested. Although the boundary was fixed it did not lie in the area suggested. According to an agreement of 1937 the eastern boundary of Ogotun with Igbara-Odo starts from the confluence of the Olokorokoro and Oruo Rivers and runs along the former to a cement pillar which marks the intersection of the boundary starting at Oke–Aba with that pillar.[4]

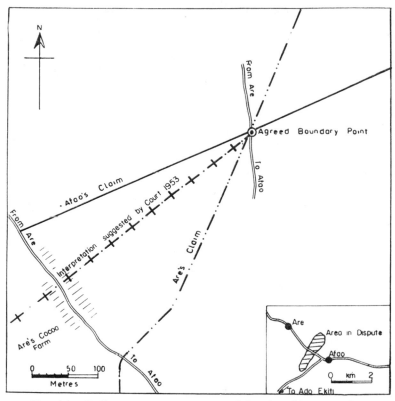

Fig. 14   *Different interpretations of the Are-Afao Boundary*

The Alatere/Oruo confluence is upstream of the Oruo/Olokoro–koro confluence (Fig. 15B). It is therefore difficult to see how the Akure suggestion could have been accepted.

Other situations could create problems more complicated than the above. This is particularly so in places where there are no natural features as in the Akure/Ogotun case. The situation in such cases can be illustrated as in Fig. 15A. Ago and Ahere have agreed on only one point, P, on their common boundary. If it is assumed that the boundary is a line through the agreed point to their boundaries with their other neighbours then it cannot be drawn until the boundaries of either with both Egure and Abule have been fixed. Suppose those boundaries have been determined and they are the lines HB and RG for Ahere and AB and EG for Ago. Then the boundary between Ago and Ahere could be any line through P to intersect the lines ABH and EGR. Since the direction of the line

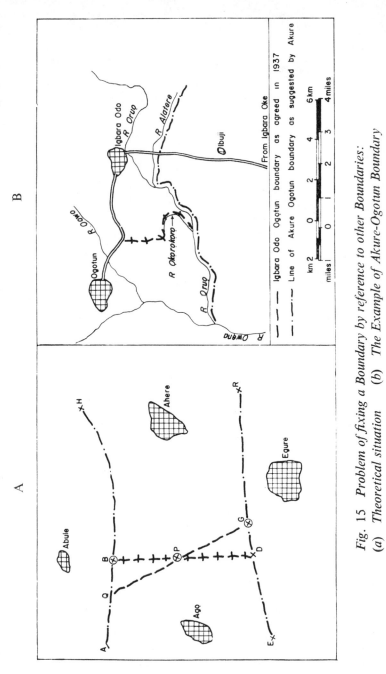

Fig. 15 Problem of fixing a Boundary by reference to other Boundaries:
(a) Theoretical situation   (b) The Example of Akure–Ogotun Boundary

was never agreed or determined by any other point beyond P there could be great dispute as to where it should pass. One solution is to suggest that the boundary should pass through B, P and G, but then the three points are not on a straight line. Another one is that it could pass through P and either B or G. In the first, the boundary would be the line BPD while in the second, it would be GPQ. In both these cases there could be opposition from the community which feels it is losing territory to the other. Greater difficulties would be experienced if the boundaries of one or both of the communities with Abule and Egure had not been fixed.

PRECONDITIONS FOR DRAWING THE LINES

Even if the straight lines were easily defined, disputes could easily arise in the delimitation of the boundary because of the conditions usually laid down by the communities. The first is that the boundary should keep everyone on his community's side of the boundary. The attainment of the objective is not difficult provided that the people had not expanded to areas beyond their community's side of the proposed boundary, and also on condition that there is no dispute on the assignment of the settlements in the borderlands.

Whether or not people pay regard to lines such as those being suggested as boundaries depend on their knowledge of the lines. Since the boundaries have not been previously delimited or demarcated no one is likely to know their location. There is therefore a high probability that expansion could take place without any regard to the line being proposed as boundary. Hence each side might expand to areas on the other side. The situation can be illustrated with the example of the boundary between Are and Afao. After the settlement of 1920 each side expanded as shown in Fig. 14. Consequently, each suggested, in 1953, a boundary which would give it control of the area where its members had settled.[5] Therefore there were two different lines, neither of which was acceptable to both sides together.

IFE/IJESA BOUNDARY PROBLEM

The Ife/Ijesa boundary dispute is one of those where both communities agreed on at least one point on the boundary. Even then delimitation of the boundary was not easy because of sharp disagreements on its location away from the agreed point.

Ile-Ife, the capital of the Ife kingdom, and Ilesa, the capital of the Ijesas are about thirty kilometres apart in the central part of Western Nigeria. Attempts were made to fix a boundary between the two communities in 1901, 1913 and 1932 but after each one, there were complaints from one side or the other against the proposed boundary. In 1913 many points were agreed upon but most of these were later rejected. In fact the only point on which there is agreement is Oke-Ora (Ora hill) in the frontier between them (Fig. 16). Therefore one might say the main problem is that of fixing the boundary away from Oke-Ora. In the following pages the various suggestions on the location of the boundary away from Oke-Ora are examined and the reasons for their rejection discussed.

Generally it can be said that the claims of each side beyond Oke Ora are based on its conception of the rights and boundaries before the British occupation. These claims are justified on the ground that the boundary thereby arrived at is the traditional boundary. According to Ife the traditional boundary passes through the Erukuru stream on the Ilesa side of Ibodi (Fig. 16). The River Erukuru is a tributary of the River Eriperi or Sasa and it does not flow through the length of the territory between Ife and Ijesa. Hence, even if Ife is correct about the Erukuru there is no indication of the boundary in areas beyond its course. Moreover, the adoption of the river as boundary would mean that the towns of Osu and Ibodi which are undisputed Ijesa towns would be on the Ife side.

The Ijesas claim that their traditional boundary with Ife is at Enuwa square in front of the present palace of the Oni of Ife in the centre of Ile-Ife.[7] They also state that a point near Itamarun where *peregun* trees are planted is on the boundary.[8] Between and beyond these two points and Oke-Ora there is no indication of the course of the boundary.

If anything at all these differences and lack of clarity suggest that if there was ever a boundary between Ife and Ijesa it was unstable. The present claims of each side are probably due to successes in war. In fact it seems likely that shere was never an agreed boundary between the two communities.

In support of this is the history of the foundation of the Ijesa kingdom and some statements at Ile-Ife. According to local tradition the founder of the Ijesa kingdom, the first Owa Obokun of Ijesaland, was the last of the sons of Oduduwa to migrate from Ile-Ife. On his departure from Ife he was presented with a sword

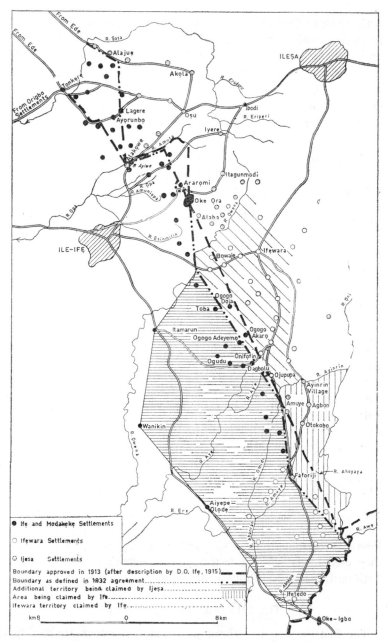

Fig. 16   Suggested Positions of the Ife-Ijesa Boundary

with which to fight his opponents and on leaving Ile-Ife he travelled to Ibokun where he settled and from there he waged war against and defeated the towns in the present Ijesa Northern Division. Later, his descendants settled at Ilesa.[9]

If this traditional account is correct it would seem odd that Oduduwa set a boundary between himself and his child. If he did set a boundary it is unlikely that he would have fixed it so close to his own town as now claimed by the Ijesas.

The above argument presumes that Oduduwa set the boundary. However, the Ijesas claim that the boundary was not fixed by Oduduwa himself, and they give three different accounts of how it was fixed. According to one version Oduduwa told Owa that he should go with the sword and wherever he struck land he should start his rule. On coming out of the palace at Ile-Ife, Owa struck the land with his sword and so laid claim to territory beyond. They explain that this is why the place is called Enuwa (*Enu ile Owa*), meaning the boundary of Owa's land.[10] According to another version the boundary was fixed as a result of war. During a war between Ife and Ijesa the latter drove the Ifes as far as Enuwa square, consequently the Ijesas ruled as far as that point.[11] A third version is that the rule of Owa as far as Enuwa square arose from the powers he assumed after the death of Oduduwa. Being the nearest child, he took over control of Ile-Ife, but the administration was conducted from his seat at Ilesa and extended as far as the palace, while his nominee, resident at Ile-Ife, controlled the rest of the Ife kingdom.[12]

These various versions agree on one thing, namely, that there was no confirmed boundary between Owa and his father at the time the former left the palace at Ile-Ife. In fact one of the views at Ile-Ife is that there was no boundary between Ife and Ijesa before the British occupation. At that time both communities used their land in common.[13] In spite of the differences on other points, the Ijesas agreed that the Ifes had a shrine on the top of Oke-Ora where they used to worship. For that reason Oke-Ora was accepted by both parties as a point on the boundary.

THE 1913 BOUNDARY AGREEMENT

The first attempt to delimit a boundary between Ife and Ijesa was made in 1901 by Major Reeve-Tucker. It would appear that the delimitation took the form of the cutting of a trace through the forest and the marking of trees along the line. The starting point was a tree at the confluence of River Oni with a small stream, Ahoyaya (Fig.16).[4] During field work in the area in August 1968 the present writer made efforts to establish the location of the line but none of the people interviewed could help. This is because the trees which were marked at the time have been cut and no map of the boundary has been traced.

Although the Ifes claim that the Reeve-Tucker line was acceptable to them, it was later set aside and another boundary agreed upon in 1913. From this it can be deduced that the Reeve-Tucker line was unsatisfactory to the Ijesas.

At a meeting held at Ibadan on 28 October 1913 the boundaries of Ijesaland were defined and the Ife/Ijesa section was described as follows:

1. From the junction of Ilesa–Akure road with Ondo boundary to the intersection of the Ondo boundary with the Oni River. Both sides agree.
2. A straight line North-Westerly to its intersection with Oke–Igbo–Ifewara road. Both sides agree.
3. The Ifewara road Northerly to a tree marked IX. Both sides agree.
4. A straight line over the summit of Oke Ora to its intersection with Itagunmodi–Ife road. Both sides agree.
5. Along this road Northerly to its junction with the section road from Iyere to Ife. Both sides agree.
6. Westerly along this road to its junction with the Ayunwe stream. Ife claims Amuta stream. In view of slight difference and since Ilesa farmers are established there Resident recommended the boundary mentioned.
7. The Ayunwe stream to its junction with Osu–Ife road. Both sides agree.
8. A straight line due North to its intersection with Orinaga–Osu road. Ilesa claims line to Agborogboro hill. Captain Humfrey and Mr Birch, who visited the ground in January, report this as too close to Ife and that they found this boundary to go through the middle of the farms belonging to the family of the late Oni. These farms border on farms which are occupied by Modakeke people who, when ejected in 1909, placed themselves under the Owa of Ilesa but did not quit their farms. As they held these farms from the Oni, the Resident informed the Ilesa chiefs that he will recommend that their claims be overruled.

9. Along the Orinaga to Osu road to its junction with Sasa River. Ilesa objected as stated above.[15]

INTERPRETATION

The main problems in the way of a correct interpretation of the 1913 agreement may be listed as follows:

(i)   the starting point;
(ii) difficulty of tracing the tree marked IX;
(iii) difficulty of identifying Osu–Orinaga road;
(iv) the objections raised by Ife and Ijesa.

The starting point was described as the junction of Ilesa–Akure road with Ondo boundary. It would appear that 'Ondo' means Ondo Province. If this is correct the intersection of Ilesa–Akure road with Ondo boundary is at River Owena, about fifty-one kilometres east of Ilesa. That area does not belong to Ife. The only possible explanation of the first clause is that the records from which the agreement is quoted refer to Ijesa boundaries and the intersection of Ijesa–Akure road with Ondo boundary is only a convenient point to start the description. This interpretation means that the starting point of the Ife–Ijesa boundary as described in 1913 would be the end of the section described in clause one of the agreement, that is 'the intersection of the Ondo boundary with the Oni River.' If this is correct then it is the point rather than the line on which both Ife and Ijesa agreed. The point is shown on Fig. 16.

The section described in clause three of the agreement is difficult to interpret. It could mean that the tree marked IX lies somewhere along the Oke–Igbo–Ifewara road. But investigations in the area reveal that no tree was marked along the road.[16] The local people recollect two marked trees, the first at the junction of the Oni River and a small tributary called Ahoyaya[17] and the second on River Owena.[18] The first of these lies to the east of the Oke-Igbo– Ifewara road and hence cannot be the one referred to in the agreement. The second marked tree lies, not on the road, but to the north of it. In the absence of any other information on the marked tree along the Oke-Igbo–Ifewara road it can be assumed that the marked tree on the Owena River was the one intended in the 1913 agreement. Even then the people interviewed could not locate the tree, it can be assumed that it was near the point at which a line drawn northwards from the Oke-Igbo–Ifewara road intersects River Owena.

In clause eight of the agreement the Osu–Orinaga road is mentioned. But during field work in the area in August 1968 no one was able to help in identifying the Osu–Orinaga road, or the settlement called Orinaga. The nearest word to Orinaga in the area is Elega, the name of a settlement on the Osu–Odesanmi–Tonkere road. It is difficult to see any similarity between the pronunciation of the two words, unless the place called Elega used to be called Ori-Elega or Orile-Elega. However, the people in the area say that neither of these names had been used for the place, and point out that the settlement is called Aba-Elega. But since that is the only place that can possibly be identified with the word in the agreement we may assume that the road mentioned is the Osu–Odesanmi–Elega road.

The Resident made a number of rulings on the objections raised by both the Ifes and the Ijesas to the boundary defined in the agreement. The Ife objection was to the adoption of the River Ayunwe as boundary, in its place the River Amuta was suggested. The Resident ruled that the River Ayunwe be adopted. The effect of this was that Arowogbade hill, on which any Oni of Ife is said to be crowned, is allocated to Ijesa. Such a situation could not have been acceptable to the Ifes, even after the Resident overruled their objection. In any case there was no indication in the records that the Ifes accepted the Resident's decision. In the same way, there was no indication that the Ijesas agreed with what the Resident said.

These various problems make the identification of the 1913 boundary difficult. The situation is further complicated by the fact that the approved boundary might have been different from that defined above. This is because the District Officer at Ife later described the approved boundary as follows:

> From Oni river to Oke Ora. From Oke Ora straight line to junction of Amuta stream and Iyere road (North-east). Thence along Amuta to its junction with Akowe–Ife road. Thence along Ife road to Ayiwe stream. Thence straight line along Reeve-Tucker boundary to Ede–Origo road. Thence along this road to Sasa river. Thence along Sasa river to its junction with Ede–Ilobu road.[19]

On the assumption that the District Officer was right, the approved boundary solved some of the problems discussed above. First, it cleared the doubts about the starting point in that it was made explicit that it is a point on River Oni. Secondly, it solved the problem of the tree marked IX simply by making no reference to it.

Thirdly, it adopted the Amuta and thereby ensured that Arowogbade hill is in Ife sphere. In the fourth place, it cleared the doubts about Orinaga by adopting the Ede–Origo road.

In spite of the above, the assumption that the District Officer was right about the approved boundary raises some problems. First, and possibly most important, are the attitudes of the Ifes and Ijesas to the approved boundary. There is no indication in the records that the two communities agreed to the approved boundary, or that they were even consulted about the changes made to the original discussion of October 1913. But even if the Ifes and Ijesas accepted the approved boundary there are other problems, namely, the starting point, the Ede–Origo road and the section described in the last sentence. The starting point is not mentioned at all, because the first sentence simply states 'From Oni River. . .' However, it may be assumed that the starting point is that in the 1913 records, namely, the junction of Ondo boundary with the Oni River.

A section of the approved boundary is said to pass through Ede–Origo road. This should be a road from Ede towards a settlement or an area in the direction of the boundary. But there is no place called Origo near the boundary area. The nearest word to Origo is Origbo, a common name for six settlements west of the boundary area. However, there is a direct route going northwards from the Origbo settlements to Ede, that route does not pass through the area under discussion. There is a possibility that the officer meant to write Osu–Origbo road. Such a route possibly passes through Ayorunbo and Lamokun to Tonkere before turning westwards to the Origbo settlements. If this were the case the boundary would be as shown on Fig. 16.

The final section of the boundary is described as along the Sasa to Ede–Ilobu road. This section would appear to be irrelevant in that Ife territory does not extend as far as Ede–Ilobu road. In the original records of 1913 that particular section was contained in the boundary between Ijesa and Ibadan.[20]

These various problems make it difficult to locate precisely the boundary agreed upon in 1913 or that which was probably finally approved by government.

REJECTION

Although one of the differences between the boundary defined at the meeting of October 1913 and the one cited by the District

Officer in 1915 favoured Ife, that community later rejected the boundary on the grounds that Ifewara[21] and Araromi[22] as well as the land south of Ayinrin River[23] were given to Ilesa.

Ifewara was founded by an unsuccessful candidate for the throne of Ife. As a result of his failure he, with his supporters, left Ile-Ife and established a settlement near Iwara, an Ijesa town, and called it Ife. The man himself took the title of Oni and his chiefs took titles of chiefs at Ile-Ife. In order to distinguish between Ile-Ife and the settlement founded by the dissidents the latter was called Ifewara (Ife near Iwara). In 1859 Ijesa attacked Ifewara and many of the inhabitants fled to Ile-Ife. In 1900 the British advised the people of Ifewara in Ile-Ife to go back to their town and many of them returned.[24] Because of the Ijesa victory of 1859 the Owa claims suzerainty over Ifewara.

The claim of Ife over Ifewara is therefore based on historical and cultural connections while that of Ijesa is based on conquest. In 1923 the administrative officers dealing with the boundary ruled that Ifewara should not be merged with Ile-Ife.[25]

Araromi is a completely new settlement founded by Modakeke elements after they were forced out of Modakeke, near Ile-Ife, in 1909.[26] The people themselves say that they settled on Ijesa land, and acknowledge the Ogboni of Ilesa as their landlord.[27]

The Ifes claimed that the River Ayinrin was their boundary with Ijesa. In support of this they argued that before the British occupation, hunters and others familiar with the area observed some conventions which indicate their recognition of the Ayinrin as boundary. At the time, any Ijesa who crossed the Ayinrin was arrested for trespass and taken to Ife; similarly any Ife who crossed the Ayinrin to the north was arrested and taken to Ilesa. They cited the example of Faforiji, the founder of the village known by that name, who came from Oke-Igbo and settled on Ife side, but who, on crossing the Ayinrin to the north, was arrested and taken to Ilesa where he was recognised as a relative of the ruling Owa.[28]

THE 1932 BOUNDARY AGREEMENT

PRELUDE

The objections of Ife to the 1913 boundary led to the consideration of another boundary more acceptable to both communities. To this end the area was surveyed and a map prepared, but all

attempts to trace the map have failed. On the strength of the survey
the District Officer at Ife remarked as follows:

> It would seem to be clear from the map that the Oni has a good
> claim to the land lying between Oke–Ora and a line on a bea-
> ring 140° to meet River Owena, while the Owa's claim in the
> southern part of the line seems to be equally well substantiated,
> though in this case there is no doubt that Famuyiwa, twice con-
> victed of tresspass in the Provincial Court in 1923 and 1928, has
> extended his area probably a good deal beyond what he could
> rightly claim.[29]

One of the proposals for a new boundary was made by Owa
and the chiefs of Ijesa as follows:

> . . . a line from Oke–Ora on Ilesaland to Aba–Loriki and from
> there to Owena River and to where the straight line joined Aba-
> Obe, and from there to cocoa Togun, and a straight line to cocoa
> Afegbe, and a straight line to Aba–Ladin and a straight line to
> Amodu's hut and a straight line to Aba–Akinsola and then a
> straight line back in Ifeland to Famuyiwa or Oke–Awo and from
> there to Faforiji's farm, as it was first suggested.[30]

They also suggested that the Ijesas should buy off Ife farmers on
the Ijesa side of the boundary and the Ifes should do the same
to the Ijesas on the other side. This suggestion shows that Ijesa
desired a boundary which would separate members of both com-
munites and hence be a cultural boundary.

The Ijesa suggestion was rejected by the Ifes on the grounds that:

> the portion given to Ife out of Ijesaland at the point Oke–Ora
> to Owena River is about four times smaller than the portion
> taken out of Ifeland for Ijesa from the point Aba–Akinsola even
> further to a point at Aba–Famuyiwa. Finally we would point
> out that Oke-Awo farm or part thereof has never been part of
> Ijesa possession.[31]

As a result of this the District Officers at Ife and Ilesa met and
suggested a boundary from Oke Ora to River Oni defined as follows:

> From Oke-Ora along pillared line to the place where the Owena
> stream crosses the path from Ife to Ifewara. Thence still along
> pillared line to Ayinrin stream on the path from Ifewara to Oke-
> Igbo. Thence along the Ifewara–Oke-Igbo path southwards to the
> Aye stream. Thence in a southeasterly direction through the
> forest to the point on the Oni river which can be found by drawing
> a line from a point described in the file.[32]

THE AGREEMENT

The suggestion made by the District Officers formed the basis of final discussions for the boundary agreement of 1932 which was signed by the Oni and six Ife chiefs and the Owa and six Ijesa chiefs. The boundary agreed upon was defined as follows:

1. Commencing from the confluence of the Oni and Awo Rivers approximately six miles north east of the village of Oke-Igbo (Ondo) by a straight line due north west to where the Amuye stream crosses the Oke-Igbo–Ifewara path immediately south of Aba-Faforiji (Ilesa).
2. Thence northwards by the Oke-Igbo–Ifewara path to where it is crossed by the Ayinrin River.
3. Thence in a north-north-westerly direction by the surveyed and pillared line to the Owena River where it is crossed by the main Ifewara–Ife path.
4. Thence by a straight line northwards crossing the Owena River by the same surveyed line to the summit of Oke-Ora.
5. Thence in a northwesterly direction by a straight line meeting the Amuta stream at a point beaconed leaving the village of Araromi in Ilesa territory. (A semi-circle of 100 yards is allowed for westerly expansion of the village.)
6. Thence westerly along the Amuta stream to where it meets the Ife–Ilesa motor road.
7. Thence westerly along the Ife–Ilesa motor road to where it meets the Aiuwe (Ayunwe) stream.
8. Thence in a straight line due north till it meets the Ede–Osu path.
9. Thence by this path in a northwesterly direction to where it crosses the Sasa River[33] [Fig. 16].

The conditions of the agreement were stated as follows:

(a) No Ifes, Ifewaras or Ijesas will be disturbed on their farms wherever they are.

(b) If Ifes wish to farm in Ilesa territory they must first of all obtain the permission of the Owa; if Ijesas (including Ifewaras) wish to farm on Ife territory the sanction of the Oni will be required.

(c) Persons farming across the above described line but whose permanent residence is either on Ife soil or Ilesa soil shall pay their taxes to the Native Administration of the district in which they permanently reside, with the exception that, in the case of cocoa farms, the tax levied on such farms shall be payable to the Native Administration on whose land such farms exist.[34]

INTERPRETATION

Unlike the earlier agreements, a map (Fig. 17) was attached to that of 1932. Normally, such a map should simplify the interpretation of the agreement, but in this case some features on the map were capable of causing dispute between the two sides. The most important of these are:

(a) mistake over the Ede–Osu road;
(b) substitution of the River Opa for the River Amuta;
(c) the Araromi arc;
(d) identification of the surveyed line between the River Owena and the River Ayinrin and of the Ifewara–Oke–Igbo road between the River Ayinrin and Faforiji;
(e) difficulty caused by the meandering course of the River Oni near its confluence with Awo River.

The last two clauses of the agreement made reference to the Ede–Osu road. Following the topographical maps of the area on scale 1:50,000, there are three routes between Ede and Osu, viz.:

(i) Osu–Akola–Alajue-Ede,
(ii) Osu–Adebola–Odesanmi–Tonkere–Ede,
(iii) Osu–Adebola–Lagere–Ayorunbo–Tonkere–Ede.

Investigations carried out at Osu in August 1968 reveal that only the first two are regarded as Ede–Osu roads. The informants mention that the last road is never used by travellers going direct to Ede, yet it was the last one that was indicated on the map attached to the 1932 agreement. This shows that the map was wrong about the northern limit of the boundary.

Although the two other roads are used between Osu and Ede, the one through Akola is recognised as the Osu–Ede road. On the strength of this it may be suggested that references to Ede–Osu road should be interpreted as meaning the Osu–Akola–Alajue-Ede road. If this is accepted if follows that the 1932 agreement should have followed that road, and the adoption of any other road may be taken as a mistake. In that case the mistake on the map means that some land and settlements which ought to have been part of Ife were grouped with Ilesa. The area involved is inhabited by Modakeke people who started farming there before they were forced out of their town near Ile-Ife in 1909. After leaving Modakeke they retained the farmlands but sought protection of the Owa of Ijesaland. However, since 1922, when Modakeke was rebuilt, most of

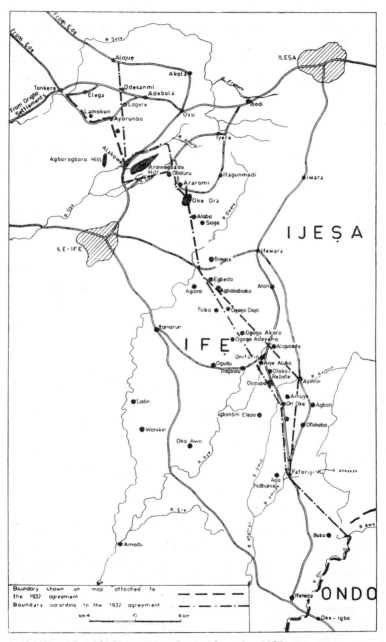

Fig. 17 Ife-Ijesa Boundary after the 1932 agreement

the farmers in the area have resettled in their former home. When the area was discussed in 1913 the Ijesa claimed up to Agborogboro hill to the west of the present boundary, but the Resident overruled their claim.[35] It is therefore likely that the original intention in the agreement of 1932 was to uphold the ruling made in 1913.

The second difficulty of reconciling the map and the agreement is caused by the mistake over the River Amuta. The river by that name crosses the Ilesa–Ife road at a point east of Alakowe, but the map indicates that the River Amuta crosses the road between Ife and Alakowe. The main river which crosses the road between Ife and Alakowe is called Opa. In other words the map was incorrect in respect of the river. The southern tributary of the Opa is called Amuni-Opa and not Ayunwe as indicated on the map. Ayunwe is a small stream rising from Arowogbade hill and crossing the road a little to the west of Alakowe village, but much nearer Alakowe than the River Opa (Fig. 16).

The adoption of the Amuta as boundary was intended to give Arowogbade hill to Ife. If the river indicated on the map were adopted, Arowogbade hill would be on the Ijesa side. This would have been unacceptable to the Ifes as it would mean that future Onis would have to be crowned on 'foreign' soil.

Another problem in the interpretation of the agreement is the Araromi arc. Araromi is in two parts, one mainly Modakeke in the west and the other mainly Ijesa on the east. The agreement stated that an arc of 100 yards should be drawn round Araromi, yet no particular point was fixed as centre for the arc. Because of this the drawing of the arc would be likely to cause dispute as people working independently of each other may have chosen different centres and so arrived at different locations for the arc.

One other difficulty in the reconciliation of the agreement and the map concerns the location of the surveyed line between Rivers Owena and Ayinrin. This is linked with the identification of the Ifewara–Oke–Igbo road between river Ayinrin and Faforiji. The problem in both cases is the point at which the line and the road join on the Ayinrin river. Following the map, the line and the road intersect on the Ayinrin downstream of the area where that river has a southerly course; this point of intersection appears to be about the location of Ayinrin village. If this were so the surveyed line would pass to the east of the villages of Oloko–Rebete, Ogogo–Akaro and Ogogo–Doja. These villages and others to the west of them would then be on the Ife side of the boundary. Acceptance of the point would also mean that the Ifewara–Oke-Igbo road in the area between Faforiji and River Ayinrin is the one passing through Agbon and Otokobo.

Field investigations in the area reveal that the interpretation made above is not correct. Enquiries at Ifewara, Ogogo-Doja, Oniforin, Aiye and Ojupupa show that the surveyed line passes to the west of Ogogo–Doja, Ogogo–Akaro, Onifofin and Ojupupa, all of which are said to be on the Ijesa side of the boundary. Similar enquiries at Ayinrin, Faforiji, Ago–Nathaniel and Ifewara reveal that the Oke–Igbo–Ifewara road does not pass through Ayinrin, Agbon and Otokobo. According to those interviewed the road passes through Atori, Alapaede, Oloko–Rebete, Ojupupa and then southwards to Faforiji. The road, which is no longer used, can be recognised at Ojupupa. These results indicate that the terminal of the surveyed line on the River Ayinrin is upstream of Ayinrin village and that Ifewara–Oke-Igbo road crossed the river upstream of Ayinrin village. The point at which both the path and the line cross the river is possibly between Ori–Oke and Ago–Bisi.

In support of this interpretation are the following points: first is the fact that the road between Ayinrin village and Faforiji was not in existence in 1932, and hence could not have been the one intended in the agreement. The road was constructed in the late 1940s. Secondly, the villages of Ori–Oke and Ago–Bisi which are to the west of the Faforiji–Ayinrin village road are acknowledged as being on the Ijesa side by both parties, this would not have been the case if the Faforiji–Ayinrin road had been intended in 1932.

Another potential point of disagreement involved the section of the boundary near the River Oni. According to the agreement, that section joins the Oni at its confluence with Awo River. But a line drawn north-westerly from the Awo will pass through a meander of the Oni before getting to the western side of the river. The problem here, therefore, is where to stop the line, whether at the point where it first touches the Oni River on the west or at another point where a line can be drawn without passing through the bend in the Oni River.

These various problems hinder the correct interpretation of the 1932 agreement and make the acceptance of the boundary difficult.

Even if there were no problems in interpreting the agreement there are many points which can be criticised in it. The most important of these are the following: the Araromi arc, the failure to pay regard to traditional rights, and the conditions of the agreement.

The decision to make the boundary pass within one hundred yards of Araromi fails to take account of the needs of the settlement and the difficulties the people would encounter in trying to keep within the boundary. Accepting that a boundary has to be set near Araromi, a more generous allowance ought to have been given for the expansion of the town. But by imposing near impossible conditions, those who concluded the agreement made it difficult for Araromi people to keep to its terms. The result is that no heed has been paid to it and the people have built beyond the boundary pillar fixed near the town.

The lack of consideration for the people near the boundary is not limited to the Araromi arc alone. Throughout its length no reference was made to traditional rights and farmlands. There was no consideration given to the fact that the straight lines described might cut through the farms of some people or split farm plots in two as it actually did. The boundary was defined as if a completely virgin forest was being divided between the two communities. This lack of regard for the rights and interests of the farmers in the area constitutes the greatest defect of the boundary and is the main reason why people have agitated for its alteration.

The main criticism of the conditions of the agreement is that they did not pay sufficient attention to the interests of the farmers near the boundary. The first condition stipulates that farmers shall not be disturbed, while the second states that permission must be sought if a person from one side wishes to farm on the other. What the signatories appear to have overlooked is that the second condition could be applied to prevent a farmer affected by the first condition from expanding his farm. For example, an Ijesa farmer covered by the first condition could be debarred from expanding his farm on the Ife side simply by making it compulsory for him to apply for permission to start new farms, and then by refusing the application when made. The same thing could apply to an Ife farmer on the Ijesa side. The main problem here lies in those cases where the farmlands of the people affected are in the territory of the community to which they do not belong. For such people to farm without restriction it would be necessary to adjust the boundary.

The third condition is also not very fair to people whose farmlands were split by the boundary because it exposed the farmers to heavy or even double taxation. Farmers who were cut off from their farmlands and crops would have to pay taxes in two places, but there was a fair chance that they would be over-assessed for income tax. This was particularly likely to occur in the case of those whose farmlands were in the territory of the community to which they did not belong. If this happened the farmers affected would demand boundary adjustment so that they could pay all their taxes in one area.

Problems Arising From The 1932 Boundary

The various problems discussed above hindered the operation of the 1932 boundary agreement. By 1936, for example, farmers had been complaining that their farmlands were split by the boundary and had petitioned against the taxation arrangements. In 1936 Chief Agoro of Ifewara laid claim to the land at Ogudu which he said measured 22 miles (35.5km) by 16 miles (24km). [36] Sixteen farmers from Ifewara also complained that they were being asked to pay tax to Ile-Ife in that year although they had paid to Ilesa in previous years. [37] Later in the same year three other farmers petitioned the Resident about the tax arrangements. [38]

Because of these complaints the Ijesas rejected the 1932 boundary. At a mass meeting in Ilesa on 11 February 1949 they passed a resolution asking that the boundary be set aside. [39] The main reason for this action was the feeling that the Ijesas lost their territory as a result of the 1932 agreement. They complained that their *oba* did not understand the purpose and course of the boundary. This point was stressed by the Owa in a letter to the District Officer in 1949:

> Before the advent of the European into this country boundaries were demarcated with rivers or streams, paths, heaps and trees such as *peregun* and *akoko*.
> In the Major Tucker description and in the subsequent boundary agreements of 1913 and 1932 geographical descriptions which were foreign to the parties concerned and could not be intelligently assimilated by them were employed. There were no explanations for their introduction and neither side knew

exactly the position of the imaginary lines 'North-West, North-East' and so on; hence the [not] infrequent cases of trespassing and the incessant feuds in their trail.[40]

Because of the complaints from Ijesa a boundary reconciliation committee was set up in 1949. The Committee had some meetings but was unable to agree on a boundary.[41] Thus the dispute remained unsolved and has continued to cause misunderstanding between the local government councils in both Ife and Ijesa areas. In a bid to have money for development each council intensified its efforts to collect rates and taxes and there was competition for the rates and taxes of those in the border areas. Many people were forced to pay to both Ile-Ife and Ilesa. From 1954 to 1958 there were 339 complaints by Ife people in the border area about tax demands from Ilesa tax collectors.[42] These people were from the villages of Alaba, Bowaje, Ogogo, Agbabiaka and many others. In each case the complainant explained that he was from Ife or Modakeke but his farm or farm house was on the Ijesa side of the boundary. The Ijesas replied that the people were only attempting to evade taxation.

The District Officers in both areas were unable to help the situation. In fact, in 1954 the District Officer at Ile-Ife told the people affected that they had to pay to both districts, although he conceded that those who live in Ife and farm on the Ilesa side need pay only rates to Ife but they must pay tax to Ijesa.[43] Later, in 1955, the tax collectors of both councils agreed that those Ifes farming on the Ijesa side should pay their flat rate to Ile-Ife and income tax to Ilesa.[44] This agreement has been superseded by another, concluded in 1958 by the Ife Divisional Council and Ijesa Southern District Council. The terms of the agreement are as follows:

(i) If a man has a house in a town which provides water and electricity then he is liable to pay water and electricity charges to the Rating Authority having jurisdiction over the place where the house is located.

(ii) A man who has a farm or other source of income is liable to pay income rate upon the income derived from that source to the Rating Authority having jurisdiction over the area in which the farm is situated.

(iii) A man who owns a house is liable to pay hunter guards rate to the Rating Authority of the area in which the house is situated.

(iv) Improvement rates are payable as for income rates.[45]

It was also agreed that a man having two farms or two houses divided between the two Authorities is liable to pay taxes in both, but assessment should be on that part of his property under the particular council area; and that the Local Government Adviser could rule that 'education rates of all affected farmers would be paid to the Rating Authority within which the majority of primary school children concerned were educated.'

Although these agreements could reduce friction between the tax collectors from Ijesa and Ife they are still too complicated for the ordinary farmer whose counterparts in other areas pay tax to only one Authority. It is likely that a farmer paying in two places will pay a higher rate than he would otherwise have done. For these reasons the agreements cannot be regarded as a solution to the problem. In any case the essence of the dispute is that some people are forced to pay taxes and rates to the Authority to which they do not belong and this is resented by all concerned. Because of this there have been complaints from the Ifes farming on the Ijesa side in the Buko area, in the southern part of the boundary, that the Ijesas were demanding tax from them. These complaints led to the passing of a resolution by the Ife Divisional Council in March 1962 requesting the government to intervene and settle the boundary dispute.[46]

BOUNDARIES DESIRED BY BOTH SIDES

Although there are demands for boundary alteration there is no agreement on the changes to be made. The Ijesas would want the boundary altered to that agreed in 1913 which they claim represents the true position.[47] However, their idea of the 1913 boundary is not the same as either that defined in the minutes quoted above or that one cited by the District Officer as being the approved boundary. According to them the 1913 boundary was as follows:

> From Oni near Oke-Igbo to River Abojupupa and thence to River Ere and to River Aye. From River Aye to Wanikin and then to Itamarun. Thence to the junction of Ifewara to Ife road with River Owena and then to River Amuta. Thence to Ife-Osu road and along that road to River Ayunwe. From Ayunwe to Ayorunbo and then to River Sasa.[48]

As Fig. 16 shows, the territory within this boundary on the Ijesa side includes a large area occupied by Ife or Modakeke. It cuts away from Ife undisputed Ife towns such as Olode and Ifetedo and Modakeke centres such as Ogudu. There is no doubt that Ife cannot accept such a boundary.

The Ifes are of the opinion that a boundary alteration would involve unnecessary trouble and cause bitterness. To avoid this they think the 1932 boundary should be retained.[49] If, however, a new one were to be demarcated, they would want the land south of River Ayinrin and Ifewara to be returned to Ife.[50] The boundary desired by Ife would not only cut off Ifewara but would include within the Ife area such settlements as Faforiji and Ayinrin.

Assuming that the approved boundary resulting from the 1913 agreement started at the intersection of the Ondo boundary with River Oni, the differences between the boundary of 1913 claimed by Ijesa and that of 1932 desired by Ife and in territorial allocations under both may be listed as follows (see Fig. 16):

(i) The starting point of the 1932 boundary is to the north of that of 1913. This means a gain of some territory to Ife and loss of the same area to Ijesa. The territory measures about 0.83 km².

(ii) From the intersection of the two boundaries near River Oni to River Ayinrin the 1932 boundary is to the west of the 1913 boundary. Thus Ijesa gained 7.54 km² from Ife.

(iii) From River Ayinrin to Oke Ora the 1932 boundary is to the west of the 1913 one. This constitutes a gain involving about 8.83 km² to Ijesa.

(iv) If the 1932 agreement is implemented fully there will be some difference between the two boundaries in the area between Oke Ora and River Amuta. The change is in favour of Ijesa which gains about 2.36 km² from Ife. The mistake discussed earlier about the adoption of River Opa instead of River Amuta gives Ijesa an extra area of about 5.93 km².

(v) If the Osu–Akola–Alajue road were used for the 1932 boundary and the Ayorunbo–Tonkere road for that of 1913, Ife would gain about 26.93 km² from Ijesa. However, the present northern limit of the boundary is that used since 1913, hence neither side has gained from the other.

If the agreement of 1932 had been implemented to the letter Ife would have gained 27.76 km² from Ijesa and lost 18.73 km² of its own territory under the 1913 agreement. This would have meant a net loss of 9.04 km² of land to Ijesa. But then the agreement of 1932 was not rightly interpreted everywhere. Hence, if only the operative boundaries are considered, Ijesa would retain all the gains mentioned above and also the area between River Opa and the Ife–Ilesa road, measuring about 5.93 km². This would bring Ijesa gains to 24.66 km². On the other hand Ife gains would be confined to those areas south of the Ife-Ilesa road; these measure only 0.83 km². Hence, by following the boundaries in operation today, Ijesa has a net gain of 23.83 km² of territory allocated to Ife in 1913.

In spite of their overall gains the Ijesas want the 1932 boundary to be altered, and although the Ifes had a net loss, they are advocating only minor changes to that boundary. The reason for this is that the Ijesas have a wrong idea of the 1913 boundary which they claim passes through points mentioned above and which would have given them more land than was actually allocated in 1913. One possible reason for the position is that the 1932 boundary splits more Ijesa farms than it did Ife farms. At Itagunmodi, Araromi and Ifewara on the Ijesa side, there are complaints that the 1932 boundary passes through their farmlands. The people affected are pressing for a change, hence it has been difficult for the Ijesas to accept the 1932 boundary.

CONCLUSION

The example discussed above shows that even where there is agreement on one (or sometimes more than one) point, there may still be great difficulties in arriving at a satisfactory boundary. The reasons given by each side for the rejection of the boundary suggested by administrators is invariably that it groups some of the land of its members with the opposite community. The arrangements for tax collection also indicate the realisation that boundaries should group members of the same community together. Of equal importance is the ignorance of each side of the advantages to be gained by accepting the suggestions of the other side. But here one must be cautious because the gain to the community can only be measured by the satisfaction of its members with the agreed boundaries. As long as some Ijesa people feel strongly about their own particular loss of territory to Ife, that community will reject the boundary. It is not the total gain by the community of territory not strongly claimed by its members that counts, but the loss of areas over which some people have laid claims and already regard as their own. The implication of this is that efforts must be made to ensure that suggested boundaries do not split the land of individual families.

Notes and References

1. File 1084 (Simple List of Ekiti Divisional Office Papers), N.A.I.
2. Are-Afao land case, Native Court, Ado Ekiti, 1953.
3. Deji of Akure to Senior District Officer, Ondo, 3 March 1950, File LR 22/1, AKDIVCO 4, N.A.I.
4. Settlement of the Igbara-Odo/Ogotun boundary dispute, 15 April 1937.
5. Are-Afao land case, op. cit.
6. Minutes of the second meeting of Ife and Ilesa representatives on Ife/Ilesa boundary dispute, held at Ilesa, 27 April 1949.
7. Owa of Ilesa, 23 March 1968.
8. Cited in a letter from District Officer, Ife, to Resident, Oyo, 27 June 1927, File 759, Oyo Prof. 1/1 (hereafter called OP/759), N.A.I.
9. G. O. Ekemode, Lecturer in History, University of Ife, 18 August 1968.
10. Owa of Ilesa, 23 March 1968.
11. G. O. Ekemode, University of Ife, 18 August 1968.
12. Mr Makinwa, Iloro Street, Ilesa, 19 August 1968.
13. Minutes of Ife Divisional Council, 8 December 1956.
14. Mr Odidi of Ifewara, 12 September 1968.
15. Minutes of a meeting held at the Residency, Ibadan (to discuss Ilesa boundaries), at 10 a.m. on 28 October 1913. The copy seen by the writer was made available by Mr Fadipe of the Tax Office, Ife Divisional Council.
16. The investigation consisted of personal interviews in all settlements between Ifewara and Faforiji in August 1968. Also interview of Mr Odidi of Ifewara whom the Ijesas regard as an authority on this boundary.
17. Bale of Faforiji, 20 August 1968; and Mr Elujobade of Ifetedo, 26 August 1968.
18. Bale of Itagumodi, 2 August 1968.
19. Cited in a letter from D.O., Ife, to Commissioner, Oyo, 28 October 1915, OP/759.
20. Minutes of meeting at the Residency, Ibadan, 28 October 1913.
21. D.O., Ife, to Resident, Oyo, 27 June 1927, OP/759.
22. D.O., Ife, to Resident, Oyo, 12 May 1930, OP/759.
23. Minutes of the Ife Divisional Council, 8 December 1956.
24. D.O., Ife, to Resident, Oyo, 15 March 1930, OP/759.
25. D.O., Ife, to Resident, Oyo, 27 June 1927, OP/759.
26. Oyo Elements in Araromi to D.O., Ife, 29 October 1941, File 1492 (Ilesa Divisional Papers), N.A.I.
27. Ibid.

28. Oni of Ife, 17 September 1968.
29. D.O., Ife, to Resident, Oyo, 30 January 1930, OP/759.
30. Owa and Chiefs of Ilesa to D.O., Ife, 12 March 1930, OP/759.
31. Oni and Chiefs of Ife to D.O., Ife, 14 March 1930, OP/759.
32. D.O., Ife, to Resident, Oyo, 12 October 1931, OP/759.
33. OP/759 (Ife/Ilesa Boundary). The agreement was signed at Ife on 11 May 1932 and at Ilesa on 12 May 1932.
34. Ibid.
35. Minutes of meeting at the Residency, Ibadan, 28 October 1913.
36. Chief Agoro of Ifewara to D.O., Ife, 14 November 1936, OP/759.
37. Petition to D.O., Ife and Ilesa, 29 July 1936, OP/759.
38. Petition to D.O., Ife and Ilesa, 11 October 1936, OP/759.
39. Minutes of mass meeting of Ijesa community held at Ilesa, 2 February 1949, OP/759.
40. Owa of Ilesa to D.O., Ife and Ilesa, 14 April 1949.
41. The committee was made up of senior chiefs from Ife and Ilesa and it met on 23 April 1949, 27 April 1949 and 28 May 1949.
42. For further details see File 1082/4 in ILEDIV (Ilesha Divisional Papers) 1/2, N.A.I. (see also file on Ife/Ilesa Boundary in Ife Divisional Office).
43. Ibid., D.O. Ife, to Awofade of Iremo Street, Ife, 12 December 1954.
44. Ibid., Chief Tax Clerk, Ilesa, to D.O., Ilesa, 24 March 1955.
45. Ibid., Local Government Adviser, Osogbo, to Secretary, Ife Divisional Council and Secretary, Ijesa Southern District Council, 17 December 1955.
46. Ife Divisional Council File on Ife/Ilesa Boundary; and *Daily Times*, 19 March 1962, p. 7.
47. Owa of Ijesaland, 31 July 1968.
48. Mr Odidi of Ifewara, 12 September 1968.
49. The Oni of Ife, 17 September 1968.
50. Representatives of Ife community meeting at Afin, Ile-Ife, 10 August 1968.

CHAPTER VI

Annexation Boundary Disputes

THERE ARE some common features between annexation and territorial boundary disputes. Both concern fairly large territories, and in both there is usually no agreement on any point or section of the boundary. The main difference between the two is that territorial boundary disputes concern ownership of the territory and its resources whereas annexation boundary disputes concern the administration of settlements and people, all or some of which had to change their allegiance from one to the other of the disputants because of disturbances during a war. The settlements involved may even deny the rights of either of the disputants to their territory at that time, although they might agree that at certain times in the past their territory had been administered by one or the other of the disputant communities. The areas or settlements, which are usually those of the losing side, may be any of the following types:

(i) areas utilised for farming, gathering or hunting but in which there were no permanent settlements (villages);

(ii) devastated settlements from which all occupants were forced to flee;

(iii) settlements of the losers but in which substantial numbers of the victors had taken permanent residence;

(iv) settlements brought under subjugation by the victors but in which most or all the original inhabitants remain;

(v) the capital and some settlements;

(vi) all settlements and hence the whole territory (Fig. 18).

It has been noted earlier that claim to territory is established by reason of first occupation. The more permanent the occupation the stronger the claim. Claims can be established if farms were previously established in an area. The farms need not be recent at all. They could have been established many years ago, and the area in question could now be under high forest. The establishment of groves or

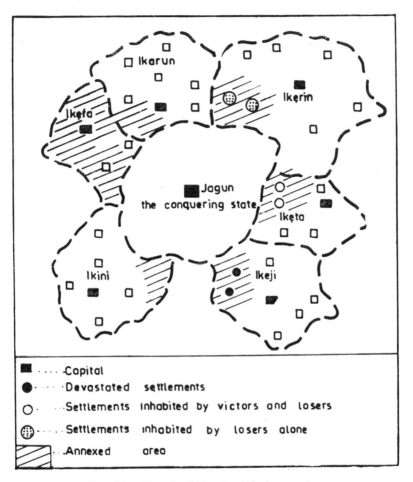

Fig. 18   *Types of Territorial Annexation*

other religious sites in an area can also be the basis of claims to
territory. In all these cases no permanent settlement need exist.
However, when such areas are affected by war the first occupants
may find themselves denied of access to them. The denial could be
permanent or temporary. It is permanent if the victors occupy
the area and start to use it. It is temporary if the victors
withdraw and the former occupants are able to return to it later.
In some cases the victors do not occupy such areas and the former

occupants do not return to them soon after the end of hostilities. Indeed the first occupants might not show interest until members of another community start to settle in the area. In that case they would ask the newer settlers to either move out or accept a tenant status. There would therefore develop a boundary dispute. Even where a third party is not involved, dispute, could arise in the delimitation of the boundary between the victors and the losers. The former may want a boundary coinciding with the farthest extent of its military campaigns or the last battleground, whilst the losers may demand a boundary coinciding with the pre-conflict contact and territorial claims. One example of this is the claim of Ijesa to Enu-Owa, in Ile-Ife town, as its boundary with Ife on the ground that during a war between them they went as far as that point.[1] Another example is the claim of Iwo to a rock near Ilawo as its boundary with Ejigbo because that was how far their fighters went on a raid against Ejigbo in 1896[2] (Fig. 19A).

The existence of a settlement in an area gives the community of the founders undisputed claim over the territory, provided of course that they were the first occupants. But many rural settlements were completely devastated during wars in the nineteenth or earlier centuries. The destruction was more of a punishment to the community than a device to eliminate their presence and claim the territory for the victors. After the cessation of hostilities the victors usually withdrew from such areas. If the devastated settlements were not reconstructed the area would return to high forest which, to all intents and purposes, were regarded as part of the frontier. A third party, neighbour to the former antagonists, could enter such a frontier, but could be challenged by either the losers or the victors. More often the losers were the ones to challenge such others and their claims have been upheld by the courts. Thus, during the Akure/Benin conflicts in the nineteenth century, Benin destroyed some Akure villages. The villages were not rebuilt after hostilities and the area reverted to high forest. When the Idanres moved to the area they were challenged by the Akures who claimed they owned the land and cited the destroyed villages to support their case. The courts upheld the Akure claims.[3]

Of greater interest in destroyed villages is the change of allegiance that could develop among the fleeing inhabitants. On taking the decision to desert the villages three options of destination are usually open to everyone: (i) a settlement of the community (the capital

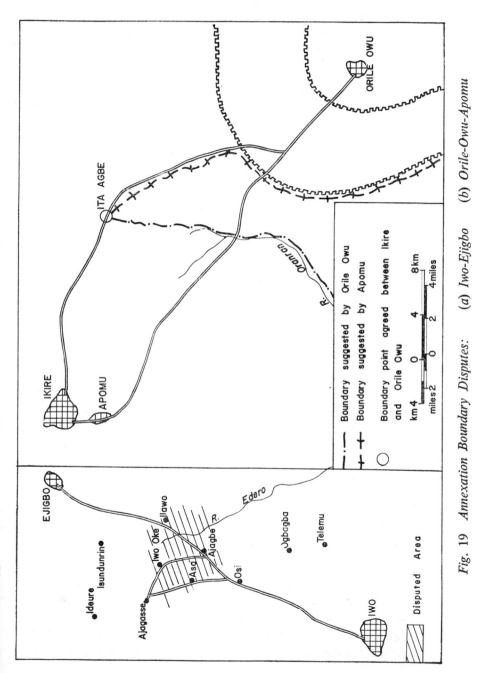

Fig. 19 *Annexation Boundary Disputes:* (*a*) *Iwo-Ejigbo* (*b*) *Orile-Owu-Apomu*

is preferred whenever it is safe) to which the villages owe allegiance; (ii) the capital or other settlement of a neighbouring community; (iii) the capital or other settlement of the advancing army. In most cases the inhabitants of a settlement or group of settlements within an area would be divided in their choice of destination but it can be assumed that members of a family would all make the same choice.

After the cessation of hostilities the refugees would return to their territory and might opt to rebuild the destroyed settlements or build new ones. In either case they can choose to revive the pre-hostility allegiance, or each returning group might choose to give allegiance to its protector community. In the event of the latter choice being made there will develop a situation whereby both the pre-hostility community and the protector communities can claim the same areas, the former on the grounds of the allegiance of the whole area before the war and of some of the people (who sought refuge in its own settlements) after cessation of hostilities. The protector communities would base their claims on the present social ties between them and many of the people in the area. A good example of the situation is the allegiance of Ilawo, Asa, Osi, Iwo-Oke and Ajagba in the area disputed between Iwo and Ejigbo (Fig. 19A). It would appear that the settlements were founded by people who owed allegiance to Ejigbo (Iwo disputes this). As a result of raids from Ilorin in the nineteenth century, people in those settlements fled to both Iwo and Ejigbo. They were unable to return until about forty years later. When they returned they rebuilt their villages, but tributes were paid to both Ejigbo and Iwo. Consequently each community claimed that the settlements should be grouped with it. Ejigbo based its claims on the situation before the war and since it ended, whilst Iwo based its own on post-hostility developments and allegiances.[4]

What has been said above concerns settlements in which resettlement was carried on only by the former inhabitants or their descendants. In some cases the victors or others sympathetic to their cause might settle in conquered settlements and bring about some changes in both the social and political patterns. Socially, they may change the dialect while politically, they may influence the pattern of allegiance and appointment of the chiefs and head chiefs in the settlement. The culture of such settlements is therefore a hybrid and the people a mixture of two communities. A good example of this is Ifewara between Ife and Ijesa. It was founded by Ife elements. When Ijesas attacked Ifewara in the nineteenth century many of them fled to Ile-Ife. Those who remained were joined by Ijesas. Today the political and social organisation is a mixture of the two systems. Although some of the present inhabitants would like to be grouped with Ile-Ife the majority appear to prefer their present merger with Ijesa.[5]

In many cases the victors withdrew from the conquered settlements. Nevertheless the settlements were required to pay tribute to the conquerors. A representative of the latter might be stationed in each settlement and the appointment of their chiefs would be subject to confirmation by the victorious side rather than by their pre-hostility community. The situation might create boundary disputes if the return of the settlements is demanded by the losing side and opposed by the conquerors. The demand for the return of settlements may be justified on the basis that the situation which gave rise to the regrouping has changed. The arguments of Ife for the separation of Ifewara from Ijesa and its merger with Ile-Ife was partly based on this stand.[6]

Where the settlements of the losing side annexed by the victor include the capital, relationships depend on later developments. The tendency was for the *oba* and major chiefs to shift to the unoccupied area where they would establish a new capital from which resistance against the victors could be organised. If the revolt was successful the capital might be shifted back to the original site. If some of the settlements occupied by the victors were not won back during the revolt, the victors would go on exercising rights over them. However, during boundary delimitation the losing side, or even the settlements themselves, could ask that the pre-hostility situation be restored. The losing side would insist that it had successfully overthrown the authority of the victors and should therefore have rights over all its former territory.

If the revolt was not successful there might be great difficulty in fixing a boundary between the two. This would be particularly so where the wars were not waged to a natural conclusion but were stopped by the British. The final outcome and relative positions of the combatants would remain unknown and consequently the rights of each side would be highly debatable. The side that had won the initial campaign would insist on retaining all areas it annexed during the war and that would include the deserted capital.

The losers would insist that they would have won back their capital if there had been no outside intervention. Moreover, the losers would claim that the destroyed capital is important for religious and cultural purposes. Even if the winning side is ready to concede the capital, there would still be argument as to how far outside the capital the boundary should be. Should it be all the former territories including the settlements or just the land surrounding the capital? These and other arguments would complicate boundary delimitation. An example of this is the dispute between Orile-Owu and Aiyedade in Osun South Division (Fig. 19B). During the nineteenth century Orile-Owu was ransacked by invading armies. The town was deserted. However, it has been resettled during the twentieth century and there is a great problem in delimiting the boundary between the town and neighbouring communities. Apomu, one of the neighbours, insists on land up to the old town walls, whilst Orile-Owu wants land up to the River Oranran.[7]

Where all the settlements in a kingdom were overrun by the winning side, the relationships are simple. The kingdom would become a vassal state which would pay tribute to the victors. Disputes would arise during boundary delimitation only if any of the settlements of the losers were to be grouped with the winning side.

OYO—OGBOMOSO BOUNDARY DISPUTE

A good example of the type of dispute arising over war-affected areas is the one between Oyo and Ogbomoso over the Ikoyi area (Fig. 20). As the most powerful kingdom in Yorubaland before the nineteenth century, Oyo brought many other communities under its own influence. Nevertheless, there was a distinct difference between the territories of the conquered communities and that of Oyo. The latter consisted of the metropolitan area inhabited by people who looked to the Alafin as their *oba* and paid homage to him. The conquered communities paid tribute to the Alafin even though individual settlements within each community paid homage to its own *oba*. It was partly from such homage that the *oba*, on behalf of the community, would send tribute to Oyo.

It is not easy to delimit the exact areas occupied by metropolitan Oyo before the fall of the empire in the nineteenth century. The main reason for the difficulty is that there are two possible explanations. First, metropolitan Oyo consisted of all areas occupied by people in settlements without crowned *obas* and who looked to

Oyo. In this sense it would include most of the settlements in the northern part of Osun Divisions as far east as Osogbo and Ede. There are conflicting accounts about the allegiance of the latter two settlements. The Ijesas claim that Osogbo was established by a member of their community[8] and the Ifes claim that the first person to settle at Ede was a member of their community from Ogi.[9] Yet both settlements acknowledged the Alafin as their *oba* and referred important matters to him even during the earlier part of the twentieth century. An example of this is the reference of boundary matters between Ifon and Ilobu to the Alafin in 1917.[10] If nothing else the evidence suggests that both Ede and Osogbo were on the frontier between Oyo and the eastern kingdoms.

The broad definition of Oyo's territory made above is not accepted by the settlements in Osun Division. It appears that they regard themselves as conquered settlements which had to pay tribute and not homage to Oyo. Thus Ogbomoso, one of the nearest settlements to Oyo, does not regard itself as part of Oyo and insists that it had a territory distinct from that of Oyo. Oyo does not dispute the stand of Ogbomoso and recognises the need for a boundary between them.

Between Oyo and Ogbomoso is Ikoyi (Fig. 20). Like many other settlements, Ikoyi took presents to Oyo in the past but it is not clear whether the presents were homage from a daughter or subordinate settlement to the *oba* of its community or tribute from a conquered community to its conquerors. The position was as follows:

> The present Oyo site used to be known as Ago–Oja. Oja was a hunter there then. . . . When Oja was here there were many villages and towns around the area. There were important bales in these towns and villages. . . . These bales in the olden days owed allegiance to the Alafin at Oyo-Ile. They used to take customary gifts to the Alafin annually during the *Bere* festival. They passed these gifts through the Onikoyi to the Alafin at Oyo–Ile. The Onikoyi was then next in rank to the Alafin among the *bales* in the kingdom.[11]

From the statement it would appear that Ikoyi was just one of the daughter settlements of Oyo and the Onikoyi was a *bale,* not an *oba.* In that case Ikoyi would belong to the Oyo community and the presents or gifts taken to Oyo would be homage rather than tribute from a conquered community.

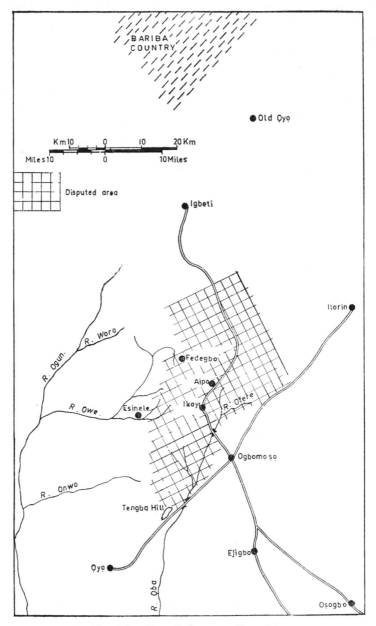

Fig. 20   Oyo-Ogbomoso Frontier

As against the above conclusion is the view that the Onikoyi was a prominent *oba* in the past who had his own territory and subordinate chiefs.[12] One reason why this viewpoint should not be taken seriously is that every ruler of a settlement is now referred to as *oba*. In the past the term *oba* was used for only rulers with beaded crowns, supposedly handed to the ancestors of the *oba*s by Oduduwa.[13] At that time other rulers were called *bale, olu* or *oloja* each of which signified a lesser role than that of an *oba* and also indicated that there was an *oba* to whom the title holder was responsible. It could therefore mean that the reference to the Onikoyi as an *oba* does not imply that he was not within the Oyo community under the suzerainty of the Alafin.

During the nineteenth century Ikoyi and the subordinate settlements were deserted because of attacks from Fulani armies from Ilorin. Some of the people went to Ogbomoso while others went to Ilorin. A few joined the Alafin at Ago-Oja where he sought refuge after fleeing from Oyo-Ile. In each of the centres the refugees from Ikoyi were given land to settle but they retained their identity and the chiefs retained their titles as shown in this statement:

> Following the desertion of Ikoyi, Siyanbola (the Onikoyi) led some of the people of Ikoyi and some of the bales in Ikoyi District in flight to Ilorin. . . . Akinlolu (Siyanbola's younger brother) also led some of the Ikoyi inhabitants in seeking refuge at Ogbomoso.
> Those who went to Ogbomoso settled in various quarters named after their original homesteads. Similarly those who went to Ilorin settled in various places named after their original homesteads. When Siyanbola got to Ilorin he continued to bear the title Onikoyi.[15]
> Igbon, Irosa and Ijoru are now part of Ogbomoso because the inhabitants of these fled to Ogbomoso when their towns were scattered. . . . [16]

At the end of hostilities the refugees returned to occupy their territory. Some of them rebuilt the destroyed settlements but many others stayed in Ogbomoso, using their old land as farmlands. Some of the Ikoyi people at Ogbomoso returned to the old site and then sent for the Onikoyi and their other kinsmen at Ilorin. These came back and the Onikoyi assumed the position occupied by his ancestors before the desertion of the town.[17] The Ilorin migrants did not all settle in Ikoyi—many of them settled in the territory north of Ikoyi and established new settlements in the area.[18]

The new settlements were not on the locations of the destroyed settlements. The Onikoyi was accepted as the *oba* by all the new settlements which paid homage to him. The *bales* in the new settlements were also appointed by the Onikoyi, for example, those of Aribaba, Igbori, Ogide, Ipekun, Alapasa, Olokoto, Odunfa and Okedoyin.[19]

The people who stayed at Ogbomoso but continued to use the land later established settlements also in the area. They, however, retained Ogbomoso as their main base and its *oba* as their overlord. In all respects they regarded themselves as part of the Ogbomoso community:

> We of Aipo family pay our tax to Ogbomoso. We have a head of family. We regard Soun as our *oba*.[20]

> I pay my tax to Ogbomoso. Those of us at Ahoro Obamo also pay our tax to Ogbomoso. I belong to Ogbomoso.[21]

> Members of Bosunla family pay their tax at Ogbomoso. Soun Ogbomoso is now our *oba*.[22]

> We all regard ourselves as belonging to Ogbomoso. We have tenants on the land. These tenants settled in some villages such as Olode, Gbara, Iporin, Iwesu, Otun-Alapo, Alaguntan and Alagbede.[23]

ORIGIN OF THE DISPUTE

When British administration was established it became necessary to determine the boundary between Ibadan and Oyo. There was much disagreement on the location of the boundary, presumably because Oyo was claiming some areas which Ibadan regarded as lying in its own jurisdiction. In any case some agreement was reached in a few areas. Thus, in December 1906, the District Commissioner remarked that '. . . the *bale* and Council in Ibadan agree with the River Obere being the Oyo/Ibadan farm boundary.'[24] At the same time the Ibadans explicitly stated that they were opposed to giving up to the Alafin any of their towns in the *area in dispute*.[25]

In order to resolve the dispute the government appointed a commission under Justice Speed in 1908 to look into the location of the boundary. Mr Justice Speed took evidence from District Officers and then recommended a boundary between the two communities. The eastern section of the boundary was defined as follows:

... Northwards along the course of the Oba River as agreed upon by the Resident and the District Commissioner, Oyo. . . . . The Boundary will then follow the Oba River till it crosses the Ogbomoso–Ilorin road for the second time.

The boundary be fixed about a mile more or less to include the road and all villages on the Ogbomoso–Ilorin road and the farmlands of Gbede within Ibadan Division[26] [Fig. 21].

When the boundary decision was being effectively implemented there were protests from Ogbomoso on the ground that it deprived them of the land effectively occupied by those who had settled permanently in Ogbomoso. Specific mention was made of Olo, Maya, Alaa and Iluju (Fig 21). They argued that in view of past history:

> Ogbomoso should be allowed to hold the lands by right of defence which amounted to conquest, and because the inhabitants came to Ogbomoso and made voluntary alliance under which they have grown into one people with our city.[27]

Following the complaints by Ogbomoso the Resident of Oyo Province toured the area to find out the allegiance of the people. Of the settlements listed by Ogbomoso only Olo refused to pay tribute to the Onikoyi. Olo's refusal was based on the fact that that village had become part of Ogbomoso.[28] The District Officer then conducted an inquiry on 21 April 1934. At the end of it he recommended that since Olo was both geographically and historically under Oyo it should[29] pay tribute to the Alafin through the Onikoyi. The Ogbomoso people protested against the recommendation and claimed that the traditional boundary was 'Ipinle, beyond Tengba hill at a little rock on the left side of the road near 161 mile pillar.'[30] They also demanded that Olo should pay taxes to Ogbomoso.

Oyo opposed the demands of Ogbomoso and went on in 1950 to complain about Ogbomoso hunters in the Ikoyi forest reserve. Ogbomoso claimed that they owed their hunting rights in the reserve to an agreement of 1936. In February 1950 the Alafin demanded the withdrawal of the Olos from the western side of the Oba River. The Olos did not withdraw. When Ogbomoso attempted to construct a road from Osundele to Ogbomoso, both Ikoyi and Oyo opposed Ogbomoso's involvement in the road construction. In 1957 there was rivalry about the appointment of an Olugbon of Igbon. The Ogbomosos appointed one and protested when the Alafin went on to appoint another.[31]

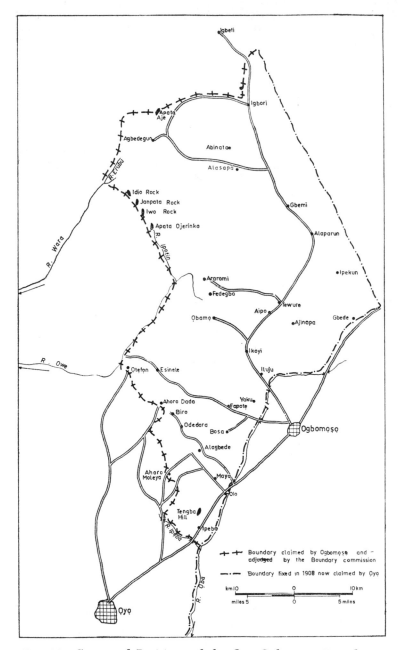

Fig. 21   *Suggested Positions of the Oyo-Ogbomoso Boundary*

The government insisted[32] on keeping the boundary defined by Speed in 1908 but later referred the matter to the Boundary Settlement Commissioner who investigated it and announced a decision in January 1971.[33]

TERRITORIAL CLAIMS

The Ogbomoso people claimed all land lying west of a line running along 'the Ipɛba stream, northwards along the Owe River, the Ipantin stream along the Iwo, Jarasale and Idio rocks thenceforth northwards to the Erubu stream and to the Ogbomoso/Igbetti boundary.'[34] The claim was justified on the ground that in the past many families which now form part of Ogbomoso community settled on the land. Among them were Maya, Fedegbo, Aipo, Obamo, Esinele, Ajinapa, Fapoto and Yakubu families. The families lived there until the Fulani wars when they sought refuge in Ogbomoso, and after the wars the families returned to the land and made further village settlements.[35] They also claimed that:

> Ever before the fall of old Oyo the territorial boundary of the Oja people and Ogbomoso has been settled by reference to the Ogun stream and Ipeba stream.
> Ogbomoso hunters who hunted at large on the area would stop at the territorial boundary so defined whilst Oja hunters would keep to their side of the boundary. Among several acts of recognition of this boundary are:
> (i) the construction by Ogbomoso of the Ogbomoso–Oyo road which runs across the area up to Ipeba;
> (ii) the recognition of Ipeba by both communities as the bordre post for the exchange of mail;
> (iii) hunters from Oyo always kept within their side of Ipeba stream whilst Ogbomoso hunters have exercised hunting rights over the whole area and have erected hunting camps for several generations along the Ogbomoso side of the boundary; and inhabitants of the area have always been on the land and exercised rights thereon as Ogbomoso people.
> The Soun of Ogbomoso by tradition had always appointed *bale*s for village settlements on the land, and always exercised rights of natural ruler thereon as head of the Ogbomoso community.[36]

Oyo's claims over the area was based mainly on the connections of the settlements with Oyo and Ikoyi before the British occupation:

> The Alafin of Oyo is the Head and overlord of all lands making up the Oyo Southern District council Area of Authority. This area at present includes Ikoyi District, Oyo Township

and villages which include Olo, Esinele, Maya, Elesun, Onidada, Biro, Odede, Igboaje, Alagbede, Aronpe, Oba, Aporan, Masifa, Bosa, Fapote, Yaku and other villages.

This area referred to above is a portion of the District administered by the Alafin from Oyo-Ile and later from Ago-d'Oyo, the present Oyo, which District includes Ogbomoso. This was prior to the advent of the British.

All throughout the period of the Alafin's stay in Oyo-Ile, all the Provincial *obas* and *bales* (including the *Bale* of Ogbomoso). send *isakole* through the Onikoyi of Ikoyi to the Alafin, and also pay homage through the Onikoyi on the yearly festival of *Bere*[37]

THE ISSUES AT STAKE

From the foregoing it is clear that Ogbomoso bases its claim on the existence of a traditional boundary between it and Oyo before the war and the rights of some Ogbomoso residents in the area before and after the wars. On the other hand the case of Oyo is based on the traditional allegiance of the settlements in the area to Oyo through Onikoyi. That being so its settlement must first resolve the following issues:

(i)   the traditional boundary between Oyo and Ogbomoso and its location;

(ii)   the rights of Ogbomoso in the area before the hostilities;

(iii) the territorial rights of individual settlements and families in the area before and after the Fulani wars;

(iv)   the nature of the relationships between Ikoyi and the other settlements in the area before and after their desertion;

(v)   the nature of relationships between Oyo and the settlements in the area before and since the wars.

Oyo/Ogbomoso Traditional Boundary: While Ogbomoso maintains that there was a boundary between it and Oyo the latter denies such boundary:

There has never been any traditional boundary between Ogbomoso and Oyo. There were traditional boundaries existing among the various towns and villages forming the kingdom but there was no such boundary existing between them and the Alafin.[38]

Both views are supported by Lloyd's opinion that subordinate towns have a clearly defined boundary with each other: 'The subordinate towns have a clearly defined boundary one with another. . . . There exists, too, a boundary with the metropolitan town though this is often difficult to describe . . . .'[39] The point to note about these claims is that boundaries exist between settlements. Since the claim is that Ogbomoso was a subordinate settlement it can be expected that there would be boundaries between it and its neighbours. If there should be any trouble at all it would be in the case of subordinate settlements adjacent to Oyo. Ogbomoso was not one of these. In support of this is the fact that the boundary claimed by Ogbomoso was between it and Ago-Oja which was to become the present Oyo:

> We have been hunting in the land long before Alafin Lawani. When we started hunting in the area the whole place was a jungle and only the brave who were not afraid could go there. The Alafin had not come to the present Oyo then.[40]
>
> Hunters from Ogbomoso hunt as far as Apata-Oloro while hunters from Oyo hunt as far as Apata-Olobi. Ahoro-Moleye to Ipeba stream is the boundary between us. This was the position before our time and it was as a result of an agreement between my ancestors (Ogbomoso) and Ogungbade, Oja's son, following frequent quarrels between Ogbomoso hunters and Ogungbade's followers. The agreement was to the effect that any game falling on the Apata-Oloro side belonged to Ogbomoso and any game falling on the Apata-Olobi side belonged to Oyo.[41]

From these statements it can be concluded that there was a boundary between Ago-Oja and Ogbomoso; furthermore, that Ogbomoso's right in its own area should be recognised even though Ago-Oja later became the seat of the Alafin who recognised Ogbomoso's rights in certain areas after he had moved to Ago-Oja as shown by his acknowledgement that Tengba hill belonged to Ogbomoso:

> I knew Tengba hill; there used to be a monkey [gorilla?] which was killing human beings. One day this monkey was killed by hunters—the children of Lagbedu of Ogbomoso. They brought the carcass to Bale Elepo of Ogbomoso who asked them to take it to the Alafin. On getting to the Alafin at Oyo, the Alafin said that the monkey was not killed on his land and that therefore it should be sent back to Elepo. Oyo was at its present site then and the Alafin was Alafin Lawani, father of Ladigbolu.[42]

There is therefore evidence that Oyo recognised certain areas as lying within the sphere of Ogbomoso. Nevertheless there is need to be cautious in interpreting it as meaning that there was a definite boundary in the way defined by Ogbomoso. The incident of the monkey carcass indicates that Ogbomoso was not certain of the extent of its territory. If it had been certain there would have been no need for the bale, Elepo, to send the monkey to the Alafin. It can, of course, be argued that he did so because he acknowledged the overlordship of the Alafin. Against this is that the Alafin sent back the carcass which he would not have done if he regarded Ogbomoso as one of his own daughter settlements. One valid deduction appears to be that the *bale* did not know the boundary between him and the Oyos. If the people near the boundary were not certain then there was no way for Ogbomoso to determine the extent of its territory. Even if the Alafin's statement is taken as meaning that Tengba hill is on Ogbomoso land, it does not indicate the boundary. He did not specify its location on Tengba hill or even away from it. It would appear that the Alafin did not accept the monkey mainly because the killers were from Ogbomoso. One can therefore infer from the incident that no boundary was agreed upon as claimed by Ogbomoso.

The above inference is valid for all other sections where Ogbomoso claims that definite agreements were reached. The specific points said to have been agreed upon included Apata-Oloro and Apata-Olobi, Ipeba stream and Ahoro-Moleye. Game on Apata-Oloro side was to go to Ogbomoso and that on Apata-Olobi was to go to Oyo.[43] There was no agreement on game between the two places. Therefore the agreement could only refer to the points. Furthermore there is no indication of which side was to have Ahoro-Moleye or how far from it the boundary should be drawn. It seems therefore that there was no agreement on a boundary in the sense in which Ogbomoso is now interpreting it. In all probability there was a zone of contact between the two sides stretching from Apata-Oloro and Apata-Olobi to Tengba hill. Hunters from both sides interacted within such a zone. The mutual recognition of Tengba hill and the fact that Ogbomoso first thought that the place was on Oyo land suggests that both sides had knowledge of it and that it represents one of their meeting points.

The foregoing interpretation conforms with what happens on other boundaries in Yorubaland, as shown in the preceding chapters. These findings contradict Lloyd's view, cited above, and all that can be said is that anyone settling boundary disputes in Western Nigeria would do well to disregard the claims of any community that a boundary was fixed between hunters because animals are not limited by imaginary lines. In any case no community has demonstrated that boundaries in the form of well-defined lines were actually agreed upon. The only boundaries that were agreed upon were between individual farmers and these were farmline boundaries.

Rights of Ogbomoso: The evidence cited above shows that the only rights of Ogbomoso in the area they claim before the Fulani wars was limited to hunting. One possible explanation is that the farming zone had not extended as far as the area. But such explanation can only be limited to the areas of Tengba hill, Apata-Oloro and Apata-Olobi, that is the southern part of the disputed zone as defined in the statements of claim cited above. The other parts were claimed by people who fled from the settlements there to Ogbomoso during the Fulani wars. In all cases the people stress the connection only from the time when they sought refuge in Ogbomoso during the wars. There is therefore the implication that they were not under Ogbomoso before the war. Ogbomoso is claiming those territories on behalf of the former refugees who have now been absorbed into its community. The point of contention is that those people have no right to transfer their land to Ogbomoso:

> It is not in dispute that those who migrated by force of circumstance to Ogbomoso and stayed there are now claiming Ogbomoso as their second home and in any event are within Ogbomoso District Council Area. What is contended is that the villages and the land they left belong to the Onikoyi, the Elesinele and the Asipa of Oyo. . . . [44]

The Territorial Right of Individual Settlements of a Community: As explained in Chapter II, a community consists of people in a main settlement, where the *oba* lives, and some subordinate ones. The land of the community consists of areas occupied by those in the subordinate and main settlements. The community as a whole is said to own the land and each individual is said to have only right of use for life, that is *usufructuary* rights in the land. This view is no doubt derived from the idea that the territory of the community is clearly defined and anyone who wants land must first receive the permission of the community leaders. But previous chapters of this study show that there is usually nothing fixed about the territory. In fact the available evidence shows that founders of the subordinate settlements, like those of the main ones, came to their location without any special permission. Many of them were hunters who later settled down to engage in agriculture. This was the case on the Ijesa/Ondo borderlands,[45] on the Ife/Ijebu frontier[46] and also in the territory between Ijebu and Ibadan.[47] Oja, the first settler in present Oyo, was also one of such founders. Each hunter continued to owe allegiance to the main town from which he set out and regarded himself as part of its community. The community's claim on the territory was based on those of the individual hunter or of others who first got there to lay claims.

The first settler in an area possibly had detailed knowledge of the territory around him. New arrivals joining him there would seek his permission and establish their own farms. But the area within which such authority was exercised was limited. The further away from the settlement a new arrival settled, the less likely was he to seek permission. At the extreme edge someone else would establish a new base and the process would start again. However, it seems the bases were not distant from each other as shown by the distances between settlements in the long-settled zones of Ekiti or Ijebu. Even in such areas the territory between the bases or settlements was not all allocated. The land on which a person settled, or that allocated to him, belonged to him and his family. No one could take it from him unless there was no heir to claim it. In the latter event land reverts to the community and any of its members may later occupy it.

The effect of the above is that evey settlement has a claim to its own territory in so far as the right is not derived as the result of a grant from the *oba*. Only if the settlement is completely destroyed and none of its citizens attempts to rebuild it can the community claim it. Where there are members of the destroyed community the ideal situation would be for each to claim the land of his ancestors. No section can claim the land of the entire settlement unless it can prove that all other sections have become extinct. The situation has long been recognised in customary practice, as was noted by Elias and Lloyd:

> . . . the real unit of land-holding is the family; and . . . the ascription of ownership of land to the community or the village is only accurate if viewed as a social aggregate.[48]
>
> The community retains reversionary rights over all the land of its members which becomes abandoned for lack of heirs. With land held by descent groups reversion is conceivable only if the whole group becomes extinct, or, as in the past was more likely, were driven from the town for rebellion. The general Yoruba rule is that land reverts not necessarily directly to the *oba* (on behalf of the community) but to whoever is supposed . . . to have granted it: thus ultimately does all land revert to the *oba*.[49]

The application of these principles to the settlements deserted during the Fulani wars between Oyo and Ogbomoso would mean that all the people who fled to Ogbomoso or Ilorin could retain their land on their return after the hostilites. No one could deprive them of the land and they could not be asked to pay rent for its use. The Alafin's demand of 1950 that Olo farmers should leave their land contravened this principle.

Ikoyi's Right in the Disputed Area: Two aspects of the problem need be considered: whether Ikoyi has any rights at all and the nature of those rights. In either case the position before and after the desertion of Ikoyi and the settlements in the area would have to be considered. There is no clear indication of the relationships between Ikoyi and the other settlements before the Fulani wars. Nevertheless inferences can be made from evidence given by each side in the dispute. According to an Ikoyi man, the settlements in the area paid homage to the Onikoyi before the wars '. . . the *bale* on the land in dispute used to bring gifts of yams and elubo to the Onikoyi every year. . . .'[50] The payment of homage signified acceptance of the *oba*. This could be due to one of two factors: either the *oba*'s community conquered the settlements or the settlements were founded by people, owing allegiance to the *oba*, who could be members of the community by birth or adoption (i.e. strangers who accept the *oba*).

Accounts given by Ogbomoso of the founding of the settlements made no reference to Ikoyi. Thus an account of Fedegbo's origin was rendered as follows:

Ajadi migrated from Efon to Fedegbo. Ajadi was a native doctor. When Ajadi settled on the land there was no one there. Oyo was at Katunga at the time. The place where Ajadi settled was called Fedegbo.[51]

Accounts of other settlements tend to deny any connection between the founders and Ikoyi. Thus, in the case of Aipo, it was stated that it was founded by an Ibariba (called Aipo) and his relations.[52] Similarly the founder of Esincle was a hunter from Ibariba who came to the area to hunt and was later joined by others from Ibariba.[53]

Despite the present denials of connection with Ikoyi only one settlement, Olo, refused to pay homage to the Onikoyi in 1934. In making the refusal Olo did not argue that it had nothing to do with

Ikoyi in the past, but that the people were now part of Ogbomoso community and should be allowed to pay their tribute there. The other settlements acquiesced in their grouping with Ikoyi and the payment of tribute there.[54] This suggests that there was some connection between the settlements and Ikoyi before the war.

If, as it is now claimed, the settlements were founded by people without reference to Ikoyi or Oyo then the connection inferred above could only have come from conquest by Ikoyi. Conquest would oblige each settlement to pay tribute to Ikoyi. In that event it can be expected that each would regard itself as independent once Ikoyi was destroyed and hence was unable to exercise control over them. The present attempt to distinguish themselves from Ikoyi could probably be interpreted in that light. However, it is to be noted that if that were the case each settlement would probably acknowlege the past domination while claiming their right to present independence. That no reference is made to any past connection with Ikoyi indicates some evasion. This suggests that they are not sure that their own version of what occurred in the past will be believed. Such uncertainty would possibly not occur if there had been wars on which they could base the connection.

One other factor makes it unlikely that the settlements had no connection with Ikoyi. This arises from certain features of the accounts of their establishment given. For example, Ajadi, the founder of Fedegbo, was a doctor.[55] It seems reasonable to expect that such a person would first have a base in a town where he would be patronised by the *oba*, chiefs and citizens. From the town base he could go out to farm and establish farm settlements. His main base would remain the town and he would regard himself as belonging to its community. The settlements founded by Ibariba hunters could possibly have been established without reference to anyone. However, Ibariba lies north of Old Oyo and the hunters would have passed through the kingdom before getting to Ikoyi area. Since they were foreigners to the kingdom they would need to owe allegiance to a part of it before they could start farming. Ikoyi, being the nearest, would appear to be a community to which they could attach themselves. There is therefore a very good chance that the various settlements were attached to Ikoyi and that they regarded themselves as part of its community before the Fulani wars. The gifts to the Onikoyi were most probably acts of homage from daughter settlements rather than tribute from a conquered community.

The above conclusion leads to a consideration of the rights of Ikoyi over such settlements. Did Ikoyi own the land and give each family certain sections of it? As previously explained, it seems unlikely that any community had so much knowledge of territory at considerable distances from it. The chances are that people left the town to seek farmlands and, by their presence, the areas they occupied were regarded as belonging to the community. The presentation of gifts was not necessarily payment of tax or *isakole*, but a contribution to the maintenance of the office of the *oba* and other community leaders whose duty it was to organise and protect the community, and hence all its members. The point was noted by Lloyd:

> All members of the kingdom may claim as much land as they need for farming and house-building, but the tribute, tax or services which they render to the *oba* are not in respect of the land but are obligations which stem from their membership of the kingdom.[56]

The *oba* or the community as a corporate body cannot therefore lay claim to the land occupied by anyone. Nevertheless, the community as a body is the only legitimate authority over unoccupied land between families and settlements. Anyone in the community can go to such unoccupied areas to farm and none of the people nearby can debar the settlement. The rights of a settlement were limited to the area effectively utilised for house-building and farming. The farmlands would include areas previously cultivated but now lying fallow. The hunting grounds which may be extensive are not usually claimable on an exclusive basis.

What the above implies is that every family has a perpetual right to the land cultivated by its ancestors but the community as a whole has control over unoccupied land between families and settlements. Applied to the present topic it means that Ikoyi as a community had control over unoccupied land between the settlements and families which existed before the war. The community can give permission to anyone to settle on any part of the unoccupied territories. That right would be exercised by the community head— the Onikoyi.

At the end of hostilities each family would be able to lay claim to the area cultivated by its ancestors. Each member of the community would also be free to go to areas not previously occupied. At the same time the community head could grant any of the unoccupied territory to adopted or naturalised citizens of the community. Therefore it was within the right of the Onikoyi to grant land to Ilorin elements who opted to join the community as was reported in evidence before the Boundary Commissioner:

> The various villages . . . are peopled mostly by Ilorin people who have come there to farm. It was the Onikoyi who gave the land to the Ilorin farmers.[57]

It must be stressed that the right of the Onikoyi to grant land is restricted to land not previously farmed by any family. If such land had been farmed the family may order eviction. On the other hand no member of a family can make a valid complaint if the land had not actually been farmed by his ancestors. In areas like Ikoyi caution needs to be exercised because many families may not be able to trace the exact areas cultivated by their ancestors. It could be that the only solution is to ensure that each family has land for its own needs before the community makes any grant to outsiders.

The Rights of Oyo: There has been no dispute over Oyo's political suzerainty over the settlements in the area before the hostilities; what is in question is that Oyo's influence over the area was any more than it exercised in other parts of Yorubaland. In other words, it is being suggested that the influence of Oyo over the area was not greater than the influence it had over Ogbomoso or Ede. If the Alafin had conceded independence to those other places he should have done the same to the settlements in the area. Oyo's reply is that parts of the area were in the sphere of influence of Oja, secondly, that some of the inhabitants of the settlements had moved to Oyo, and lastly, that the other settlements were under Ikoyi which still acknowledges the suzerainty of Oyo.[58] The relationships between the settlements and Ikoyi have been discussed above. The extent to which one can accept Ogbomoso's claim of a definite boundary between Oja and itself has also been discussed. If, as already explained, there was no definite boundary between Oja and Ogbomoso, claims to territory in the common frontier can be established only by permanent occupation. Each side would have rights over the land occupied by its own people. Therefore the Oyos or *bale* of Oja could claim land on which settlements were founded by those who owe allegiance to them. One such settlement is Esinele.

The claim over Esinele by Oyo is based on two grounds. First, that Esinele was founded by people who owed allegiance to the Alafin before the wars:

> The Elesinele is a *bale;* he is also an *eso* to the Alafin. The *Eso*s are the Alafin's military commanders. Ajagbe was the first Elesinele; then came Oluyide, Olujaiye and Olugbohun. Olugbohun brought the title from the homestead of Oyo town. Atiba was the Alafin then.[59]

A second reason for Oyo's claims to Esinele is that some of its citizens moved to Oyo during the hostilities. Apparently there were two attacks on the settlement. On the first occasion the people fled to Oyo. The people who fled to Oyo must have returned under Olugbohun to settle the place or defend it. They failed and took refuge in present Oyo and in Ogbomoso. This interpretation is based on the following evidence: that Olugbohun was the first Elesinele and that he was a military commander;[60] and also the statement that:

> Two wars scattered Esinele. I don't know after which of the two wars Olugbohun came to Oyo. I don't know the *bale* at the time Esinele was first evacuated. I don't know to which place the Esinele people fled when it was first evacuated.[61]
>
> I learnt from my father that when the various *ahoro* at Oke Oba could no longer contain the Fulani warrior, Ahoro Esinele, and the other *ahoro* fled to Ogbomoso during the second Fulani war.[62]

The essence of the situation is that the people of Esinele are now found in both Oyo and Ogbomoso. Ordinarily there should be no dispute about land in that each family can lay claim to land occupied by its ancestors. However, there is a problem because, in the past, Oyo had claimed that those resident in Ogbomoso should pay *isakole.*[63] The claim is based on the assumption that Oyo owns all the land. As already shown, Oyo does not own all the land, the individual families have a right to land cultivated by their ancestors.

As against the Oyo claims, the people in Ogbomoso want to lay claim to all the land on the ground that they had a boundary with Oyo which placed the disputed area on their side. It has been shown above that boundaries did not exist and each family can only claim areas cultivated by its ancestors. Land not cultivated before the destruction and flight during the wars belongs to the community. That community could be one of three: the descendants of people of Esinele, the Ogbomoso community or the Oyo community. The descendants of people of Esinele could claim unoccupied land on the basis that it belonged to their ancestors. However, there was no definite boundary of Esinele land and what they did not cultivate could have been occupied by any member of the community to which they belonged before the wars. This is based on the fact that such a community would have been the acknowledged owner of land lying between its daughter settlements. Therefore the descendants as a whole cannot claim any area. The unoccupied land belongs to the community of which the descendants are now a part. Difficulties arise because there are two such communities—Oyo and Ogbomoso. The latter's claim rests on the descendants of Esinele now living in Ogbomoso. If that be the case, Ogbomoso cannot have more than the claim of those descendants, which is the area cultivated by their individual families. It would appear, therefore, that Oyo, as the community to which the people belonged before the war and to which some of the descendants now belong, should have undisputed rights over areas not cultivated by any family before the Fulani wars.

IMPLICATIONS FOR A SETTLEMENT

From the above it would appear that a settlement of the dispute should take cognisance of the following principles:

(1) The descendants of each of the families which settled in the area before the wars have a right to land cultivated by their ancestors and could cultivate such land themselves or through their tenants. In either case they do not have to pay *isakole*.

(2) Land not cultivated before the wars belonged to the community of which the people were a part at that time. Any member of the particular community can settle on such land or expand his farm into it without payment of *isakole* to anyone. The community, through its *oba* and chiefs, could also grant part of such land to any group they may think fit and on conditions agreed between them. The conditions may include the payment of *isakole*.

(3) The administrative grouping of the area should, as far as possible, reflect the present community affiliations of the people and ensure that the land occupied by those on each side is grouped with the appropriate community, i.e. the

land of those in Oyo should be grouped with the people in Oyo and the same with Ogbomoso.

(4) Where the third principle is not possible each block or settlement should be grouped with the community to which the majority of the people now owe allegiance. In such a case those not on the side of their community should *never* be asked to pay *isakole* and provision should be made for them to have unrestricted rights over their land which should be clearly defined.

ADJUDGED BOUNDARY

The Boundary Settlement Commissioner who decided the boundary in 1971 took a different position from that suggested above. Notable among his conclusions[64] were the following:

4. That each of the towns and villages on the land in dispute, except Ikoyi, was being ruled by its own *bale*. The Onikoyi was an *oba*, superior in rank to any of the *bales* . . . .

5. That each ruler, however, be he an *oba* or *bale* had dominance over the territory comprised in his domain and was not a tenant either of the Alafin or of the Onikoyi or of anyone else. . . .

10. That there is no scintilla of evidence before me from which I could reasonably hold that the Onikoyi (i.e. the Ikoyi community) owned or owns any part (except Ikoyi) of the land in dispute.

11. That similarly there is no evidence before me, apart from the ancient status of the Alafin, from which I could reasonably hold that the Alafin (i.e. the Oyo community) owned or owns any part of the land in dispute.

12. That consequently, I find that title to the land over which each town or village was situated was in the ruler of the place and his subjects whose long possession has never been denied but rather admitted by all sides.

13. That as a result of the Fulani wars . . . all the towns and villages on the land in dispute were deserted and their rulers and inhabitants fled to Ogbomoso and established various compounds there. The Onikoyi and some of his subjects, however, fled to Ilorin . . . .

16. Esiele (or Esinele) and Ikoyi were among the towns on the land in dispute that fled to Ogbomoso and have equally, thereby, subjected themselves to the traditional jurisdiction of Soun of Ogbomoso. . . .

20. That the descendants of the original owners still own and are still in possession of the lands inherited from their

forebears, although some parts of the lands are now occupied by tenants placed thereon by the Onikoyi.

In his final conclusion the Commissioner stated that:

I am satisfied, and I so hold, that from the welter of evidence before me the people of Bosunla, Fapoto, Fedegbo, Obamo, Aipo, Dada, Yaku, Esinele, Ikoyi and other towns and villages on the land in dispute placed themselves under the protection of the *bale* of Ogbomoso at some time during the wars of the nineteenth century and thereby became subject to him. They have all therefore become part of Ogbomoso Community and their land now belongs to that Community.[65]

He then delimited the boundary between the two communities as:

From the confluence of Oba River and Ipeba stream and running along the bank of the Ipeba stream in a general north-westerly direction for a distance of approximately 55,000 feet to Ahoro-Moleye. Thence the boundary continues in a general north-easterly direction for a distance of approximately 36,000 feet to a point marked Peg forty-nine on Plan No. AB3589. The boundary then proceeds along the Biro-Ahoro–Dada-Oniya-Gboguro road for a distance approximately 47,500 feet to a point on Onimo stream where the said stream crosses the said road. The boundary then runs along the bank of the Onimo stream to its confluence with the Owe River and then continues in a general north-easterly direction along Owe River passing through Olohunhun stream, Oloku stream and Gbogun stream to a point at the confluence of Owe River and Ipatin stream at a distance of approximately 75,000 feet. From this point the boundary runs along the bank of the Ipatin stream to Apata-Ojerinko and in a general north-westerly direction passing through Iwo Rock and Janponta Rock and then along the Idie stream to Idie Rock and then to Apata–Alaru for a distance of approximately 66,500 feet. The boundary then continues in a general westerly direction along the bank of the Onikansan stream to the confluence of Onikansan and Erubu streams for a distance of approximately 13,200 feet. From the confluence the boundary runs in a general north-easterly direction along Erubu stream to its confluence with Epete stream. Finally the boundary runs in an approximately northern direction for a distance of about 18,000 feet to the boundary with Igbeti.[66] [Fig. 21].

A CRITIQUE OF THE DECISION

The Commissioner's findings appear in many cases to be based on a sound knowledge of Yoruba custom and customary law. However, he sometimes overlooked some basic ideas of Yoruba administrative practices and territorial organisation. For example, his fourth finding cited above is sound in theory and practice but the inference he appeared to have drawn from it contradicts known practices in the region. His inference is that the settlements were independent of each other and this is explicitly stated in the fifth finding. The position is that each kingdom was divided into local government units in the form of the subordinate towns. Although each subordinate town was independent in internal affairs the *oba* of the kingdom had overall control of external relations and capital punishment. As Lloyd rightly noted:

> The rights of the *oba* in respect of his subordinate towns included the right to legislate throughout the kingdom; though the rulers of the subordinate towns might make their own rules so long as they did not conflict with those of the kingdom. The rights of the *oba* in respect of certain animals extended throughout his kingdom. The subordinate towns were not empowered to hear cases of treason or homicide—these were referred to the *oba*'s court. The boundaries of the kingdom were the *oba*s boundaries, and any dispute over them lay between the two *oba*s concerned and not between neighbouring subordinate towns of each kingdom.[67]

Another inference from the fifth finding is that the territories of the settlements were clearly defined. The previous chapters of this book and the early section of this chapter make clear that this could not have been so. The only situation in which the commissioner's inferences could be true is if all the settlements, including Ikoyi, looked to one *oba*. If so that *oba* would be the Alafin. Even then each of the settlements would not be independent in the way the commissioner implied. It would appear, as earlier argued, that the settlements belonged to a single community and that was probably the Ikoyi community. That community had rights over uncultivated land between its settlements or other areas occupied by its citizens.

One unfortunate aspect of the findings is the failure to realise that witnesses frequently exaggerate their claims and are anxious to prove subservience where none existed in the past. For this reason they frequently interpret homage by one settlement as *isakole*. *Isakole* is a rent payable by tenants who could be from another community or another family. Members of a community can claim land for their needs provided no other member had previously done so. It was not therefore necessary for the subordinate towns or villages to be tenants on land of their own community as was being suggested in the fifth finding. In short one must query the tenth finding where it is stated that there is no evidence that the Ikoyi community had rights outside Ikoyi town.

The twelfth finding is mis-leading if only because it overlooks the arguments advanced earlier that land belongs to individual families. Much more important is the apparent contradiction between the thirteenth and the sixteenth findings. In the former he held that some people in Ikoyi fled to Ilorin, whilst in the latter he stated categorically that Ikoyi and Esinele went to Ogbomoso and thereby accepted the suzerainty of the Soun. Apart from contradicting himself on the destination of Ikoyi refugees he also did so on the matter of suzerainty, for elsewhere in the findings he noted that Ikoyi accepted Ilorin's suzerainty:

> It is generally accepted by all witnesses who gave evidence
> . . . that Onikoyi Siyanbola fled from Ikoyi with some followers
> to Ilorin. But it was this same Onikoyi, who, before the last
> desertion of Ikoyi, took it away from allegiance to the Alafin
> of Oyo-Ile and made it a vassal state of Ilorin.[68]

In view of all this it would appear that the commissioner failed to take full cognisance of the 'welter of evidence' before him. In fact he did not prove beyond any doubt whatever that the whole area accepted the Soun as their overlord. If they did one may ask why it was necessary for some of the Ikoyis to recall their *oba* from Ilorin, resettle their own town and even prefer now to accept the Alafin as their overlord.

The bases of the judgment apart, it is to be regretted that the delimited boundary paid no attention to individual farmlands but followed the old mistakes of using straight lines which might cut across farmlands and lead to rejection of the boundary. This happened on the Ikere/Akure[69] and the Ife/Ijesa[70] boundaries and has made acceptance difficult.

CONCLUSION

The discussion of the Oyo/Ogbomoso boundary brings out clearly the features of annexation boundary disputes. The arguments advanced by each side are quite different from those in other cases. The solution would tend to be more legalistic as it depends on the rights of each claimant before and after the war which led to annexation. Such legal rights require deep knowledge of customary administrative law and territorial organisation. It is therefore incumbent on anyone called to participate in the settlement of such disputes to have sound knowledge of the rights and obligations of individuals, villages and the community (as represented by the *oba*) in territories. Attention must be paid to the foundation of each settlement, the allegiance of the founders and the extent to which people in each village or settlement now accept the former community. It is to be regretted that in the above example the counsel for Oyo made no attempt to produce evidence of earlier attachments between Ikoyi and the other settlements being claimed by Oyo. Much more regrettable is the fact that the Boundary Commissioner made no attempt to elicit evidence in that regard but instead blamed Oyo for not producing it. If boundary disputes are to be permanently settled judgments on them must be based on truth which an arbitrator must painstakingly establish. The arbitrator, be it a court or a Boundary Commission, must not depend only on the evidence which counsels present. The court is for justice, it is unbiased. Counsel representing their clients want unfavourable evidence suppressed and where the opponent is not hard working vital evidence may be overlooked. Justice will be miscarried. It is the duty of those responsible for settling boundary disputes to ensure that all essential evidence is presented and that justice is not miscarried.

Notes and References

1. Owa of Ilesa during an interview with the author, 1969.
2. Oluwo of Iwo in evidence at the inquiry into the Iwo/Ejigbo boundary dispute, January 1938. File 1391 Vol. II, Oyo Prof. 1/1, N.A.I.
3. See Chapter IV.
4. 'Inquiry into the Iwo/Ejigbo Boundary Dispute, 26–31 January 1938', File 1391 Vol. II, Oyo Prof. 1/1, N.A.I.
5. Omolade Adejuyigbe, 'Ife/Ijesa Boundary Problem', *Nigerian Geog. Jnl.* 13 (1970), p. 27.
6. Oni of Ife during an interview which the author had with him in August 1969.
7. Olowu of Orile-Owu to Resident, Oyo Province, 13 February 1939, File, OY 2279 Vol. I, Oyo Prof. 1/2, N.A.I.
8. A. Oloyede, 'Rural-Urban Relationship of Odo-Otin District and Osogbo', Unpub. B.A. Essay, Geography Department, University of Ife, June 1969, p. 6.

9. Information by Oni and elders of Ife and Edunabon, 5 May 1968.
10. See correspondence on this issue in File 4309, Oyo Prof. 1/1, N.A.I.
11. S. A. Ogunmola, in evidence before Commissioner for Boundary Settlement, 1970. See Western Nigeria Boundary Commission, *Findings of the Ogundare Boundary Commission of Enquiry into the Boundary Dispute Between Oyo and Ogbomoso given on the 29th Day of January,* 1971 (hereafter referred to as the Ogundare Commission).
12. A. Akinwale, in evidence before the Ogundare Commission, op. cit.
13. G. J. Afolabi Ojo, *Yoruba Culture: A Geographic Analysis* (London: University of London Press, 1966), pp. 126–7.
14. The boundary discussions were aimed at ensuring the placement of the tributary settlements under Ibadan. See, for example, Resident, Ibadan Province, to District Commissioner, Oyo, 12 December 1906, File C 390, Oyo Prof. 1/206, N.A.I.
15. S. Ayinla, in evidence before the Ogundare Commission, op. cit.
16. A. Dongare, in evidence before the Ogundare Commission, op. cit.
17. See the evidence of Y. Aremu, J. Y. Atanda, S. Amao and Y. Ajape before the Ogundare Commission.
18. Ibid.
19. Ibid.
20. A. Aipo, in evidence before the Ogundare Commission.
21. O. Alabi, in evidence before the Ogundare Commission.
22. D. Adeleye, in evidence before the Ogundare Commission.
23. R. Babalola, in evidence before the Ogundare Commission.
24. Resident, Ibadan, to District Commissioner, 22 December 1906, File 1174 Vol. I, Oyo Prof. 3/772, N.A.I.
25. Ibid.
26. 'Report of the Speed Boundary Commission on Ibadan/Oyo and Ibadan/Ife Boundaries, 20 August 1908', File No. 4866, Oyo Prof. 1/1, N.A.I.
27. Bale and Chiefs of Ogbomoso to Resident, Oyo Province, 21 February 1934, File OY 1331, Oyo Prof. 1/2, N.A.I.
28. See File OY 1331, Oyo Prof. 1/2, N.A.I.
29. 'Report of an Inquiry into the Oyo/Ogbomoso Boundary Dispute, 21 April 1934'.
30. Bale and Chiefs of Ogbomoso to Resident, Oyo Province, 30 June 1938.
31. There were many petitions between 1938 and 1950. All of them about the rejection of Ogbomoso or the acceptance of Oyo. See File OY 1331, Oyo Prof. 1/2, N.A.I.
32. Civil Secretary, Western Nigeria, to Resident, Oyo and Ibadan, 31 March 1953.
33. Ogundare Commission, op. cit.
34. Statement of Interest by Ogbomoso Community before the Ogundare Commission.
35. Ibid.
36. Ibid.
37. Statement of Interest by Oyo Community before the Ogundare Commission.
38. S. A. Ogunmola, in evidence before the Ogundare Commission.

39. P. C. Lloyd, *Yoruba Land Law* (Ibadan: Oxford University Press, 1962), p. 49.
40. O. Isola, in evidence before the Ogundare Commission.
41. Ibid.
42. Ibid.
43. Ibid.
44. Akerele, chief counsel for Oyo, in final submission before the Ogundare Commission.
45. Sole Administrator, Ondo Division, to Permanent Secretary, Ministry of Local Government, Ibadan, 15 February 1967, File G.419 Vol. II, Ministry of Local Government, Ondo.
46. Resident, Ijebu Province, to Resident, Oyo Province, 5 October 1927, File 07839 Vol. I, Oyo Prof. 3, N.A.I.
47. See report by A.D.O., Ibadan, on the cause of the dispute between Ijebu and Ibadan farmers in File OY 815 Vol. II, Oyo Prof. 3, N.A.I.
48. T. O. Elias, *Nigerian Land Law and Custom* 2nd ed. (London: Routledge and Kegan Paul, 1953), p. 91.
49. P. C. Lloyd, op. cit., p. 66.
50. G. Olukokun, in evidence before the Ogundare Commission.
51. J. A. Oluokun, in evidence before the Ogundare Commission.
52. S. A. Aipo, in evidence before the Ogundare Commission.
53. K. Omowale, in evidence before the Ogundare Commission.
54. See File OY 1331, Oyo Prof. 1/2, N.A.I.
55. S. A. Aipo, op. cit.
56. P. C. Lloyd, op. cit., p. 66.
57. S. A. Aipo, op. cit.
58. Statement of Interest by Oyo Community before the Ogundare Commission.
59. Y. Afolabi, in evidence before the Ogundare Commission.
60. Ibid.
61. Ibid.
62. K. Omowale, op. cit.
63. 'Report of Meeting with Olo people by District Officers, Ibadan and Oyo, on 3 March 1950', File 4866, Oyo Prof. 1/1, N.A.I.
64. The Ogundare Commission.
65. Ibid.
66. Ibid.
67. P. C. Lloyd, op. cit., p. 49.
68. The Ogundare Commission.
69. See pp. 31.
70. See pp. 105-126.

CHAPTER VII

Superimposition Boundary Disputes

OF ALL types of boundary disputes discussed in this book, the superimposed type is the most difficult to define. The difficulty is due to the fact that many boundaries can be easily described as superimposed, depending on the viewpoint being considered. For example, a community which lays claim to territory in another administrative unit would consider the existing boundary as being superimposed on territorial rights. In a situation like that in Western Nigeria the community may have none of its members on the territory being claimed. In such a case as this many scholars may argue that the boundary is not superimposed. A community which has some of its citizens on the opposite side of the boundary would also consider the boundary superimposed. In some cases the people affected have settled beyond their own community's side after the boundary had been fixed, that is to say the boundary antedates their settlement (antecedent boundaries). For example, the Idanres did not start to settle north of Alade until after their boundary with Akure was fixed there in 1898, hence the boundary (if it may be so called) antedates the settlements. Even then the Idanres laid claim to areas on which their people settled and much of the attempts of government officials to resolve the dispute in the 1920s centred around ensuring that the Idanre settlements were on their community's side of the boundary. Akure rejected all the proposals because the boundary would be superimposed on its territorial rights.[1]

The preceding paragraph suggests that two types of superimposition can be identified, i.e. on the territory (territorial superimposition), and on people who have similar cultural traits (cultural superimposition). In either case there is need to differentiate antecedent patterns from those which existed at the time the boundary was being delimited. However, problems exist in discussing patterns which pre-dated the boundary. In the case of territorial claims the problem is caused by the lack of boundaries and the indefinite nature of the areas which belonged to each side. It is therefore difficult to say that a boundary was fixed in disregard of territorial claims. The Akure/Idanre dispute cited above is a good example: the Akures were not in physical occupation of the area and the Idanres did not admit Akure's rights over the territory. Each claimed the area. In view of this problem, disputes about land over which ownership was not certain at the time of boundary making cannot be described as superimposed in that the rights of each side were not evident.

Territorial superimposition concerns farmlands on which there is no permanent settlement. It also includes areas over which a party has got judgment but which is not occupied (for example forest reserves) and is cut across by the boundary. In this case the judgment must have been given before the boundary delimitation. Since no boundary disputes arose before boundary delimitation in the present century there are few (if any) territorial superimpositions arising from the disregard of court judgments. The main ones concern farmlands and other territories which were separated from their users by boundaries fixed between different commmunities.

Cultural superimposition is also difficult to determine. In the first place a community may lay claim to settlements which do not wish to join it even though they share its culture and history. Among the examples here are Ifewara and Oke-Igbo, south-east of Ife Division (Fig. 16). The Ifes would want both settlements to join their Division, but neither of them has shown much willingness to do so.[2]

Secondly, a community may not give active encouragement to a settlement across its boundary which demands union with it. The demand would be based on cultural ties with the community to be joined. Thus Ekiti has not given active support to Igbara-Oke which demands that it be transferred from Akure District and be merged with Ekiti[3] (Fig. 4).

Thirdly, there could be demand that a community be sub-divided into two. The reason is usually internal dispute within the community. If the division is made, the smaller one might be too small to constitute a separate administrative unit and hence might be merged with a neighbouring one with which it has fewer ties. This would result in a boundary which is superimposed on the cultural landscape. Thus, due to dispute among various sections of Ikale, the Osoro section demanded separation from the main body early in the twentieth century. Since it was too small to stand on its own the section was merged with Ijebu-Ode District. Later the dispute with other Ikales was settled and the Osoro group demanded merger with the main body of Ikales in Okitipupa Division.[4] That request has not been granted at the time of writing (April 1974), due mainly to opposition from Ijebu-Ode.[5]

A fourth situation is that in which the boundary cuts across the homeland of a community and people on both sides demand alteration. An example of the last case would be the situation on the Ondo/Ikale boundary after 1928. The adoption of the Oniserere–Irele road as boundary in 1928 meant that there were many Ikales on the Ondo side and many Ondos on the Ikale side. In each case there were demands by the people within the affected areas and their respective communities (particularly the Ikales) for union[6] (Fig. 9).

These four situations could be described as superimposed boundaries by many scholars. However, it is to be noted that in the first two there was no mutual recognition of oneness by both sides. Since no group of people can be described as a community unless they jointly recognise their oneness it would be inadvisable to consider the first and second situations as superimposed boundaries. The third type is more difficult to place. At the time of boundary making the community oneness was absent because of the dispute. Yet, not long after that, the demand for union came. If superimposition is based on the situation at the time of boundary delimitation then the third type would not be a superimposed boundary in so far as it reflected demands at the time. If, on the other hand, superimposition is based on mutual acceptance by both sides then the third type would be one because both sides later demanded union and in any case the internal dispute was not a denial of oneness but a request for sub-dividing a single community. The fourth situation is, of course, the classic example of the superimposed boundary.

From the foregoing it can be suggested that a boundary may be regarded as being superimposed when it separates a community from any part of the land it had effectively occupied (or of which it had been adjudged the owner) before or at the time the boundary was fixed; or when the boundary separates a settlement from the community of which it considered itself a part and which regarded it as a component at the time the boundary was fixed.

CAUSES OF SUPERIMPOSITION

Superimposed boundaries are due to three factors, namely, (1) lack of detailed knowledge of the cultural patterns, territorial rights and physical features of the borderlands; (2) desire on the part of boundary makers to adopt particular features as boundaries; (3) conflict within cultural or community groups resulting in sub-division and grouping of each part in different administrative units.

INACCURATE KNOWLEDGE

When government officials started to delimit inter-community boundaries early in the twentieth century they made efforts to enquire about the community attachment of settlements in the borderlands. Nevertheless mistakes were made, due primarily to conflicting claims and hastiness in resolving them. A good example of this type is the boundary between Oyo and Ibadan in the area of Fiditi and Iware-Ikereku. Fiditi was founded by refugees from Ijaiye, a town destroyed by Ibadan armies in the nineteenth century. The town accepted the authority of Ibadan rather than that of Oyo. Yet, when the boundary between the two areas was fixed in 1908, Fiditi was grouped with Oyo on the grounds that it was 'half Ibadan and half Oyo'.[7] In fact it was distinct from both but was politically under Ibadan.[8]

Lack of detailed knowledge about territorial claims was due mainly to the interpretation of boundaries desired by neighbouring communities. Usually each side wanted a boundary passing through widely separated points. The practice was to join the point by straight lines without any investigation of the pattern of occupance in the intervening section. Usually the resulting boundaries cut across some people's territory. Thus on the Ibadan/Ijebu boundary both sides agreed in 1908 that Mamu and Apata-Olowe lie on the boundary. That boundary transferred a large area occupied by Ibadans, including the undisputed Ibadan village of Araromi, to the Ijebu side.[9] The Akure/Ikere boundary agreement of 1954 has not been generally acceptable for the same reason. The straight lines joining the agreed points cut across the farmlands of people on either side. Consequently there has been dispute among affected farmers.[10] The Ife/Ijesa agreed boundary of 1932 was rejected by the Ijesas because it cut through their farmlands. Soon after the agreement was signed, Ifewara farmers complained that the boundary grouped their farmlands on the opposite side.[11]

Inaccurate and insufficient information about the physical features being used has often led to superimposed boundaries. This is particularly true of rivers, about which two types of inaccuracy could occur. The first concerns the direction of flow of the stream and the second, its name. An example of incorrect information about the course of streams is that of the Rivers Opa and Owena on the Ijebu/Ife frontier. The definition of the Ife/Ijebu boundary in 1909 assumed that the River Opa was a tributary of the River Owena and that the latter flows into the River Oni. It therefore described the boundary as follows:

> . . . Ijebu-Ode–Isoya Road to its intersection with River Opa. The Oni River to its intersection with the Northern Boundary of the colony of Lagos.[12]

At a later date the definition was improved as follows:

> . . . Isoya–Atikori road to its intersection with River Awpa [Opa]: river Awpa and River Awwennaw [Owena], River Awni [Oni][13] [Fig. 7].

Defined as such, the boundary (if it can ever be plotted) would give all land south of those rivers to Ijebu. Yet the Ifes had evidence of earlier occupation in that area. The adoption of the rivers as they exist (Fig. 7) would not have constituted the same type of problem. Because of the definition the Ijebus tried to occupy land in the area allocated to them and the Ifes objected. Even after the true position was known, a boundary corresponding with the supposed courses of the rivers was suggested by the Lieutenant Governor.

> . . .thence northward along this road [Isoya-Atikori] to its intersection with the Opa River, thence in a south easterly direction to the intersection of the Abeku–Oke–Igbo road with the Oni River[14]. [Fig. 7B]

The mistake which arose from the incorrect idea of the direction of flow of the rivers was being perpetuated, and hence a superimposed boundary was being suggested.

Incorrect information about the names of rivers could also lead to superimposed boundaries. The main reason for this is that the proposals leading to boundary agreements and the agreements themselves were usually prepared by government officials who depended on information supplied by others. In some cases rivers were wrongly named, with the result that the one specified in an agreement would be different from that on the accompanying map which would be the operative boundary. Thus on the Ife/Ijesa boundary the agreement specified River Amuta. The map accompanying the agreement was wrong with respect to the River called Amuta. The one named Amuta on the map was actually the River Opa[15] (Fig. 16). The boundary is therefore superimposed on the territorial claims of Ife—at least as they understood it in 1932.

ADOPTION OF PHYSICAL FEATURES

One common practice of boundary makers in Western Nigeria was the adoption of well-known physical features as boundaries, the most common being rivers and paths. Unfortunately these features seldom separate one community from another. In fact paths never separate communities even though they may be adopted as boundaries between members of the same community. The reasons for this have been explained in Chapters I and II. The adoption of the Abeku–Fowoseje–Obutu–Jagun–Alafara–Olomo road as the boundary between Ife and Ijebu (Fig. 7b) has led to disputes between them, particularly as to the control of the settlements along the road.[16] Similarly the adoption of the Irele–Oniserere road as boundary between Ondo and Ikale in 1928 created a superimposed boundary (on Ikale).[17]

The adoption of rivers as boundaries was more successful than that of paths and has greater support in customary practice. But then people sometimes crossed rivers and settled on the other side. Even when boundary makers knew that the river they adopted was not a cultural division they sometimes insisted on keeping it because rivers are regarded as natural boundaries. This was partly the reason why the Oyo/Ogbomoso boundary was fixed along the River Oba (Fig. 21). It was felt that the River Oba was a natural boundary as shown by the following recommendation:

> The Boundary line will then go northwards along the course of the Oba River. This is so obviously the best natural boundary. . . . .[18]

INTRA-COMMUNITY CONFLICT

Conflict within a community can lead to superimposed boundaries. Usually one section expresses a desire to separate from the others and be on its own. If the separatist section is too small to constitute a separate administrative unit it may be merged with a neighbouring community. The resulting boundary will be clearly superimposed on the cultural landscape. One example at the community level is that of Ikale in Ijebu Division mentioned above. At higher levels, particularly in the grouping of communities into divisions and provinces, many more examples can be found but these need not concern us here.

SUPERIMPOSITION DISPUTES

It has been explained in Chapter III that superimposition does not, in itself, lead to disputes. Assuming that mistakes were made no dispute would arise if corrections are effected when the mistakes are discovered. Disputes arise because correction is opposed by the beneficiary community or by the government. The argument of the beneficiary community is that the existing boundary was made in recognition of the *status quo* at the time and that both communities agreed to it. They always point to the series of discussions preceding the boundary delimitation. As against that, the claimant community will argue that it was not consulted or that it did not appreciate the implication of the agreement. Irrespective of the opposition of the claimants, the beneficiary will insist that the boundary separates the territory of one community from another and, that being so, will make demands such as follows:

(1) that members of the claimant community on the affected area should either accept tenant status or vacate the land. The demand of Oyo that any Olo not prepared to pay *isakole* should leave the Western side of River Oba is a case in point;[19]

(2) that members of the claimant community in the affected area should pay taxes to the beneficiary. This is perfectly logical on the part of the beneficiary in that it was expected to administer the area and provide amenities there. However, the affected people may not share the aspirations of the beneficiary, particularly in the provision of amenities for its capital or contribution for projects like grammar schools, town halls and the like;

(3) that royalties on timber and other natural resources should be paid to the beneficiary community or its *oba*. This follows from the contention that the existing boundary was meant to divide the territory of one community from

another and the fact that royalties are paid to the land-owners.

Not only are these demands opposed by the claimant community but also there is demand that the affected area be transferred to its administration and the boundary altered accordingly. The appeal is usually to the government which delimited the existing boundary and can order an alteration. But very often the government is not prepared to make the necessary alteration. Two related reasons are usually advanced to support the governments position in such cases. The first is that the boundary is easy to recognise and the second that it is an administrative boundary which does not affect the territorial rights of the communities on either side. As the Lieutenant-Governor, Southern Provinces, remarked in the discussion on the Ife/Ijebu boundary.

It is the policy of the Government to make administrative bound-aries coincide with tribal ones but where there are rival claimants to the land, Government must lay down its own inter-provin-cial boundaries without prejudice to the ownership of the land.[20]

The claimant community is not always satisfied by these argu-ments, first, because it has its own administrative unit and does not see how its demands conflict with the position of the govern-ment, and secondly, because of the attitude of the beneficiary com-munity over ownership of the affected area as outlined above. Behind the demand for boundary alteration is the desire of every community to keep its citizens under its own administration. There are many reasons for the desire. First is the fact that each community constituted a traditional administrative unit. Even within a kingdom each village constituted a separate local or internal administrative unit, as is rightly noted by Lloyd: 'The subordinate towns enjoyed what might be termed in modern parlance, internal self-govern-ment.'[21] The revenue accruing to the community administration under the traditional system as well as under the Indirect Rule system of the colonial period and its successor, the Local Council, depended on the population of its area of jurisdiction. Therefore no community wants to lose population to its neighbours. Also, the administration of customary law varies slightly from one com-munity to the other. Hence people in areas affected by boundary superimposition do not want to be under 'alien' administrators of justice. The second reason is related to the above, namely, that since people were expected to pay taxes according to the boundaries fixed by government the claimant was losing revenue and its people were adversely affected in the administration of customary law. There was also the fact that payment of royalties on natural resources depended upon which side of the government 'administrative' boundary the resources were located. In other words the above assurances by the government were at best meaningless and at worst harmful to the interests of the claimant community in so far as their authority over the territory was not profitable to them.

The government tried to reduce the effect of superimposition by making regulations on tax collection and the payment of royalties. Sometimes the arrangements covered the administration of customary law. The arrangements usually provided that residents in the affected area could pay their taxes to the town to which they belonged.[22] However, these were not always successful or satisfactory. In many cases the implementation of the agreement has meant that some people pay taxes to the two communities. Much more important is that such arrangement does not always take into account the provision of amenities for the inhabitants of the affected area.

The provision of amenities is usually within the boundaries fixed in the twentieth century. If people in an area pay their taxes to the community across the boundary there is need to specify who will provide amenities there. The community to which they do not pay taxes would be reluctant to provide the amenities and the one which collects taxes would be precluded by regulations from crossing the boundary to provide the amenities. Because of these difficulties the community which is adversely affected by superimposed boundaries has always insisted that the boundary be changed to reflect the cultural pattern.

The Example of the Ife/Ede Boundary Dispute

Many of the problems discussed above are exemplified by the boundary dispute between Ife and Ede over an area to the north of the River Sasa near Edunabon (Fig. 22A). Edunabon is one of six settlements collectively called Origbo in the north-western part of Ife Division. Traditionally, Edunabon and all other Origbo settlements owe allegiance to the Oni of Ife who has sovereign right in the whole kingdom.

According to local history the metropolitan territory of the Ife kingdom extended as far as the River Osun in the west and north.[23] As a result of Fulani attacks on Oyo settlements in the nineteenth century, many refugees fled from the Oyo kingdom and crossed the River Osun to reside in or near settlements on Ife territory.[24] Among such settlements were Ede and also Modakeke (which was established on the outskirts of Ife).

During the wars of the late nineteenth century the refugees from the Oyo kingdom supported Ibadan against Ife and Ekiti. The result was that when peace was finally established the settlements on Ife territory, in which the refugees were in the majority, were regarded as within the control of Ibadan.[25] When British administration was established the boundary between Ife and Ibadan was fixed such that all such refugees except those in Modakeke were under Ibadan. The boundary was along the River Sasa.[26]

The main defect of the Sasa as boundary was that it cut off to the Ibadan side, much of the territory of the Origbo settlements which were, and still are, in Ife Division. The worst affected of these settlements was Edunabon[27] whose citizens had farms to the north of the River Sasa and as far as the River Aworo (Fig. 22).

The defect of the boundary would not have mattered much if Ibadan and Ife had agreed on the interpretation of the boundary fixed by the British. But they disagreed. Ife, particularly Edunabon people, had the opinion that the agreement had no effect on their rights to farmlands north of the Sasa. Ibadan, on the other hand, interpreted the boundary as meaning that all land to the north of the Sasa belonged to them. Because of the interpretation the people of Ede (the Ibadan tributary town nearest to the boundary) demanded that Edunabon farmers should vacate the area they (Edunabon) occupied north of the Sasa. The Edunabon people refused to do so. Thus was started the dispute about the area which government officials called the Edunabon enclave.

ATTEMPTS AT SETTLEMENT

After prolonged argument two government officials recommended in 1913, that the Edunabon farmers should be allowed to remain on their farms between the River Sasa and the River Aworo provided they paid tribute to the *bale* (head chief) of Ibadan.[28] This did not settle the dispute because the Edunabons were unwilling to pay the tribute and the Edes were unwilling to accept anything short of total withdrawal, as was shown in their demand of 1916 that the Edunabons should be made to withdraw from the area.[29]

About that time a political officer attempted to solve the problem by pointing to a tree, about six kilometres north of the River Sasa, up to which the Edunabons could farm. The tree was located very close to the point where the River Aworo crossed the Ede–Edunabon path [30] (Fig.22). The Edunabons interpreted this to mean that their boundary with Ede had been altered from the Sasa to the Aworo. The interpretation was made clear in 1920 when the Oni of Ife claimed that the Aworo was the boundary[31] and by the Oni's protest against the attempt by Ede to start roadworks near the

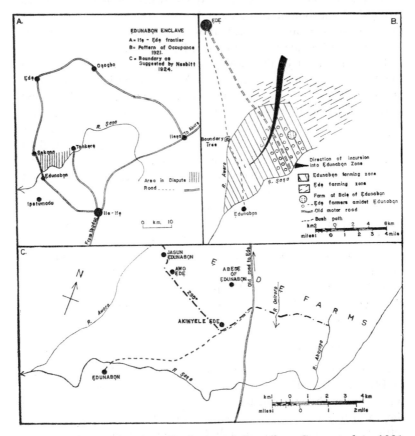

Fig. 22   The Edunabon Enclave and Boundary Suggested in 1921

Sasa.[32] In that protest the Oni pointed out that the Edes should start their roadworks from the River Aworo.

The above solution was not accepted by the Edes who continued to press for the withdrawal of Edunabon farmers and who started to enter the area claimed by Edunabon.[33] The attempt by the Edes to farm in the disputed area caused the Edunabons to petition the government to prevent the Ede incursion. This led to intervention by the District Officers, at Ife and Ibadan, who made efforts to find a suitable boundary between the two communities.

The first of the efforts was a boundary starting at the point where the Aworo stream crosses the Ife–Ede path and running eastwards to join the old Ife–Ede motor road and past it before turning south to join the River Sasa (Fig.23).[34] However, the boundary did not separate the communities for it left some Ede farms on the Edunabon side. In suggesting the boundary the District officer at Ife argued that the Ede farmers who would be left on the Edunabon side were recent arrivals in the area and that they could remain in the area only if they were ready to accept Edunabon as landlords. The suggestion was not approved.

DEMARCATION 1924–1925

The second attempt to fix the boundary was started in 1924 when Mr Nesbitt the Assistant District Officer at Ibadan, was asked to survey the disputed area with a view to finding a boundary which would separate Edunabon farms from those of Ede. He surveyed the section between the old Ife-Ede motor road and recommended a boundary (Fig.23). The representatives of both Ede and Edunabon at the occasion agreed that there were no Ede farms to the south and no Edunabon farms to the north of the surveyed section. They also agreed to the conditions laid down about the whole length of the boundary which were that:

(i) The boundary line is a farm-line boundary and not in any sense a Divisional boundary. The Sasa remained the Divisional boundary.

(ii) Any Ede people who had farmed to the south of the line in the past can remain but no new Ede must start farming south of the line.

(iii) The line makes no difference to the payment of *isakole* (land rent).

(iv) The Oni of Ife and the Timi of Ede may each send messengers

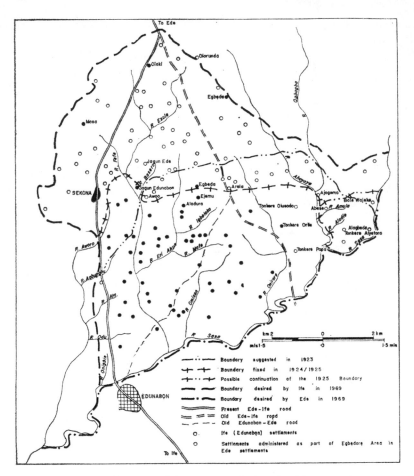

Fig. 23   *Suggested Positions of the Ife-Ede Boundary*

into the area to call their own people but the whole area
is still under Ede and Ibadan.[35]

The section between the old Ife–Ede motor road and the Aworo
stream was surveyed in 1925 by the Assistant District Officer at
Osogbo. During the survey he found the line suggested by Nesbitt
to cut through 'the midst of Edunabon farms and leave Ede farms
to the North'. He discovered that Ede and Edunabon farms were
mixed and that in many places the only recognised boundary was
the local farm path. Consequently, the officer recommended that the

boundary should follow the local farm paths accepted as boundary by both sides. In places where there were no farm paths he set a boundary by cutting a trace through the bush.[36]

The boundary arrived at during the demarcation of 1925 had only one slight defect. In one instance it put an Ede farm on the Edunabon side. The name of the owner of the farm was not stated, but it was probably that of Akinleye of Ede indicated on the map prepared by Nesbitt in 1924 (Fig.22). Apart from that one case, there was no other error made in this demarcation exercise.

The two sections of the boundary surveyed by Mr Nesbitt in 1924 and the Assistant District Officer at Osogbo in 1925 were approved by the Resident, Oyo Province, on 6 April 1925. In giving his approval the Resident added that the enclave will be under the Ede court and stated: 'I would insist on the provision that no further Edes shall be allowed to farm or increase their farms in the Modakeke [Edunabon] enclave'.[37]

PROBLEMS ARISING FROM THE BOUNDARY AGREEMENT

The problems arising from the above agreement may be considered in two ways: first, the location of the boundary line, and secondly, the interpretation of the terms laid down by Mr Nesbitt and approved, with additions, by the Resident of Oyo Province.

PROBLEMS OF LOCATION

The main difficulty in locating the boundary is due to the fact that the map attached to the demarcation of 1925 cannot be found and also to the presence of Modakeke elements in the eastern part of the area being claimed by Edunabon. Because of the loss of the map prepared in 1925 the only detailed map of the area, as understood at the time, is that drawn by Mr Nesbitt in 1924. But the Nesbitt map is wrong about the extent of both River Aworo and River Ahoyaya, the two main rivers on the boundary.

On the Nesbitt map (Fig. 22c) the River Aworo is shown as flowing from north of Jagun-Edunabon. But the topographical map on scale 1:50,000, based on air photographs, shows that the Aworo rises south of Jagun-Edunabon while another stream, named Araga, rises near Sekona and flows northwards to join the River Isule. It is clear that the River Araga was assumed to be the northern continuation of the Aworo.

The mistake creates a problem about the location of the boundary on the watershed between the Araga and the Aworo Rivers because that area was not surveyed by the Assistant District Officer at Osogbo in 1925. Therefore, to determine the boundary in the area, it will be necessary to carry out surveys so that the boundary between the farms of Jagun-Edunabon and those of Sekona can be established. It is the farmline boundary that ought to be accepted in the area.

The mistake about the Ahoyaya is that it was shown as flowing to the Sasa. During fieldwork in the area it was found that the river flowing to the Sasa is called Ogbagba and River Ahoyaya is only one of its western tributaries.

Since the map prepared in 1925 cannot be traced the boundary demarcated then cannot be located. In an attempt to do so reliance has been placed on attachment of farmsteads to the two communities concerned. The position as in July 1968 is shown in Fig. 23. Since there is no dispute about such attachments, it is certain that a survey party can locate the boundary by plotting the boundaries between the farms of settlements near the line indicated on the map.

Another difficulty regarding the location of the boundary is caused by the presence of Modakeke elements in the Tonkere area to the east of the enclave. The Modakeke elements owe no allegiance to either Edunabon or Ede and they prefer to associate with Ode-Omu. They cannot therefore, be easily grouped with either of the parties to the dispute. This presents a problem in the determination of the eastern boundary of the disputed area in that any attempt to fix a boundary in the Tonkere area could mean either grouping the Modakeke villages with one of the parties to the dispute, or isolating them as an enclave in the area, or dividing them between the two sides. In order to avoid any of these, Nesbitt did not demarcate a boundary in the area in 1924 and as yet that has not been done. But those who attempted a settlement before Nesbitt envisaged that the boundary of the enclave should end on the River Sasa, and it would appear that the boundary intended cut off some Modakeke villages on the Edunabon side.

INTERPRETATION OF THE TERMS

Another problem of the boundary approved in 1925 concerns the interpretation of the conditions attached to it. Quite clearly the conditions were designed to minimise the adverse effects of superimposing the administrative boundary on the cultural pattern. According to the Resident, Oyo Province, the enclave was to be under the Ede court while both the Oni of Ife and the Timi of Ede could send messengers to the area. Also no Ede could go south of the line but no mention was made of the movement of Edunabon people to areas north of the boundary.

In so far as the area was under the Ede Court it may be assumed that the administration of the area was under Ede. This would be in keeping with the Divisional boundary. However, the right of the Oni of Ife to send messengers to the area made him responsible for the welfare of his subjects (Edunabon farmers) in the area. This right of the Oni detracted much from the influence of Ede in the area in so far as the Indirect Rule system ensured that people continued to pay homage to their respective *oba*s. Hence it was an anomaly to place the area under the Ede court.

The anomaly referred to above is more glaring in the case of the collection of taxes and tributes. Although the area was under the Ede court people in the enclave paid their taxes to Ile-Ife. This was disclosed in 1929 when the District Officer at Ile-Ife wrote to the Resident of Oyo Province saying:

> Up to the present year the Edunabon people farming in the enclave across the Sasa have paid income tax on cocoa trees there to Ife. This year, however, the tribute clerks from Ede are asking them to pay at Ede. The question has not previously arisen and nothing was said about this in the settlement.[38]

In reply the Senior Resident, Oyo Province, wrote to the District Officer at Ibadan on 30 July 1929 that:

> It was decided formerly that all disputes and tribute collection within this enclave shall be dealt with through the Oni of Ife and tribute should be collected by Ife. Will you therefore instruct the Ibadan tribute clerks not to collect any tax within this enclave and to refund what has already been collected within this enclave.[39]

Following the instruction the District Officer at Ibadan refunded the tax collected in the enclave. This is shown in his letter to the Resident on 22 August 1929. 'The sum of £12. 2s. 8d. has been remitted to the District Officer, Ife, being a refund of 1928 taxes wrongly collected by Ibadan tribute clerks.'[40]

The instruction of the Resident cited above gave full control of the area to the Oni. There were, however, some farmers who were not from Edunabon and who did not pay tribute to Ife before the Resident gave the order. Such areas did not pay to Ife even after 1929. One such example was Momo's village (now called Abese), which was founded and inhabited by people from Ode-Omu. In 1931 the villagers complained that they were being asked to pay tribute to Ile-Ife. When the District Officer at Ife investigated the complaint he reported that the Oni of Ife 'admitted that Momo's village was under Ode-Omu and had always paid tribute through Ode-Omu, nor did he make any claims that Momo's village pay to Ife.'[41]

The position of the people of Momo's village and others like them led to a reconsideration of tribute collection in the area. It was finally suggested that only Edunabon people and others living within the enclave and who did not have permanent residence elsewhere should pay taxes to Ile-Ife. The suggestion was accepted by Ibadan.[42] This meant that those who farmed in the enclave but were from Ede or Ode-Omu should pay taxes to the towns to which they owed allegiance.

The above agreement was altered slightly in 1934. The alteration affected those who had no attachment outside the enclave and it was that as from mid-1936 such people should pay taxes to Ibadan. This was because of objections raised by Ibadan to the collection of such tributes by Ife. The original proposal, which was accepted by Ibadan, was made by Ife on 19 June 1934: 'At the end of two years, it should be necessary for Ibadan, so long as Sasa remains the boundary between us, to collect tribute from those of Modakeke who have no town houses in Ife or in other words those of them who reside permanently in the enclave.'[43]

REVIVAL OF THE DISPUTE

As a result of the above agreement, people from both sides lived peacefully side by side until the reorganisation of local government administration in Western Nigeria in the 1950s. As a result of the reorganisation new councils were created at Ede and Edunabon. According to the Instrument establishing it the area of authority of the Ede District Council was the area of jurisdiction of the Ede court; similarly the area of authority of the Edunabon/Moro Local Council was the area of jurisdiction of the Edunabon court.

According to the order of the Resident of Oyo Province, made when the boundary of the enclave was approved, the enclave was to be under the Ede court. In practice, however, the farmers in the enclave took their cases to the court at Ife and later that of Edunabon, and so the effective court within the disputed area was that at Edunabon.

In an attempt to exercise authority in the enclave the Ede District Council demanded taxes from the farmers [44] and claimed the right to issue permits for cutting timber.[45] The Edunabon farmers in the enclave petitioned Ife Divisional Council and demanded that the Ede District Council be warned against molesting them. They also demanded that forest guards from Ife Division should come to the enclave to stamp logs. As a result of this the Secretary of the Edunabon/Moro Local Council wrote the Secretary of Ede District Council on 30 October 1961 to demand that the people who farm within the enclave should not be molested by officials of Ede District Council.[46]

Because of the attempts by Ede to claim the enclave, the Edunabon people have in turn claimed that they used to own the land as far as the River Osun, and that they want part of the land now occupied by Ede farmers. The area they now claim[47] is indicated on Fig. 23.

A POSSIBLE SETTLEMENT

A settlement of the dispute must solve two main problems, first the ownership of the territory, and secondly, the location of the divisional boundary. These two problems are interconnected in the sense that the first affects the second. However, it is necessary to treat them separately because of the history of the dispute. Hitherto, the claims of Edunabon to the enclave have been considered separately from the location of the administrative boundary.

The problem of ownership of the territory has to be considered from two sides: that of Ede and that of Edunabon. Ede is claiming the boundary as far as the River Sasa on the ground that the river was adopted as boundary between Ife and Ibadan in 1908. The logic of the Ede claim is that all areas on their side of the boundary belong to them. Three main points may be advanced in support of the claim being made by Ede:

1. The refusal of the government to alter the boundary after they discovered that Edunabon people farm north of the Sasa. The refusal suggested that the government felt that people under Ife did not belong to the area north of the River Sasa.

2. The Resident's instruction in 1925 that the enclave should be under Ede Native Court suggested an acknowledgement of the rights of Ede in the area.

3. The agreement reached in 1934 between Ife and Ibadan that the latter should collect taxes from those permanently resident in the enclave indicated that Ife recognised the overlordship of Ibadan (and hence of Ede) in the area, and that the Edunabons were there under special permission.[48]

As against the Ede claim is that of the Edunabons that they used to own the land as far as the Osun and that they would now like to claim not only the enclave but also a part of the area occupied by Ede farmers. The reasons given for the claim may be summarised as follows:

(i) The Edunabon people were farming in the area before Ede citizens came, this was before the adoption of the Sasa as boundary. At that time Ede had no claims on them and did not make any.

(ii) The instruction given by the Resident in 1929 that Ibadan should not collect tax in the enclave and the refund by Ibadan of tax previously collected in the area indicates recognition by both the government and Ibadan (and hence Ede) that Edunabon farmers were there by right rather than by special permission. If Edunabons had settled there with the permission of Ede or Ibadan the latter would have insisted on the traditional *isakole* (land rent).

A close examination of the reasons reveals that the Edes base their claim on the adoption of the River Sasa as boundary and it is from this initial claim that other points arise. On the other hand the Edunabons base their claim on traditional history and *de facto* occupation of the enclave as well as on historical rights over the territory between the Rivers Osun and Sasa.

The fact that the government authorised and approved the demarcation of a 'farmline boundary' between Ede and Edunabon and also allowed Ife to collect taxes and tributes or homage in the Edunabon enclave suggests that the government recognised that the boundary was wrong. It is certain that if administrators were not convinced that Edunabon had genuine claims to the enclave they would have refused to allow Ife to collect taxes there. Furthermore the resritction placed on the advance of Ede farmers south of the farmline boundary and the acceptance by Ede of such restrictions suggests that Ede realised that the Edunabons were in the enclave as a result of traditional rights. The government's insistence on placing the area under the Ede court appears not to have any significance, rather it shows that they were unwilling to change the Divisional boundary.

The attempts by Ede to exercise authority within the enclave need to be seen as a desire not to refuse a gift. This latter point is supported by the fact that by 1968 the tax office at Ede acknowledged that the enclave belonged to Edunabon.[49] No attempt is now made by Ede to collect taxes within the enclave. It is suggested that Ede would not have given up their attempts to collect taxes in the area if they were convinced of the rightness of their action. In view of these considerations it would be more appropriate to regard the enclave as Edunabon territory over which Ede has no claim.[50]

The above conclusion affects only the enclave as demarcated in 1924. But the Edunabons are now claiming more than the enclave. The area they now want to add to the enclave is occupied by Ede. In 1924 they did not ask that the area be included in the Edunabon sphere and they then expressed satisfaction with the boundary as demarcated by Nesbitt. For these reasons it is difficult to justify the claims of Edunabon to the area north of the 1924 boundary.

The suggestion that the claims of Edunabon to ownership of the enclave ought to be upheld raises the question of the boundary between Ife Division in which Edunabon is presently located and Osun Central Division in which Ede is located.[51] Hitherto, the Sasa had been the boundary and it could be argued that so long as the Edunabons are allowed to farm in the enclave there is no need to alter the Divisional boundary. In support of this is the fact that the Sasa is more easily recognised than the boundary demarcated in 1924. Furthermore, the retention of the enclave in the Osun Central Division does not affect Edunabon in any sense. The people would be free to pay their taxes to Edunabon or Ife and they would be free to go to Edunabon or Ife. The essence of this argument is that the administrative location of the area is not important.

But the administrative location of the enclave is important, particularly from the point of view of the provision of amenities to the villages in the area. If it remains in the Osun Central Division it would be the responsibility of that division to provide amenities such as the improvement of roads, maintenance of dispensaries, and opening of schools. There would be no problem if the farmers there pay their taxes to the Osun Central Division. But, as already noted, the farmers prefer to pay their taxes to Ife Division. The right and proper authority to provide amenities in any area is that one which collects the taxes in the area. At present this authority in respect of the enclave is the Ife Divisional Council.

If Ife Divisional Council is to collect the taxes and provide the amenities it is obvious that the area should be grouped with Ife Division. This would mean the adoption of the boundary approved in 1925 as the Divisional boundary between Ife and Osun Central Divisions.

EGBEDORE VILLAGES WITHIN THE ENCLAVE

The villages in the enclave from which Ife could not collect taxes, even after the favourable order of 1929, are those inhabited by Modakeke people and which have since been grouped in Egbedore District in Osun Southern Division which embraces Ode-Omu and Gbongan with their surrounding villages. These villages: Afonle, Abinu, Tonkere-Papa, Tonkere-Aiyetoro, Abese, Oloba, Amosun, Alagbede and Bale-Wajeko (Fig. 23) are located to the east of the enclave and are therefore separated from Egbedore District with which they are grouped. The reason for grouping these villages in Egbedore District was that like Ode-Omu they were founded by Modakeke refugees from Ife.[52]

If, as suggested above, the enclave is grouped with Ife Division the Egbedore villages will become an enclave sandwiched between Osun Central, Ijesa Southern and Ife Divisions. If the fragmentation of administrative units is to be avoided the villages will have to join either Ede or Edunabon District.

In making a decision on the issue it is necessary to remember that the people in the villages are of Modakeke extraction and Modakeke is in Ife Division in which Edunabon District is located. The main road between the villages and other areas is the Edunabon–Tonkere road, built and maintained by Edunabon. For these reasons it may be better to group the villages with Edunabon rather than with Ede District.

The merging of the nine villages with Edunabon will mean that the boundary between Ife and Osun Central Divisions will be changed from the River Ogbagba to the farmline boundary between the villages and the Ede communities nearest to them. Such a boundary will be similar to the one indicated on Fig. 23.

CONCLUSION

As the foregoing shows, the point to be decided in superimposed boundary disputes is whether the boundary fixed by government officials shall take precedence over local history and *de facto* patterns of occupance. It calls into question the validity and importance to be attached to boundaries fixed by government officials in the present century. Probably the main evidence against those boundaries is that supplied by the government itself, namely, that they do not reflect territorial ownership but are fixed to suit the convenience of its own officials such as court judges and District Officers.[53] Bearing this point in mind it cannot but be suggested that no importance ought to be attached to such boundaries except in places where they coincide with local wishes and reflect patterns of occupance.

However, patterns of occupance must be shown to precede the boundary, and ownership of the territory by the occupants must be demonstrated before a boundary is described as superimposed and alterations made. In most cases the necessary evidence can be deduced from actions taken by the disputants and the government after the boundary was delimited.

Notes and References

1. See Chapter IV.
2. Oni of Ife during an interview which the author had with him in August 1969.
3. Information collected at Akure in August 1969.
4. B. J. A. Matthews, 'Assessment Report on the Ikale District', File O/C. 143/1914, Ministry of Local Government, Okitipupa, pp. 50-1 and 230–7.
5. Awujale of Ijebu-Ode to D.O., Ijebu-Ode, 12 December 1967.
6. P. R. Foulkes-Roberts, 'Report on the Ondo/Ikale Boundary Dispute, 1935', File 31615, C.S.O. 26.
7. Resident, Oyo Province, to Secretary, Southern Province, 19 June 1936, File 72/1927, Oyo Div. 2/14, N.A.I.

8. Ibid., especially paragraph 12.
9. File J.27/1923 Vol. II, Ijebu Prof. 6/6, N.A.I.
10. Deji of Akure to Ogoga of Ikere, 26 August 1954, File LR 23/2, AKDIVCO 4, N.A.I.
11. Chief Agoro of Ifewara to D.O., Ife, 1 January 1936, File 759, Oyo Prof. 1/1, N.A.I.
12. Public Notice, *Southern Nigeria Gazette*, 24 February 1909.
13. Government Notice No. 69, *Nigeria Gazette*, 12 June 1919.
14. Secretary, Southern Provinces, to Resident, Oyo Province, 9 September 1928, File 07839, Oyo Prof. 3, N.A.I.
15. See Chapter V.
16. Treasurer, Ife Divisional Council, August 1969.
17. P. R. Foulkes-Roberts, op. cit.
18. E. A. Speed, 'Report on Ife/Ibadan and Ibadan/Oyo Boundaries, 20 August 1908', in File 4866, Oyo Prof. 1/1, N.A.I.
19. Alafin of Oyo to Olo farmers, 14 February 1950, File 4866, Oyo Prof. 1/1, N.A.I.
20. Secretary, Southern Province, to Resident, Oyo Province, 6 September 1928, File 07839 Vol. I, Oyo Prof. 3, N.A.I.
21. P. C. Lloyd, *Yoruba Land Law* (Ibadan: Oxford University Press, 1962), p. 49.
22. B. J. A. Matthews, op. cit., pp. 228–9.
23. Information from the Oni of Ife, March 1968.
24. I. A. Akinjogbin, 'The Prelude to the Yoruba Civil Wars of the 19th Century', *Odu: University of Ife Journal of African Studies* I, 2 (1965), p. 44.
25. S. Johnson, *History of the Yorubas* (Lagos: C.M.S. Bookshop, 1919), p. 549.
26. Recalled in letter from District Officer, Ife, to Acting Senior Resident, Oyo Province, 28 Oct. 1921, File 1171, (Simple List of Oyo Prov. Papers,) (Numerical Series S.O.P.P. 1171), N.A.I.
27. Idem.
28. D.O., Ife, to Commissioner, Oyo Province, 5 May 1916, S.O.P.P. 1171, N.A.I.
29. Idem.
30. D.O., Ife, to Acting Senior Resident, Oyo, 28 October 1921, S.O.P.P. 1171, N.A.I.
31. Oni of Ife to Resident, Oyo, 20 August 1920, S.O.P.P. 1171, N.A.I.
32. Oni of Ife to Resident, Oyo, 18 December 1929, S.O.P.P. 1171, N.A.I.
33. D.O., Ife, to Resident, Oyo, 28 October, 1921, S.O.P.P. 1171, N.A.I.
34. D.O., Ife, to Resident, Oyo, 10 May 1923, S.O.P.P. 1171, N.A.I.
35. A.D.O., Ibadan, to D.O., Ibadan, 10 October 1924, S.O.P.P. 1171, N.A.I.
36. A.D.O., Osogbo, to D.O., Ibadan, 20 March 1925, S.O.P.P. 1171, N.A.I.
37. Resident, Oyo, to D.O., Ibadan, 6 April 1925, S.O.P.P. 1171, N.A.I.
38. D.O., Ife, to Resident, Oyo, 25 April 1929, S.O.P.P. 1171, N.A.I.
39. Resident, Oyo, to D.O., Ibadan, 30 July 1929, S.O.P.P. 1171, N.A.I.
40. D.O., Ibadan, to Resident, Oyo, 22 August 1929, S.O.P.P. 1171, N.A.I.
41. D.O., Ife, to Resident, Oyo, 10 October 1931, S.O.P.P. 1171, N.A.I.
42. D.O., Ibadan, to Resident, Oyo, 21 October 1931, S.O.P.P. 1171, N.A.I.

43. Oni of Ife to D.O., Ife, 19 June 1934, S.O.P.P. 1171, N.A.I.
44. Minutes of Ife Divisional Council meeting, 29 August 1959.
45. Minutes of Forestry Committee, Ife Divisional Council, 3 March 1962.
   Also Secretary, Edunabon Progressive Union, to Secretary, Ife Divisional Council, 14 August 1961.
46. Secretary, Edunabon/Moro Local Council, to Secretary, Ede District Council, 30 October 1961.
47. Bale and chiefs of Edunabon during an interview the writer had with them on 19 July 1968.
48. This was cited by the Timi of Ede during an interview the writer had with him on 19 July 1968.
49. This was revealed during an interview with the treasurer and rate collectors of Ede District Council on 19 July 1968.
50. This is already recognised by farmers in the area adjacent to the enclave.
51. Osun Central Division is one of the four newly created units into which the old Osun Division has been split.
52. The origin of these villages was confirmed during field investigation in the area in July 1968 and also during interviews with the *bale* and chiefs, of Edunabon on 16 July 1968, and with the Secretary, Egbedore District Council, and chiefs on 22 July 1968. See also D.O., Ife, to Resident, Oyo, 10 October 1931; and Tonkere Chiefs to Resident, Oyo, 26 August 1937, S.O.P.P. 1171, N.A.I.
53. See statement by Lieutenant-Governor, Southern Provinces, on purpose of administrative boundaries, in G. J. Matthews, op. cit., pp. 226–7.

CHAPTER VIII

Approaches to the Settlement of Boundary Disputes in Western Nigeria

The settlement of boundary disputes among the Yorubas of Western Nigeria has received government attention since the end of the nineteenth century but most particularly since the beginning of the twentieth century. The methods adopted in settling the disputes may be enumerated as follows:

(1) investigation and recommendation by political officers,
(2) arbitration by political officers,
(3) court judgment,
(4) adjudication by a Boundary Settlement Commission.

The aim in this chapter is to discuss the operation of each method and examine the extent to which it can effect a lasting settlement of boundary disputes.

INVESTIGATION BY POLITICAL OFFICERS

One of the earliest activities of colonial political officers in Western Nigeria was the investigation of the boundaries between adjacent communities. Initially, the investigations were motivated by the need to know the limits of the territory of each community and the jurisdiction of its *oba*. The investigations led to boundary delimitation or the establishment of boundary marks. The latter could be trees on which special marks were made, as was apparently the case on the Ife-Ijesa boundary in 1901;[1] or they could be a collection of stones at some points (stone cairns) as was done at Alade on the Akure/Idanre boundary in 1902.[2] One consequence of the early investigation was to make each community aware of the territorial claims of its neighbours. The boundary delimitation carried out amounted to a sudden stabilisation of territorial claims. Since the claims of neighbouring communities did not always coincide, there

184

were disputes as to the location of the boundary.

Government accepted the responsibility of resolving the boundary disputes and empowered its political officers to settle them. Thus one of the duties of the Resident was the settlement of boundary disputes between communities in a province:

> Disputes as to tribal or communal boundaries will be settled executively by the Resident or if the communities belong to different Provinces, by a joint inquiry by the two Residents subject to the decision of the Lieutenant-Governor, and final appeal to the Governor to whom the Lieutenant-Governor would refer any case of special importance. If such a decision is ignored or wilfully contravened it will be enforced by the executive.[3]

In settling a boundary dispute the Resident normally relied on investigations and recommendations by the District Officers in charge of the disputant communities. To this end each District Officer investigated the claims of the community under him. The two District Officers then met to effect a reconciliation of the claims of both communities. After the reconciliation they would make a joint recommendation which would be sent to the Resident and each of the communities for consideration. If the Resident agreed with the recommendations he would approve them even if one of the communities did not accept them.

In their investigations the District Officers relied on information given by the *obas* and chiefs as well as on fieldwork in the boundary area. The fieldwork could involve the traversing of parts or the whole of the disputed area. During this, evidence would be collected on the pattern of occupance and the proprietary rights of all the people in important locations along the route. In some cases the communities might be asked to cut (jointly or separately) a trace or traces through which the District Officers would pass or walk.

There are many instances of the type of investigation mentioned above. In the Ibadan/Ijebu boundary dispute an officer traversed the area in 1911 before suggesting a boundary.[4] The comments by the Resident, Oyo Province, on the demands by both Ijesa and Ife on the boundary suggested to them in 1913 were based on field investigations carried out by government officers. A report of one such investigation by Lieutenant G. H. Bell ran as follows: 'After going over the Reeve-Tucker Boundary, I went with Ilesa messengers over the boundary which the Owa of Ilesa claims, this runs down the Aiwe [Ayiwe] River to a pile of stones which it was stated

Captain Blair had placed there, thence the boundary runs to the top of Oke-Ogborogboro. From this point, we proceeded along a cut line which ran in varying directions until it came to the point where the Osu River runs into the Sasa.'[5] Similar field investigations were undertaken on the Akure/Idanre boundary in 1926 and many other times before the matter came to court in 1939.[6] The various suggestions on the Ondo/Ikale boundary were made after field investigations. This is clearly shown by the comments of the investigators, for example, that of Foulkes-Roberts in 1935:

> From Ayadi I visited the Ikale settlements called Olotin, Oloda, and Kindoro, to the west of the Owun Lamudifa. I did not visit Logbe . . . .[7]

Although each community justifies its territorial claims by reference to history, the boundary recommended by most political officers paid more attention to the existing pattern of land occupance. The practice is well shown by the remarks of the Resident, Oyo Province, on the Ife/Ijesa boundary[8] and by the following observation by the District Officers investigating the Akure/Idanre boundary dispute in 1926:

> Broadly speaking it would appear that villages to the south of Kindoro's farm are inhabited by Idanre farmers who attend Idanre Native Court, while villages to the north are inhabited by Akure who attend Akure Native Court.
> We are therefore of the opinion that the boundary between the Idanres and the Akures should be fixed somewhere in the vicinity of Kinoro's farm and the apparent division of Idanres and Akures which is to be found near this point leads us to believe that a decision in this sense will, when their natural disappointment in the failure of their respective claims has abated, be accepted by both sides.[9]

The boundaries suggested by political officers were generally accepted immediately they were proposed but many were later rejected. Many reasons account for this state of affairs. One of these is that the communities first thought that the proposed boundary was fair to both sides even though they did not normally study its details. Indeed the communities might not fully appreciate the implications of the suggestions until the demarcation and implementation of the boundary. This point was stressed in the comment of the Oni on the rejection, by Ife, of the River Osun as boundary with Ede. He stated that he did not understand the agreement of 1908 (by which the River Osun was made the boundary between Ife and Ibadan) to mean that people on the Ibadan side had exclusive right to their side along the whole length of the River Osun.[10] Similarly, the Owa of Ijesa complained that the 1932 boundary agreement between Ife and Ijesa adopted terms whose meanings were not comprehended by them.[11]

The rejection of the boundaries suggested by political officers was due largely to the fact that sufficient attention was not paid to the pattern of occupance along the course of the boundary. The practice was to base the boundaries on the generalised pattern of territorial occupation and define them by straight lines linking certain points. In many cases the boundaries so defined cut across the farmlands of some people or families who would disregard the boundary and who could instigate their community to reject such a boundary. For example, the Ijesa rejection of the 1932 boundary agreement with Ife occured after the Ijesas realised that the boundary divided the farmlands of people on the Ijesa side, particularly those at Ifewara.[12]

Much more often suggestions by political officers have been rejected because they paid no attention to the historical patterns of occupance. The disregard of non-contemporary patterns of occupation is due to the acceptance of the view that a boundary should group together people who share common characteristics.[13] Because of this they could accept only the existing patterns of occupance. The party whose claims (as supported by its own conception of the historical pattern of occupation) are overruled usually rejected the suggestions. Thus the Ikale of Aye rejected the boundary settlement of 1904 with Ondo on the ground that it did not accord with their own claims which were based on their past occupation of areas on the Ondo side.[14] Similarly the Ijebus rejected suggestions on their boundary with Ibadan because the proposed boundary failed to recognise the historical pattern of occupation.

SETTLEMENT BY ARBITRATION

When a boundary dispute cannot be settled as a result of investigation and suggestion by District Officers, recourse is usually had to arbitration. The arbitrator is normally a political officer who is specially assigned to take evidence from both parties and suggest a boundary.

The main differences between settlement by investigation and settlement by arbitration may be listed as follows: first, settlement by arbitration is by a single officer whereas that by investigation usually involves more than one. Second, settlement by investigation may not involve bringing the two sides together in one place while in the case of arbitration both sides have to meet at some stage. The arbitrator may be given power to summon witnesses who are not members of the disputant communities but this was not generally so when political officers undertook to settle by investigation. Usually the tendency is for arbitrators to sit as courts and take all relevant evidence. The main difference between arbitration and court procedure is that lawyers do not appear before arbitrators and any cross-examination is done directly by the parties on both sides. Also, the arbitrator usually takes evidence near the disputed area whereas courts sit at special locations. An arbitrator normally tours the disputed area to see things for himself whereas the officer presiding in a court rarely engages in such tours of disputed territories.

The boundaries suggested by arbitrators bear a closer relationship to the pattern of occupance than those by political officers who carry out settlement by discussion. Nevertheless, boundaries suggested by arbitrators were sometimes rejected, particularly at the demarcation stage when their defects become obvious. The reason is that the boundaries are usually in the form of straight lines linking some agreed points. It is therefore possible that the boundaries split individual farmlands between the agreed points.

Arbitrators usually try to forestall the rejection of their suggestions by making the disputants agree beforehand that they will abide by whatever recommendation is made. The agreements may make provision for the treatment of farmers who might find themselves on the wrong side of the boundary fixed by the arbitrator.

An example of a boundary fixed by arbitration is that between Ikere and Akure in 1954. Before the arbitrator took evidence he got both sides to agree to accept his decision. Furthermore both sides 'agreed that there should be no disturbance of farms which, in accordance with the final decisions, may lie within the boundary of the other's district. Both agreed that no isakole would be levied since, historically, the Deji and Ogoga are brothers born of the same father and mother.'[16]

During his fieldwork in the disputed area the arbitrator noted the pattern of occupance by the two sides. For example, he observed that, in the area of Orokun hill, only Ikere farms are along the northern slopes whilst Ijus (on the Akure side) farm only on the eastern slopes. Also, whilst in the field, he got both sides to agree on certain points, namely, Eleru hill, Elekuru hill, Ota-Ore, a point on the Iju–Ikere road $2\frac{1}{2}$ miles north of Iju, and Orokun hill. The boundary was defined by straight lines linking the agreed points.[17]

Soon after the decision the Akures complained that contrary to the prior agreement their people on the Ikere side were being maltreated. Consequently they rejected the boundary.[18] The arbitrator recommended that the protests of Akure should be disregarded.[19] However, the Akures did not change their views and at the time of writing the boundary is not finally settled.

In some other cases the recommendations of an arbitrator were rejected soon after they were announced. The explanation for the rejection could be found in the non-compliance of the suggested boundary with the conception of one of the parties as to its historical rights. The rejection by Ondo (reported in Chapter II) of the decision of an arbitrator on the Ondo/Ikale boundary in 1922, was due largely to such reasons.

JUDICIAL SETTLEMENT OF BOUNDARY DISPUTES

A community which is not satisfied with the suggestions of political officers on a boundary may refer the matter to a court of law. In the early stages the cases were referred to the Provincial Courts where legal representation was not allowed. The disputants gave evidence directly and each side cross-examined the other. At a later stage boundary cases were referred directly to High Courts where the parties could be represented by counsel.

The communities which refer boundary cases to the High Courts usually employ counsel through whom they present their cases to the court. Cross-examination of the witnesses is carried out by the lawyers rather than by the members of the opposing communities. The presiding judge may ask witnesses to clarify some statements but he normally does not cross-examine a witness. Another major feature of court cases is that each side must prepare a surveyed map of the disputed area and present it in evidence before the court. One significant aspect of the judicial settlement of boundary disputes (in common with all other disputes) is that the judge must base his decision on evidence actually presented in court. Normal judicial practice precludes the judge from taking into consideration evidence or information not produced during the hearing in court.

The system of cross-examination by lawyers precludes the members of the communities from asking questions on new evidence or information adduced by the opposite side. Yet the extent to which a counsel can cross-examine witnesses of the opposite side depends largely on how effectively he has been briefed by his own clients. Fortunately most communities brief their counsel so well that a counsel knows as much as the whole community before going to court. But when a counsel is inadequately briefed vital questions may not be asked during cross-examination. It is not unusual for judges to comment that the evidence adduced by one side was not challenged by the other and then proceed to pronounce judgment on the basis of the unchallenged evidence.

The judge's knowledge of the area in dispute is often limited to the survey plans produced by each side. The plans usually show the boundaries of the area being claimed by each side. Details of the pattern of occupation within the disputed area are not usually given on the plans. The effect of this is that the judge has little option but to award the disputed area to one of the parties. Yet in the majority of cases the best solution would be to divide the disputed area between the two communities.

Court judgments are usually given on the assumption that the communities had agreed on a boundary in the past. It is also assumed that the boundaries pass through specific points as indicated by one of the communities. Consequently court decisions usually involve the creation of boundaries linking specific points which may be many kilometres apart. Such boundaries are liable to cut across the farms of some people or split villages into two. If that happens the people affected will not accept the boundary and will seek all opportunities of getting the judgment set aside.

The judgment of a lower court may be challenged on appeal to a higher court. When a dispute has gone to the highest court no appeal is possible and the decision given becomes binding on all concerned. It may therefore be assumed that judicial decisions on boundary disputes represent a final settlement. Unfortunately the fact that no further appeal is possible does not mean that the adjudged boundary is accepted by the losing side. In many cases the losing side remains unhappy and will explore other ways of preventing the implementation of the court's judgment. Mention was made in Chapter IV of Idanre's opposition to the demarcation of the boundary fixed between it and Akure by the court in 1943. The argument was that the boundary was unacceptable and that since Idanres had been in occupation of the area their rights of free occupance should not be disturbed.[20] They went to the extent of taking up arms to prevent the beginning of demarcation. During the demarcation they refused to co-operate with surveyors who had to cut traces through their farms.[21] As far as can be ascertained by the writer, the Idanres have not given formal approval to the demarcated boundary. When the Boundary Commission was constituted the Idanres got the case listed for hearing. The same non-acceptance of judicial decisions is shown by the revival of the boundary dispute between Ise and Emure. It was settled in court in 1937. An appeal was made to the West African Court of Appeal which upheld the decision of the lower court in favour of Ise.[22] The case has been listed before the Boundary Commission and Emure is making every attempt to get the earlier judgment set aside.

The type of finality involved in judicial decisions on boundary disputes encouraged many communities to take their claims to court. But the resort to court action has many side effects. First, it involves much recrimination between the communities. The long duration of court cases coupled with the fact that, according to a Yoruba saying, people who have taken their conflict to court for settlement do not become friends after the court case, means that relationships between the communities remain strained long after the court decision. The second effect is that boundary cases in court are very costly in both time and money. The time cost includes the long period spent on attending court sessions over a period which may be of many years. The money cost includes the cost of survey and the charges by counsel. At the time of the fieldwork for this study counsel did not normally charge less than the equivalent of two thousand one hundred naira (₦2,100) to appear in a boundary case. In many cases the charges could be two or three times that amount. In addition to the professional charges counsel usually make other claims for research, travelling and other expenses. A community involved in a boundary dispute may therefore spend up to twenty thousand naira (₦20,000) or more before judgment is given. Even then the community may lose that case.

SETTLEMENT BY THE BOUNDARY COMMISSION

In order to avoid many of the problems arising from the judicial settlement of boundary disputes the government decided to set up a commission which is charged with the settlement of boundary disputes out of the regular courts. To this end the Boundaries' Settlement Law was passed in 1956. However, the Commission did not function until 1968. The main provision of the Boundaries' Settlement Law are:[23]

4. The Governor in Council may by order refer to a Commissioner for determination of the boundaries or any part of the boundaries between the area of two or more local government councils or communities.

   (1) Where the boundary or boundaries to be determined are described in the Instrument or Instruments relating to the councils or in any law or other instrument or document relating to the communities concerned by reference to any boundary of the area of jurisdiction of a chief, the Commissioner shall, subject to subsection (2) of this section, settle the boundary so described

       (a) in the case of a local area, the line which he finds to be the limit of the proprietary interests of that area;

       (b) in the case of the area of jurisdiction of a chief, the line which he finds to be the limit of the jurisdictional interests of that chief.

   (2) Notwithstanding the provisions of subsection (1) of this section, the Commissioner may, if he considers that grave administrative inconvenience would be caused if the boundary between two council areas, at any part of it, were fixed in accordance with the provisions of that subsection, settle as the boundary such other line as appears to him to be suitable having regard to administrative convenience and the proprietary interests of the areas or the jurisdictional interests by reference to which the boundary is defined. . . .

6. Where an Order has been made under section 4 referring the determination of any boundary to a Commissioner the Commissioner shall. . .

       (b) hear all such evidence relevant to the enquiry as may be offered by any person;

       (c) permit any council or community or any other person who satisfies the Commissioner that he is in any way interested in or concerned with the boundary which is the subject of the enquiry to be represented by counsel at the enquiry; . . .

(e) make an inspection of the land which the boundary to be determined will traverse; . . .

10. (1) For the purposes of hearing and determining appeals under this law there shall be an appeal tribunal which shall consist of the Chief Justice and two other Judges of the High Court.

(2) An appeal shall lie at the instance of any Council, community or person affected to the appeal tribunal against the finding of a Commissioner relating to the boundary or any part of the boundary determined or to any rights or interests in or over land of such Council, community or person. . . .

(4) Except with the leave of the appeal tribunal no appeal shall lie after the expiration of six months from the delivery of the finding of a Commissioner. . . .

11. (3) Upon the conclusion of the hearing of the appeal, the appeal tribunal shall deliver its decision and either

(a) confirm the finding of the Commissioner with respect to the matter upon which the appeal is taken; or

(b) vary, to such extent as may be stated in the decision, the finding of the Commissioner. . . .

(5) No appeal shall lie from the decision of the appeal tribunal. . . .

14. (1) . . . the determination of a local government or community boundary, or any rights or interests in or over land . . . shall, notwithstanding anything contained in any Instrument or judgment, be final and conclusive as to that local government or community boundary, or those rights or interests in or over land.

The provisions of the Boundaries' Settlement Law indicate the way the government expects that boundary disputes shall be settled in the State. Judging by section four of the law and the administrative set-up and practices in the State, the normal procedure would appear to be as follows:

(1) a community or council should inform the Divisional Officer in its area that there is a boundary dispute between it and a neighbour;

(2) the Divisional Officer should inform the Ministry of Local Government of the existence of the dispute;

(3) the Ministry of Local Government should then communicate with the Executive Council which shall decide whether or

not the dispute shall be listed for hearing by the Boundary Settlement Commissioner and advise the Governor accordingly (the normal procedure does not necessarily apply during a military régime when some communities may write directly to the Military Governor).

The different channels through which a case has to pass before getting to the Boundary Commission is likely to delay the settlement of boundary disputes. One would think that since the Commission is one of the legal means of getting redress in Nigeria there should be no restriction of access to it by citizens or communities in the State. As the law stands now, it is quite possible for the Governor, acting on the advice of the Executive Council, to refuse to refer a case to the Commission. If that happens the parties concerned will have no option but to take the case to the regular courts. In that event one of the objectives of passing the Boundaries' Settlement Law will have been defeated.

A more fundamental aspect of the Law is the power of the Commission to settle boundary disputes and the way of effecting the settlement. Sections 6(b) and (c) of the Law empowers a Boundary Settlement Commissioner to take evidence and the parties to be represented by counsel. There is nothing different from the practices in regular courts in those provisions. Therefore a Boundary Commissioner is liable to make mistakes similar to those made in judicial settlements.

A major difference between the Commission and the ordinary law courts is that a Boundary Commissioner is required by section 6(e) of the Law to inspect the territory the boundary is to traverse. Unfortunately the purpose of the inspection is not specified: there is no indication of what the Commissioner should observe. As a result, the usefulness of the inspection is bound to be very limited. This opinion is supported by the type of traverse inspection made before the decision was reached on the Oyo/Ogbomoso boundary which the Commissioner reported as follows:

On 13 November 1970 the land in dispute, including the boundaries claimed, was inspected. Representatives of both communities and their counsel were present at the inspection. Various places were visited including Ahoro-Dada, Oniyan Village, Yawota Village, Esinele and Ikoyi. The Oba River, Onimo Stream and Owe River were also visited. The inspection which lasted about eight hours ended at Ogbomosho.[24]

The area in dispute and which was inspected in eight hours covers more than 1,500 square kilometres. Obviously then, not much could have been gained by the inspection. This itself is very obvious from the statement of the Commissioner. For example, not much could have been gained from the visit to the Oba, Onimo and Owe Rivers. There is no indication that any additional fact, besides those presented at the hearing, was gained by the flying visits to some villages. In short, the type of inspection undertaken by the Commissioner could not contribute to a better understanding of the boundaries being claimed.

The intention in the preceding paragraph is not to deny the usefulness of fieldwork in disputed areas. Indeed, it is the opinion of the present writer that detailed fieldwork should precede the settlement of any boundary dispute. The fieldwork should seek to understand the pattern of human occupance of the disputed area and, if possible, the ownership of the farmlands within it. In the case of villages efforts should be made to establish the allegiance of the population to either of the disputant communities. Fieldwork of this sort cannot be undertaken within a few hours. Furthermore lawyers, who are the only people so far appointed as Boundary Settlement Commissioners, are not trained to undertake the type of spatial or geographical surveys which such fieldwork requires.

Another aspect of the Boundaries' Settlement Law is the system of appeal. The appeal tribunal is much like the regular court of appeal. What is of interest in the appeal tribunal is that its decision shall be final on all boundary disputes. The finality is, by itself, not a bad thing since there must necessarily be an end to litigation on boundary disputes. The only questionable aspect of it is that no provision is made for any discussion with the parties. This means that throughout the process of settling a boundary dispute by the Boundary Commission the battle is to be fought purely on a legal basis. If the Boundary Commissioner is a legal practitioner then it might be better that the appeal tribunal should consist not only of judges but also of experts in other disciplines. The inclusion of experts in non-legal disciplines would mean that the final declaration on a boundary dispute would take account of other factors in addition to legal issues. Such a final decision should consider the geographical, social and historical aspects of the problem.

It could be argued that the consideration of non-legal factors ought to take place before the Boundary Commissioner rather than at the appeal stage. Such an argument is no doubt valid. However, if social, historical and spatial factors are to be considered at the first hearing, then the structure of the Commission would have to be reformed. A possible review would be to appoint more than one person to hear evidence and suggest the solution of any boundary dispute. The people appointed would have to include experts in law, history and geography.

A commission comprising people such as those suggested above will not be pre-occupied with questions of strict legality; therefore it may not be necessary for each party to be represented by counsel before the Commission. In other words a revised law may have to make provisions similar to section five of the 1933 Law on the settlement of intercommunity boundaries. The section states that:

> No legal practitioner shall appear or act for or assist any party in any inquiry . . . unless he is a member of one of the tribes which are parties to the dispute, is personally interested in its settlement and receives no remuneration for his services in the inquiry.[25]

A revision of the Law along the lines suggested above would make the Boundary Commission more of a fact-finding body than a judicial commission. That being so, members of the investigating panel would be able to question anyone they think could help them, rather than depend on counsel or the communities to summon witnesses. The panel would also be free to consider any relevant information collected from archives or elsewhere. Furthermore, the panel would be able to undertake detailed social surveys to determine the patterns of occupance and the social interaction of people in the disputed area.

The powers of the Boundary Commission on the settlement of boundary disputes is worthy of comment. The intention of section 5(1) of the Law is clearly to ensure that a boundary separates two communities. Section 5(1) (a) requires that the boundary shall be the line which a Commissioner 'finds to be the limit of the proprietary interests of that area.' *Proprietary interests* is defined, in the case of a village, as 'the right of disposition of interests in land of any person or authority on behalf of the inhabitants of such area.' In the case of a district, *proprietary rights* is defined as 'the right of disposition in land of any person or authority on behalf of the natives of any area of jurisdiction of a chief, village, village group, clan, town or other area traditionally associated with that customary court or district area.'[26]

As against section 5(1), section 5(2) empowers a Commissioner not to fix a boundary in accordance with proprietary rights if he considers that grave administrative inconvenience would thereby be caused. The point here is the determination of what constitutes 'grave administrative inconvenience'. The provisions of section 5(2) also makes one wonder about the purpose of the boundaries being fixed: are they administrative or communal boundaries? It is necessary to clarify the purpose in order that a permanent settlement of boundary disputes shall be effected. In the past the Government regarded administrative boundaries as those which separate the jurisdiction of political and other officials appointed by it, whilst communal boundaries were those which separate the land or territory of adjacent communities.

The area of jurisdiction of government officials was based on the political units into which the government divided the country. The political units comprised areas which could easily be administered from the headquarters where the political officer resided. The ease of administration (i.e. administrative convenience) was determined partly on the basis of effective control through indigenous political leaders (*obas* or chiefs) and partly by the ease of identification of the boundaries. The area controlled by an indigenous political leader was defined as the territory occupied by people owing allegiance to him even if they do not have proprietary rights over parts of it.[27] This meant that the administrative boundaries were delimited on the basis of allegiance to traditional rulers or the availability of easily identifiable physical features rather than on the basis of ownership of territory. Therefore, in places where members of one community occupy land which is claimed by their neighbours or where the physical feature chosen does not lie at the communal boundary, there will be differences between communal and administrative boundaries. In the past the government was of the opinion that administrative boundaries had nothing to do with the ownership of land. One must therefore ask whether boundaries fixed in accordance with section 5(2) of the Law shall not affect the proprietary rights of the communities.

The provisions of section 5(2) are the more disturbing in view of section fourteen of the Boundaries' Settlement Law which provides that the boundary so fixed shall 'be final and conclusive as to that local government or community boundary or those rights or interests in or over land.' This would appear to mean that a boundary fixed on the basis of administrative convenience shall decide the rights of people over land. If that is the case then boundaries fixed in accordance with section 5(2) are not likely to be accepted by the community which is adversely affected. This view is based on developments in the past when communities have rejected administrative boundaries where attempts have been made to deny them proprietary rights on land they claimed on the opposite side of the boundary. The most notable of such rejections include the Ife/Ede boundary which was rejected by Ife when they were being denied proprietary rights on land north of the River Sasa.[28] Similarly the Ikales rejected the administrative boundary fixed between them and Ondo in 1928 because it would make them lose their rights on land on the Ondo side of the boundary. It therefore seems highly probable that boundaries fixed in accordance with section 5(2) of the Boundaries' Settlement Law will be rejected by the side which is adversely affected.

The foregoing criticism of the Boundaries' Settlement Law is the more justified because of the way the Commissioners operate at present. A Commissioner is accorded the rights of a High Court judge. He depends entirely on evidence brought before him by the disputants through their lawyers. He does not engage in any independent research. He blames counsel for not producing evidence which he considers could have helped the cases of their clients. Thus in the Oyo/Ogbomoso dispute the Commissioner remarked that: [30]

> . . .no evidence has been led to show links between the present day Oyo and Ikoyi such as were shown in the case of Ogbomoso.
> One would have expected that this witness would be led to give evidence on the founding of Ikoyi and how Onikoyi assumed ascendancy and/or ownership over the land in dispute. On the contrary the witness gave an account of how Ogbomoso became associated with the land in dispute.
> Chief Akerele in his written address attached certain documents not in evidence before the Commission. This, to say the least, is an improper way of introducing evidence not properly tendered. I am not going to take cognisance of the said documents.

These statements are understandable because the Commissioner was following the rules of procedure obtaining in the High Court. He was not acting as an investigator whose object is to find out the truth and who should accept any relevant information no matter when or by whom produced. Such an investigator would have asked the questions he considered relevant to establish the links between Oyo and Ikoyi. He would also have asked the witness referred to in the second quotation above the questions he considered necessary to determine how Ikoyi acquired her rights over the disputed area. Finally a researcher would have been happy to go through the documents tendered by Chief Akerele to see if they held any new information. But in the interest of fair play and justice the procedure in the courts of law requires that the judge shall be a passive assessor of all that is said. In this case such passivity may not help the establishment of the truth.

The adoption of a passive attitude by the Boundary Commissioner is unfortunate because it means that a boundary decision will depend not on all the facts (most of which ought to be established by direct interview and research), but on the competence of the counsel for the parties. Yet when a decision has been reached the attitude of the communities is dictated by what they know (or perceive) to be the facts rather than by what their counsel say. Since the objective of the Boundary Commission is to make the communities accept the boundary, no effort should be spared in finding out each side's notion of the facts. Such efforts can only be effectively made by independent inquiry and research, not by total dependence on counsel who may be too busy or, in fact, incapable of undertaking such an exercise.

ADDENDUM

Since writing the above critique of settlement of boundary disputes by the Boundary Settlement Commission, the Western State government has appointed a committee under Mr Justice Akinola Aguda to review the working of the Commission. The committee met from January to March 1975 and recommended some of the changes suggested above. However, at the time of going to press the reaction of the government to the committee's suggestions has not been announced.[31]

Notes and References

1. See the 1913 definition of the Ife/Ijesa boundary in Chapter V.
2. Evidence in the Akure/Idanre boundary case (*Deji of Akure* v. *Owa of Idanre*), Suit No. 40/1939, Benin Judicial Division.
3. F. D. Lugard, *Political Memoranda* (London: Waterlow, 1919), p.400.
4. See File J27/1923 Vol. II, Ijebu Prof 6/6, N.A.I.
5. Appendix A of the minutes of the meeting held at the Residency, Ibadan, on 28 October 1913 on the boundaries of Ijesaland.
6. See Chapter IV.
7. P. R. Foulkes-Roberts, 'Report on the Ondo/Ikale Boundary Dispute, 1935', File 31615, CSO 26, N.A.I.
8. Minutes of a meeting at the Residency, Ibadan, op. cit.
9. Assistant District Officers, Ado-Ekiti and Ondo, to District Officers, Ondo and Ado-Ekiti, 27 November 1926, File 843, Ondo Prof 1/1, N.A.I.
10. Oni of Ife to Resident, Oyo Province, 18 December 1929, File 1171, Simple List of Oyo Provincial Papers, (Numerical Series), N.A.I.
11. Owa of Ilesa to D.O., Ife-Ilesa, 14 April 1949.
12. Chief Agoro of Ifewara to District Officer, Ile-Ife, 14 November 1936. File 759, Oyo Prof 1/1, N.A.I.
13. Minutes of a Meeting at the Residency, Ibadan, op. cit.
14. Lapoki, Bale of Aye, to District Commissioner, Ondo, 2 February 1905, File C 15/1921, Ministry of Local Government Divisional Office, Ondo.
15. The suggestions were made at a joint meeting of the Residents of Oyo and Ibadan Provinces in June 1924. See File 815 Vol. I, Oyo Prof. 3, N.A.I.
16. Inquiry held by Mr C. H. Richardson, District Officer, to decide the boundary between Akure District and Ikere District, 14–24 July 1954.
17. Ibid.
18. Deji of Akure to Ogoga of Ikere, 26 August 1954, File LR 22/3, AKDIVCO 4, N.A.I.
19. C. H. Richardson to Provincial Adviser, Ondo Province, 2 March 1957, File SDC 1/8 Vol. II, Ekiti Southern District Council, Ikere.
20. *Owa of Idanre* v. *Deji of Akure*, Suit No. B/36/1948, Supreme Court, Benin Judicial Division; File A.N.A. 23A, AKDIVCO 2, N.A.I.
21. For details of the problems encountered during the survey, see File 318 Vol. IV, Ondo Prof 1/1, N.A.I.
22. Emure/Ise boundary dispute. See *Obasorun* v. *Odusina*, Suit No. W/19/1937, West African Court of Appeal.
23. Western Nigeria, *The Laws of the Western Region of Nigeria* 1959 Vol. II (Ibadan: Government Printer pp.), 9–19.
24. Western Nigeria Boundary Commission, *Findings of the Ogundare Commission of Enquiry into the Boundary Dispute Between Oyo and Ogbomoso given on the 29th Day of January*, 1971.
25. Western Nigeria, *The Laws of the Western Region. . .*, op. cit., Vol. III, p. 57.
26. Ibid., Vol. II.

27. Minutes of a meeting at the Residency, Ibadan, op. cit.
28. See Chapter VII.
29. See Chapter II.
30. Western Nigeria Boundary Commission, op. cit.
31. Western Nigeria, *Report of the Committee on the settlement of Boundary Disputes* (Ibadan: Ministry of Justice, 1975).

CHAPTER IX

Towards A Permanent Settlement of Boundary Disputes

IT WAS suggested earlier (Chapter III) that the primary objective of studies of this type is the solution of boundary problems. The previous chapter has shown that none of the approaches hitherto adopted in effecting the solution of boundary problems is totally satisfactory. The aim in this concluding chapter, therefore, is to examine ways of achieving a permanent settlement of boundary disputes in Western Nigeria.

There is no doubt that a major aim in the settlement of boundary disputes is to make both sides accept the adjudged boundary. The attainment of that objective can be viewed from three perspectives, namely: the mechanism for effecting settlement of boundary disputes; the objectives of settling boundary disputes; and the bases of delimiting boundaries.

MECHANISM FOR SETTLING BOUNDARY DISPUTES

The review made earlier of the four channels by which boundary disputes were settled in the past shows that none of them is entirely satisfactory. Even so, an indication of the right channel for the settlement of boundary disputes can be obtained by examining the reactions to boundaries settled by each of the four channels. Very often disputant communities accept boundaries suggested as a result of investigation by a political officer or by an arbitrator. For example there were such acceptances on the Ife/Ijesa boundary in 1932,[1] the Ibadan/Ijebu boundary in 1931[2] and the Akure/Ikere boundary in 1954.[3] The rejection of the boundaries came when the implications of the agreements were known or when it was realised that they cut across farmlands. By contrast, the boundary disputes settled in court and by the Boundary Commission are rarely fully accepted.

In the case of court decisions the losing side feels itself cheated and often refuses to accept the implications of the judgment. In the case of the Boundary Commission all the boundary disputes reportedly settled so far have been rejected and appeals have been lodged with the Appeal Tribunal.

The right channel for the settlement of boundary disputes can therefore be ascertained by considering the features in which the political and arbitration methods differ from those of the courts and the Commission. Such consideration should make it possible to identify the good aspects of the first set of methods which can be incorporated into a system of settling these disputes.

One common feature of the political and arbitration methods is that the communities are involved. Suggestions on the settlement of a boundary dispute made by political officers were usually discussed with the communities. In the arbitration approach the two communities expressed themselves freely and could cross-examine those representing the other side. In the judicial approach the disputants are called as witnesses and they are given little opportunity to ask questions directly. The judge does not visit a disputed area, therefore his knowledge of it is based on maps submitted by the disputants. If one of the maps does not correctly represent the features of the landscape on which decision is to be based, the judge may not be aware of this fact.[4] Furthermore, courts depend on counsel to lead evidence in support of the cases of their clients. It is common knowledge that counsel advise their clients on which evidence should be given before a court. In the case of boundary disputes such practice may lead to the suppression of vital information, especially if the counsel for the opposite side is not particularly competent. These features of the judicial approach make it the most unacceptable of the methods for settling boundary disputes in Western Nigeria.

Although the principles underlying the Boundaries' Settlement Law are good (see Chapter VIII) there is much that needs be done to correct its defects and operation. In the first place the disputant communities must be more directly involved in suggesting and discussing the solution of their problems. One step in this direction is to allow the communities to present their evidence directly to the Boundary Settlement Commission and be free to ask their opponents any questions they wish rather than to depend on counsel. However, it should be realised that mere involvement of the communities does not guarantee that all the necessary facts will be forthcoming. In many cases none of the disputants is able to produce all the facts, some of which may be in government files or in the archives. Because of this, the commission should carry out its own research into past decisions on any particular disputed boundary and the contemporary patterns of land occupance in disputed areas. As previously suggested, such an exercise would be better performed if the commission consists not only of legal practitioners but also geographers and historians. With this approach the commission would be seen as an administrative fact-finding body whose recommendations should be discussed with and explained to the disputant communities. When the recommendations have been accepted by the government the boundary should be gazetted. If anyone of the communities is not satisfied with the decision it can appeal to the Boundary Appeal Tribunal. The decision of the Appeal Tribunal should be final.

OBJECTIVES OF SETTLING BOUNDARY DISPUTES

Whatever the mechanism for the settlement of boundary disputes, permanent solution will not be achieved unless the objectives of the boundaries are clearly stated. The preceding sections of this study indicate two objectives: the first is that boundaries are designed to separate administrative units created since the beginning of colonial rule (districts, divisions and provinces); the second is that the boundaries are to separate different communities.

A major purpose of many of the boundaries delimited by government officials was to separate the area of jurisdiction of one officer from another. Thus, during the discussions on the Ikale/Ondo boundary, the government stated that the main purpose of the delimited boundary was to separate the area of jurisdiction of its own officers:

> This boundary had nothing to do with the ownership of land but with the jurisdiction of two commissioners of the Provincial Court.[5]

A similar opinion was expressed during the discussions on the Ife/Ijebu boundary:

> ... where there are rival claimants to the land, Government must lay down its own inter-provincial boundaries without prejudice to the ownership of the land.[6]

The view was reflected in a number of government decisions on disputed areas. Thus, in the settlement of the Ife/Ede boundary dispute in 1924, the government made a distinction between the communal and the administrative boundaries:[7]

1. (a) The boundary line was a farmline boundary and not in any sense a Divisional boundary.
2. (b) The Oni of Ife and the Timi of Ede could each send messengers into the area to call their own people but the whole area was still under Ede and Ibadan.

According to these conditions a farmline boundary was a communal one and should not be confused with the administrative or divisional one. Since the second condition gave both communities rights in the area it can be assumed that the phrase 'under Ede and Ibadan' refers not to local control but to that of the government officials in those two places.

The attempt to make a distinction between administrative and communal boundaries creates a great deal of misunderstanding because the communities do not fully appreciate the differences between the two types of boundary. Before the colonial administration each kingdom and the community on which it was based was independent of the others. Anyone settling within the area controlled by a community owed allegiance to its *oba* and paid tribute or *isakole* (if he was an outsider) to him. During and since the colonial period tribute has been replaced with taxes. However, the administrative boundaries fixed by government were designed not only to separate the area of jurisdiction of political officers but also tax collecting areas. Thus people on one side of the boundary are expected to pay their taxes to the headquarters of the community on that side. In places where administrative and communal boundaries do not coincide the tax arrangements have meant that some communities were not collecting taxes from their territory grouped with the adjacent administrative unit. Consequently there has been persistent protest against administrative boundaries by the communities which are adversely affected by them.

The protest on the administrative grouping of disputed areas has arisen because of the difficulty of reconciling two principles applicable to the creation of administrative units. The first principle is that an administrative unit should be made up of a single community of interest. This principle has been expressed in various forms by different scholars. For example, Dickinson advised that 'since boundaries there must be, the need of the future is to establish political regions in such a way as to harmonise as closely as possible with . . . existing regional fabric of society.'[8] The regional fabric of society being 'an area of human association which we know to exist, although it cannot be defined by exact boundaries.' The need for culturally homogenous political units, that is, political units whose boundaries reflect social and cultural differences in society is shown by Hartshorne's statement that: 'In short, regional heterogeneity creating difficulty for political organisation is solely that of cultural heterogeneity.'[9]

The basis of the principle is that any political unit exists to cater for the economic and social development of its citizens. Both of these are best served where there are no great differences between the various parts. Cultural differences create problems because it may be difficult for the government to cater for all the cultures within its jurisdiction in every item of legislation. Indeed the tendency is for legislation to reflect the practices of the most important culture group or groups. That being so, the minor cultures would complain of neglect, and if the conditions were favourable they might demand separation. The greater numerical strength of the dominant cultures also means that they would constitute the majority to benefit from any welfare service provided by the government. This would also make the minor groups complain. The effect of the complaints would be to make it difficult, though not impossible, to administer culturally heterogeneous political units. Scholars therefore urge that the ideal situation is that a political unit should comprise people who belong to the same culture or interest group.

Applied to the present topic, the principle implies that each area must be grouped with the community with which the inhabitants have cultural ties. For example, in the Akure/Idanre dispute (Chapter IV) the Alade area should be grouped with Idanre rather than with Akure, since socially and historically the people there look towards the former town, build their town houses there and send their children to school there. The general applicability of the principle in Western Nigeria is shown by the fact that in many other parts of the state people demand that rural areas should be grouped with the town or community with which the inhabitants share cultural affinities. The demand of Edunabon for the control of the areas which some of them occupy north of the River Sasa,[10] of the

Ikales for the Arinjan area of Ijebu Division on the grounds that the people are Ikales,[11] or of Ogbomoso for areas around Ikoyi in Oyo Division[12] are examples of the principle in Western Nigeria.

The second principle used in the creation of political units is that a state should control the territory which belongs to it. This means that everyone on a state's territory should come under the administrative jurisdiction of the state. This is the more so with sovereign states. The basis of this principle is that unless a community or state administers its own territory it cannot control the exploitation of its resources or compel users or inhabitants to comply with laws and regulations relating to the use of the land. The difficulty of enforcing compliance with regulations would be increased if the users belong to a community which is likely to support them in any disagreement over the use of the territory. For example, the only way to ensure that tenancy agreements are complied with is for the landlord to have power of eviction over those who default in the discharge of their tenancy obligations. Such power of eviction can be more easily exercised if the territory or property and the landlord are under the same administrative unit and hence within the jurisdiction of the same courts applying the same laws. Applied to the present topic the second principle implies that a community should control all its territory, irrespective of the fact that parts of it may be occupied by people from neighbouring communities. This interpretation is the more relevant in view of the fact that in the past the various communities were in different sovereign states, each of which controlled its own territory.

Nobody can seriously challenge the basic argument of the second principle which is that a community or person must be able to control the use of his property and is entitled to derive some benefit from it. However, there is need to re-examine the view that such control or benefit cannot be ensured unless the owner himself administers the property. The view does not apply to individual property where it is usual for an owner to employ an agent to manage his property. The agent ensures that tenants comply with the conditions of the tenancy and that those who default are evicted. It is realised that in cases where the owner and the tenants are in two different sovereign states such agency management may be difficult, particularly if the landlord wishes to adopt policies resented by the tenants and their government. In such a situation, the laws of the state in which the property is located and of which the tenants are citizens can be changed to the detriment of the foreign property owners. However, where the property owner and the tenants are within the same state, no great problem need be experienced. Property owners can always protest if the government plans to enact laws deterimental to their interests.

Since no local administrative unit within a state can enact laws radically different from those of other units, and each is usually a local arm of the state government, people in different local administrative units within the same state can be regarded as being under the same government. It would, therefore, not matter greatly if the landowners and their property in a state are not within the same local administrative unit. This is the more so if disputes on the property can normally be referred to a court which does not implement customary laws — the latter may differ slightly from one community to another. This argument implies that the property of a community need not be within its own local administrative unit for the community to exercise effective control over its use and derive benefits from it. If this modification of the second principle is accepted it would mean that a disputed area need not be grouped with the landowners.

The implication of the modification suggested above is that an area should be grouped for administrative purposes on the basis of the cultural affinities of the people but that adequate protection should be given to the landowners so that they derive some benefit from their territory. The first protection is that the landowners must be able to charge and collect *isakole* from people using their land and also collect royalties on natural resources (timber and minerals) from the area. In order to ensure payment, the council with which the area is grouped should be asked to collect and pay the amount (after deduction of expenses) to the landowning community. Greater efficiency can be attained if the total amount due to the landowners in any year is charged on the income of the council which administers the affected area and the date for payment fixed. The council can then be sued for non-payment. It is therefore the responsibility of the council to collect the funds from the tenants.

Control of the use of the land can be done through a system of inspection by the landowners and agreements on the areas that can be farmed by the tenants. A system similar to that of reservations in residential areas can be adopted. The reserved areas will be those where the tenants cannot farm. Once the tenants have exhausted the area allocated to them further expansion must be outside the disputed area. The size of individual farms within the non-reserved areas shall not then be the concern of the landowners except for the purposes of assessing *isakole*. According to these suggestions, an area which has been the subject of a dispute will be administered by the community to which the inhabitants have cultural and historical allegiances. They will be able to pay their taxes to the council on which they will depend for the provision of social amenities.

The solution in the preceding paragraph does not take account of the possibility of citizens of the landowning community settling in the disputed area. For example there could be some Akure citizens within the area formerly disputed with Idanre, and adjudged to belong to Akure, but whose main population is from Idanre. Such Akure citizens could insist that they too would like to be administered by their own community in whose urban centres they have their houses and where they send their children to school. The landowners may, because of that demand, be unwilling to accept the solution. This aspect of the problem can be solved in one of two ways: first, by the government insisting that the people must agree to being administered by the community of the tenants. Such a decision can be defended on the ground that administrative grouping has to be based on the cultural affinity of the majority of the population. The defence will stand provided the number of landowners is small. When they constitute an important proportion of the population it may be difficult to overlook their demands. In any case, they would go on pressing that their own community should come to their aid and this may re-open the problem of administering the area.

An alternative method of dealing with the problem created by the presence of members of the landowning community in such an area is to allow them to pay their taxes to the community to which they would also normally go for matters dealing with local customary law. For other purposes, they should be regarded as being in the jurisdiction of the council administering the area. This could be justified on the grounds that their town houses are in the community's main town and that the farms are merely their working places. But it means that they would enjoy the facilities provided by the council administering the area to which they do not pay their taxes. The situation may not create a problem in places where

the landowners constitute a small proportion of the population because the loss in revenue to the administering council would not be
substantial. The position would be different where the population
so treated is large and the revenue loss is considerable. A possible
solution in the latter situation could be the transfer of the affected
settlements to the administrative units of the landowners.

BASES FOR DELIMITING BOUNDARIES

Before disputes on communal boundaries can be satisfactorily
settled two different issues must be clearly understood. These are
(1) membership of a community, and (2) the rights of a community
to land.

A necessary condition for the determination of the boundaries
of a community is the identification of its members. Ideally the
identification should not be difficult since it depends on the claims of
the people. In practice the spokesman of the community might
make claims which are not subscribed to by some of the members
of his group. The possible differences could occur:

(1) where some settlements disagree with their inclusion in the
     community;
(2) where some groups which desire to be included within the
     community are left outside the territory being claimed;
(3) where people in a settlement belong to two different commu-
     nities and each side wants to be grouped with its own com-
     munity.

In many cases a community may claim some settlements which
do not wish to be grouped with it. The reasons given to support
the claim are usually historical. Examples of such claims include
that of Ife over Ifewara, Araromi and Alakowe on the borderlands
with Ijesa;[13] also Akure's claim over Alade on the boundary with
Idanre;[14] and Imu, claimed by Ikale, on the boundary with Ondo.[15]
In each of the cases the settlement does not accept inclusion with
the community concerned. The basis of the claim could be that:

(a) the founder of the settlement originated from the claimant
     community;
(b) the founder of the settlement was given land by the claimant
     community;
(c) the settlement was conquered by the claimant community.

In all cases the settlement would deny the bases of the claims and give other explanations to support its exclusion from the community. The decision on the different claims could affect the attitude of either party to the dispute. The claims are difficult to decide because the denial of association with a community could be based on recent political developments rather than on historical facts. It is usual for a settlement which desires independence to deny any connection with its erstwhile political capital. An example of such a denial is that of Ifewara vis-à-vis Ile-Ife. Ifewara was founded by a migrant from Ile-Ife who passed through Ilesa before getting to the present site of Ifewara. In an attempt to assert its rights over the settlement, Ife opposed the attempt by the head chief of Ifewara to wear a crown in 1916.[16] In 1943, when the attempt was revived, Ifewara admitted owing allegiance to Ilesa and prayed the Owa to allow their head chief to wear a crown.[17] The Owa of Ijesaland accepted their homage and granted their head chief permission to wear a crown and said: 'I have made it clear to the Loja and the *bale* that the beaded crowns as they were should be worn by them as sub-chiefs to me and they cannot be recognised [as being] as important as those of the natural rulers of the Western Provinces.'[18] The Owa's permission was not approved by the Resident because of opposition from Ife.[19] Later, in 1958, Ifewara claimed independence of Ilesa and wanted their own territory to be clearly delimited and distinguished from that of Ijesa: 'We the undersigned are in origin of Ifewara extraction of Ife now domicile in Ifewara town [*sic*] which by reason of the interdivisional boundary had been located to Ijesa Division, Oyo Province. We hereby submit and humbly solicit for your enquiry and final determination of the long standing subject of the Ifewara boundary with Ife and Ilesa. . . .'[20]

Sometimes, people in a settlement may change their allegiance to a community in the course of the determination of a boundary dispute. This was the case in the Oyo/Ibadan boundary dispute where the people of Ikereku once declared that they were under Iware.[21] At a later stage they claimed that they were independent of that settlement.

Such denials make it difficult to decide the membership of a community and thereby delimit its boundaries. Yet in many cases boundary agreements have been rejected because the settlements claimed by one side had been grouped with its neighbours. An example of this is the rejection by Oyo of the boundary delimited between them and Ogbomoso by the Boundary Commission in 1971.

In some cases the spokesmen for a community may suggest a boundary which excludes some settlements which regard themselves as part of their community. This was the case in 1915 when the Olubadan of Ibadan suggested that the Ibadan/Ijebu boundary should pass through Igikola[22] (Fig.6). That boundary cut off some Ibadan settlements among which was Araromi. Such suggestions are usually withdrawn once the allegiance of the settlements are known, but the opposing community usually will insist on their implementation.

Sometimes settlements in some border areas might be inhabited by members of the two neighbouring communities. This is more likely to happen under annexation boundary disputes and in places where people who had fled to different communities return to re-establish devastated settlements. During boundary delimitation each set of returnees might want the settlement grouped with the community in which it sought refuge during the hostilities which led to the evacuation of the settlement. This was the case with Esinele on the Oyo/Ogbomoso borderlands. During hostilities in the nineteenth century people at Esinele fled to both Oyo and Ogbomoso. After the hostilities both sides returned and when the Oyo/Ogbomoso boundary was being delimited each asked that the new Esinele should be grouped with the community in which it had sought refuge.[24]

From the foregoing it is clear that a permanent solution of boundary disputes requires that the means of determining membership of a community and allocating the settlements should be explicitly stated. Such a statement should clarify a number of issues some of which are:

(a) The ties between the settlement and the community from which its founder originated and also that through which he passed: It has to be noted that the latter community bases its claims on ownership of the territory on which the settlement was founded. But, as previously argued, it is highly improbable that any one community had exclusive claim over land in the frontier. Therefore it may be wrong to allocate a settlement simply on the basis of such claim unless the claimant of the territory can show evidence of permanent occupation before the foundation of the settlement.

(b) The present allegiance of the inhabitants of the settlement, particularly the proportion claiming ties with either side:

In this regard a distinction would have to be made between tenant farmers and landowners. In allocating a settlement tenant farmers should be regarded as belonging to the community of their landlords.

(c) The appointment of head chiefs before and since the beginning of colonial administration: Usually village head chiefs are appointed by the community to which the territory belongs. However, in considering pre-colonial appointments a distinction would have to be drawn between *bale* (or *olu* or *oloja*) who is the village head chief and the *ajele* who was appointed by a conqueror as his representative in a defeated settlement.

RIGHTS OF A COMMUNITY

Once the membership of a community has been decided it will be necessary to examine their proprietary rights over the disputed territory. In this regard it will be necessary to take notice of both the past and the present rights to the land. As the preceding chapters show very clearly most boundary disputes deal with the rights of the communities to the land. The determination of the rights becomes difficult because:

(a) a community may claim rights based on past occupation;
(b) a community may base its case on the fact that its rights had never been challenged and that it had never paid *isakole* to the claimant to the land;
(c) a community may base its claim on the right to inherit a part of what belonged to a common ancestor.

One of the commonest arguments of disputants is that they used to occupy the area in dispute. It has been argued that evidence of permanent occupation in terms of a settlement is required to justify such claims. But unless permanent occupation is proved it will be necessary to determine (1) the duration of occupation, (2) the length of the period since the area was left vacant, (3) the attempts to assert rights over the area since the settlement was evacuated.

It is possible for a community to make a brief stop at a point in the course of its migrations. There may be no permanent settlement at such a point. There could be other brief occupations of various sites. For example, the Ikales claim Gbekelu because one Abodi fell ill and stayed there during a journey to Ile-Ife.[25] In view of this it will be advisable to stipulate the nature of the settlement and its duration. It may be necessary to fix a minimum period of stay on a site—say a generation—before a claim to ownership of the area can be accepted.

Whatever the duration of the permanent settlement, account will have to be taken of the period since the area was left vacant. Sometimes a settlement may be evacuated during a war or because of a move to another side. The former inhabitants would still think of the old site as belonging to them. However, the inhabitants might have left the place for a long time without returning to it to farm or take physical possession. In their absence the place could revert to virgin forest and a new group could occupy it. The question, therefore, is whether the latter occupants ought to be denied ownership simply because the first occupants had a settlement there. In order to solve such problems it will be necessary to stipulate the length of absence after which a community may lose its rights to a territory.

The length of absence is relative and would have to be considered in the light of the attempt by the first occupants to assert their rights in the area. If they have continuously asserted their rights over the area by hunting there or collecting royalty on timber or *isakole* from farmers, it may be inadvisable to consider their occupation as ended at the time the settlement was deserted.

The payment of *isakole* is an acknowledgment that the rights over the land belong to the collector of the *isakole*, whilst the person making the payment is a tenant. Consequently in some boundary disputes a community may claim that it used to receive *isakole* from the opponent. The latter would deny that it had ever made such payment. The point here is that in many such cases a confusion is made between *isakole* (the land rent) and tribute (paid by a settlement to the *oba* of its community).

Isakole is paid as a form of recognition of non-ownership of proprietary rights, whilst tribute is paid as a kind of homage. Settlements within a kingdom jointly maintain the *oba* of the community and give him presents on important occasions. This is tribute. It is a mark of recognition that all the settlements accept the *oba* as their ruler. It does not in any way indicate that the settlements bringing the tribute are subservient or subordinate to the other. Neither does it mean that the inhabitants of the various settlements regard themselves as tenants of the *oba* or of the people in the headquarters. All members of a community have it as a birthright to cultivate and use any territory which has not been occupied by other members. In some cases the right to the territory was acquired by the ancestors of the individual concerned. In other cases, especially in the frontier areas, it is the individual himself who acquired the rights. Whichever the case, the settlements founded in each area are in duty bound to help maintain community projects and support the *oba*.

The above situation is accepted in principle and is implemented so long as all the settlements remain together under the *oba*. If, however, one settlement attempts to claim independence of the others the rest might lay claim to the land and argue that the secessionist used to pay *isakole* to the *oba*. The attempt to claim independence has arisen since the creation of many local government units from single kingdoms of the past. In an attempt to assert rights over timber royalties or tax collection from the border areas each Local Council within each kingdom has demanded boundaries between itself and its neighbours. This has often led to counter-claims in which the headquarters of the old kingdom claims not only the border-lands but also the territory on which the other settlements are founded.

If a settlement established its independence of the community of its founder it may still lay claim to part of that community's territory. The claims would be justified on the ground that since they have a common ancestor each of them is entitled to a part of the property of that ancestor. That being so, the land of those ancestors should be split between the settlement and the rest of the community. This type of argument was advanced by Ifewara to justify its claim to parts of the territory between it and Ile-Ife.[26] But the argument could equally be advanced by settlements which have a different Local Council from the headquarters of the community or kingdom to which they originally belonged. Accepting that the territory ought to be partitioned, the only just solution is to give each side ownership of the area it effectively occupies and any uncultivated land should be divided proportionately between adjacent individuals and settlements.

The establishment of the rights of a community over territory occupied by another must therefore state the following:
   (i)   the origin of the founders of the settlement in dispute;
  (ii) the connection between the founders of the disputed settlement and that of the claimant;
 (iii) how the connection between the two settlements was esta-

blished;

(iv) any disruption to the connection;

(v) the type of contribution by the disputed settlement to the claimant and how and when payment was made;

(vi) disruptions to the payment (if any) and the reasons for them;

(vii) steps taken to re-establish payment since the end of the situation leading to its disruption.

CONCLUSION

The foregoing discussion shows that if boundary disputes in Western Nigeria are to be permanently settled to the satisfaction of all concerned the following conditions, among others, ought to be fulfilled:

(i) the causes and nature of the disputes must be known;

(ii) the purpose of the boundaries being delimited must be clearly stated. Where administrative and communal boundaries do not coincide, provision must be made to protect a community's interest in any part of its land grouped with the adjacent administrative unit;

(iii) the machinery for settlement must not be based exclusively on strict legality but must be flexible enough to take account of customary law and practices as well as current knowledge about traditional boundaries;

(iv) boundary definitions must not be ambiguous.

In addition to the four conditions, the boundary must be marked or demarcated in a way that is easily recognised in the field. At present the practice is to fix cement pillars at various sections of the boundary. The advantage of cement pillars is that they are not easily destroyed. However, cement pillars have the disadvantage that they can be overgrown by vegetation and therefore not easily located by those working at some distance from them. It may therefore be preferable to supplement cement pillars with the traditional boundary trees such as *peregun, akoko* or *atori*. Such trees can be planted at regular intervals so that they are visible to those on either side of it along the boundary. In that way anyone will be able to identify the trees, and hence the boundary, in the field.

In an agrarian community like that of Western Nigeria land is a very precious resource, to be used by the present generation and preserved for those yet to be born. Therefore no individual, family or community wishes to concede any piece of its land to another. In such a situation boundary disputes are likely to occur when two communities or families meet on their common frontier. Whilst the settlement of such disputes must take account of due processes of the law, it should be primarily based on the establishment of all relevant facts and on due regard for past and present patterns of occupation. The suggestions made in the various sections of this book are designed to indicate how such settlement can be effected.

Notes and References

1. See Chapter V.
2. See Chapter I.
3. See Deji of Akure to Ogoga of Ikere, 26 August 1954, File LR 22/3, AKDIVCO 4, N.A.I.
4. For example the two maps (BK 8016 and IFO 2949) presented in the Ajawa/Lagbedu boundary case (Suit No. HOS 59/67) in Osogbo High Court, differed as to details of features on the landscape, particularly the rivers named Laregede and Ito.
5. B. J. Matthews, 'Assessment Report on the Ikale District, Okitipupa Division', File O/C 143/1914, Ministry of Local Government, Divisional Office, Okitipupa.
6. Memorandum from Secretary, Southern Provinces, to Resident, Oyo Province, 6 October 1928.
7. Assistant District Officer, Ibadan, to District Officer, Ibadan, 10 October 1924, File 1171, (Simple List of Oyo Provincial Papers, Numerical Series), N.A.I.
8. R. E. Dickson, *City Region and Regionalism. A Geographical Contribution to Human Ecology* (London: Routledge and Kegan Paul, 1947), p. 7.
9. R. Hartshorne, 'Morphology of the State: Areas of significance for the State' in *Essays in Political Geography*, ed. C. A. Fisher (London: Methuen, 1968), p. 29.
10. See Chapter VI.
11. C. I. Gavin, 'An Intelligence Report on Ikale District of Okitipupa Division, 1934'.
12. Western Nigeria Boundary Commission, *Findings of the Ogundare Commission of Enquiry into the Boundary Dispute between Oyo and Ogbomoso given on the* 29th *Day of January*, 1971.
13. See Chapter V.
14. See Chapter IV.
15. See Chapter II.

16. Mentioned by Oni of Ife to Senior District Officer, Ife/Ilesa Division, 16 February 1948.
17. Bale of Ifewara to Owa of Ijesa, 13 October 1943.
18. Owa of Ijesa to Resident, Oyo, 18 October 1943.
19. Oni of Ife to Senior District Officer, Ife/Ilesa Division, 16 February 1948.
20. Ifewara Community in a letter addressed to the Divisional Adviser, Ilesa, 7 July 1958, File IL 1528, Ministry of Local Government Divisional Office, Osogbo.
21. See account by Mr Birch of interview with Ikereku in January 1919 cited in report by the District Officer, Oyo, on his tour of Ikereku/Iware disputed area, 30 September 1932, File 72/1927, Oyo Div. 2/14, N.A.I.
22. See report by District Officer, Oyo, of his interview in September 1932 with people on the Ikereku/Iware disputed area, File 72/1927, Oyo Div. 2/14, N.A.I.
23. Letter from Olubadan, File J 51/1950, Ijebu Prof. 6/3, N.A.I.
24. Ministry of Justice, Western Nigeria: *Findings of the Ogundare Commission of Enquiry into the Boundary Dispute Between Oyo and Ogbomoso given on the 29th Day of January, 1971.* See Evidence by Yesufu Afolabi, James Adewale Afonja and Kehinde Omowale.
25. P. R. Foulkes-Roberts, 'Report on the Ondo/Ikale Boundary Dispute 1935', File 31615, C.S.O. 26, N.A.I.
26. The explanation was given in reply to a question posed to Ifewara by the, Oni of Ife on 8 June 1937, File 759, Oyo Prof. 1/1, N.A.I.

INDEX